What is Education?

Edited by A. J. Bartlett and Justin Clemens

EDINBURGH
University Press

Edinburgh University Press is one of the leading university presses in the UK. We publish academic books and journals in our selected subject areas across the humanities and social sciences, combining cutting-edge scholarship with high editorial and production values to produce academic works of lasting importance. For more information visit our website: edinburghuniversitypress.com

Edinburgh University Press Ltd
The Tun – Holyrood Road
12(2f) Jackson's Entry
Edinburgh EH8 8PJ

Typeset in 10.5/13pt Monotype Baskerville by
Servis Filmsetting Ltd, Stockport, Cheshire, and
and printed and bound in Great Britain by
CPI Group (UK) Ltd, Croydon CR0 4YY

A CIP record for this book is available from the British Library

ISBN 978 0 7486 7532 6 (hardback)
ISBN 978 0 7486 7534 0 (webready PDF)
ISBN 978 0 7486 7533 3 (paperback)
ISBN 978 0 7486 7535 7 (epub)

Contents

Acknowledgements

The editors would like to sincerely thank all the contributors for their commitment to this collection. The strange simplicity of the question seemed to manifest untold symptoms in many collaborators and colleagues over the time this volume took to complete, and so to those who managed to 'work through' we offer our gratitude and appreciation. We also thank our excellent and inspired translators, Elke Wakefield, Robert Boncardo and Laura Lotti. We would especially like to thank Carol Macdonald at EUP for her unwavering support, even as we tested it at every turn. A. J. Bartlett would like to thank Angela Cullip. Justin Clemens would like to thank Helen Johnson.

Thanks to Sunday Rose for her work on the bibliography.

This publication was supported by a Faculty of Arts Publication Subsidy scheme from The University of Melbourne.

Foreword

Alain Badiou

This book sets itself a difficult and essential task: nothing less than opening a new epoch of thought on the practice of what education is.

A new epoch after three others: first, positivist education, the authoritarian transmission of a constituted knowledge. Next, the leftist and postmodern critique of positivist education in the name of the freedom of subjects, their personal integration, the diversity of cultures, the creative value of revolts against every form of imposed universalism. Finally, throwing itself into the opened breach, the contemporary 'education' system, which organises in some way a free submission to the enchanting flexibility of liberal capitalism, and making use of diverse means, fixes its place.

The meditations of this research are multiple. Nevertheless, it brings to light a common determination: all true education does not only, nor even principally, rest on already-known knowledges, but on the Idea by which the becoming knowledges are organised. It is from the point of impasse of established knowledges, and ultimately of the dominant order, that true education is animated.

But to do this, it is necessary to exceed the three previous stages. To the positivist, one objects to its conservative closure, foundation of its false authority. To the critique borne by the new sociology, one objects that, in liquidating the principle of universality, it has prepared the way for a quasi-total grip of liberal capital on the education system, thought no longer being anything more than the mirror of the circulation of commodities, money, and the uninterrupted appetite for the 'novelty' of what's offered. To liberal education, finally, one objects that its imperative, 'live without Idea', definitively brings back education to what one could call a positivism of empty freedom.

To recreate education is therefore also to entirely pass beyond the three ideologies that have constrained and finally destroyed it: the positivist, the critical, and the liberal. To support this passage, A. J. Bartlett and Justin Clemens find the oldest name there is: Socrates-Plato. The whole collection can certainly vary this reference, not think of it, abandon it. It remains that the aim is the same, the care identical, and that the consequences are also homogenous: to restore education to its ideal point of invention returns, I repeat it simply, to nothing less than changing the world.

Introduction: What is Education? A Polemical Question

A. J. Bartlett and Justin Clemens

And we give to dominant opinion the strength of a strange beauty.

Alain Badiou

What is Education? is the deceptively simple question that we asked the contributors to this collection to address. Happily – and somewhat disturbingly – in each case no further elaboration proved necessary. All the contributors, themselves researchers and educators, seemed to appreciate immediately the logic of the question. For, in a contemporary situation replete with educational institutions and saturated by discourses 'of education', it is nevertheless necessary to take up once again the question of education. Despite this global institutionalisation and saturation there remains a lack, something critical to the history, thought and practice of education that education itself requires to be sought out. It is a somewhat paradoxical situation: never before has education been so ubiquitous and yet evidently so lacking. And in some sense this ubiquity has made the lack even more profound than previously, when formal education – institutional and theorised – was of almost no consequence to the organisation of states.

What we at once inferred from our contributors' responses is that what appears today of education is, to put it simply, not. What there is of education that makes it recognisable across epochs – invariant despite the vicissitudes of states, forms of rule, the power of money, or the charms of fashion – is today lacking under that name locally, as well as within the global system that functions in its name. The wager of this collection is that this lack exists, has a history, can be articulated in itself and affirmed as what is at the core of education here and now, as it has been before. Hence, the question *What is Education?* is a wager which declares that education exists, it must be found, refounded. The contributions to this volume, each in their own way, take up this wager as what is at stake for education locally and globally.

Context and Currency

This introduction will not summarise the variety of ways in which our contributors find and have found education. Rather, assuming that the contributors recognise this question as critical to what can be thought of education – which is to say theoretically and practically, without reduction of one to the other, thus neither a positivism nor a (social) constructivism – this introduction seeks to situate the question within its proper philosophical context. This is quite simply because education must be a matter of knowledge – of its production, its transmission, its use. Yet it is also a matter of the very framework or structure or logic of this knowledge. Every education transmits not just the content of its curriculum but also the form of the very knowledge it transmits. Broadly positivist educational theories in the twentieth century generally sidelined this aspect of education by concentrating on the 'objective' conditions of knowledge and transmission: 'just the facts, ma'am!' we might mark as its motto. This is to say that such theories accept that a body of knowledge exists that is critical to the reproduction of existing society; and not only positions within this society, but the very structure that guarantees these positions. This objective knowledge is then transmitted objectively, such that those subject to it will come to occupy these existing positions and thus reify and reproduce the structure itself.[1] This is a formulaic remark, of course, but it remains accurate and we would say that there remains in this discourse some utility beyond the utility it serves.

While this discourse has never gone away – indeed there are voices raised today that pine for its return – it has waned, usurped in its position as dominant discourse by what is usually called the 'new sociology' of education.[2] The new sociology dominates theoretically and thereby within educational policy too, which has translated itself into various practices familiar to students and teachers since the 1980s.[3] The new sociology is broadly constructivist in its philosophical framework even if it has mostly eschewed philosophy as such, as belonging to the positivist problem. The new sociology established its criticisms of positivism by suppressing in educational thinking and practice the very things central to its critique: the relations between knowledge, power, domination, hierarchy and stratification, and so on. In other words, it targeted the relations between social reproduction and the means of transmission, in effect arguing that schools and educational institutions broadly were the means of protecting status quo.

A whole new language was developed in this critique, which in some ways nonetheless broke down an already open door. After all, the positivist vision of education wanted much the same things: access to knowledge, equality and freedom. But the successful argument of the new sociology was that positivism was not a real education, that it falsified and misunderstood the stakes. In effect, then, the new sociology also held that education was lacking. Through empirical studies, diverse theoretical engagements – political, psychological, epistemological – the new sociology exposed the mechanisms of omission and selection involved in setting curriculum, exposing what came to be called the 'hidden curriculum' composed of ideological assumptions, political and economic commitments, notions of privilege and, critically, as an outcome of these factors, the pedagogical methods whereby students from different class backgrounds are a priori assigned to set positions in the structure by education itself. The same, moreover, was argued with relation to gender and race.[4]

The institutions themselves were subjected to the same critique, showing the variety of means at the state's disposal – accreditation, funding, staffing, architecture[5] – for directing and determining what they call today 'student outcomes'. These critiques were and are powerful – and when genuinely applied are still revelatory even in our cynical times. The unpleasant irony is that these critiques have in turn contributed to that very cynicism which, through repetition, is linked to a certain 'passive nihilism'.[6] More broadly speaking, the new sociology, which is coincident with and in many ways dependent on both critical theory and the so-called poststructuralist turn in contemporary theory, around the same time savagely criticised the state as a figure of authority making claims of a universal nature. If there is little doubt as to the necessity of this move, critical cynicism becomes nihilism at the point where any attempt to think universality is a priori deemed to be authoritarian, oppressive and dominating. Moreover, this attack on universality thereby renders it not only untenable, discursively and theoretically speaking, but also finally, unthinkable. In short, something is proscribed from knowledge a priori and so from what is education itself.

We admit that this summary works with very broad brushstrokes.

But let us also insist on the accuracy of its tenor; not least because, as we shall see in more detail below, every educational programme is bound up with fundamental propositions. The problem for the new sociology in thinking education, as for the generally postmodern tenor it supports, is that of making something new. Critique has opened up a multiplicity of worlds, so to speak, against the determinations of the One, but short of leaving everyone to their own devices, no new possibilities for collective action are thinkable because a priori any such thought is rendered impossible (that is, as an essentially false, inimical and pointless universal). The assumption is that any claim to universality repeats the worst. In the 1970s and 1980s this retreat from ideas, from their metaphysical heritage and from revolutionary frameworks like Marxism (including the ultimate implosion of the 'communist states') left a sort of void into which the only organised rationality still standing – capitalism – skipped happily. And it did so without any opposition to these critiques: capitalist enterprises, like almost everyone else, were not interested in going back to the future as such. Rather, what we now call neoliberalism – which was an educational project in its inception – ostensibly took as its own the ideological critique of the postmoderns.[7] Like the new sociology, neoliberalism celebrated the hollowing out of the state; liberation from constraint; freedom of choice, communication and information; flows, change, adaptation and resilience; the globalisation of networks against the universalisation of ideas; and so on. For neoliberalism, as for the new sociology, with the right knowledge individuals can make their way, can transform themselves from nothing to everything (if you don't mind the allusion).

Neoliberalism very rapidly became both content and form of the curricula it promulgated, and it did so partly by adopting many of the critical insights of 'radical' theory and putting them into practice. Just as Wall Street traders famously celebrate Marx's birthday – that great teacher of Capital! – in education, the critical ideas of the constructivist were being put into practice on the basis of their emancipatory promise: 'freedom from' is the neoliberal pass. We cannot detail the coincidence here and nor are we setting up critical theory as some sort of scapegoat in all this. We want only to remark that, within new sociological educational theory, as it developed and was incorporated into the policy frameworks of states and territories, its critical aspects become instrumentalised in the service of capital itself.[8]

Capitalism is after all the single greatest force for exploitation that has ever existed. In addition to its fundamental penchant for resorting to primitive accumulation whenever possible, its ideological mobility is unparalleled. It has exploited critical theory, constructivism, the new sociology, brilliantly. In many ways, this is a natural process. As states and territories seek knowledge of education for policy, they look to their own educational institutions, and adopt and adapt what they can. For example, what better way to reproduce in a subject the necessary knowledge of the existing state of things than to be able to 1) know their background, the psychological development of the child, its individual desires, its material needs, its talents and failings; and 2) know the ways and means and methods of making this happen as education, which is and remains the promise of freedom or of subjective transformation as such (but into what?). The point is that now the new methods, the new critiques have become themselves servants of the dominant order. Education functions as one of the central sites for the service of order. Indeed, with the markedly increased chatter about education over the last several years – heard at every school gate and middle-class dinner party – education has become the site of socioeconomic reproduction as at no other time.[9] In the new sociological critiques, something profoundly amenable to neoliberalism is insisted upon – and that is its relation to knowledge, or rather to knowledge in truth. In other words, its commitment to some form of the ineffable.

Education in this sense is now global, and this education is sold equally to all as the royal road to the only true freedom. But note that at the very point of its triumph, neoliberalism overreaches. To sell education as the only freedom is to mark the intrinsic, historical and conceptual link between education and freedom. This marking out, which occurs in a variety of ways within the discourses on education – transmission and transformation being crucial – is in a certain sense its very aporia or impasse. For if one were to ask the question of this freedom, then the question of what conditions or limits it would necessarily arise; if one were to ask after the form of this education, what constrains it and what determines it would necessarily arise; and if one were to ask after the form or conditions of this relation, its history, ideology, epistemology and its state power would necessarily arise. In other words, by means of its own marking out, the lack of education in the contemporary world of education would necessarily be set out. Our question, if nothing else, recognises that the implications of this impasse must be taken up, once again.

Having polemically described the dominant situation of education as we find it in its most determined global forms today – that is, as a form of critical neoliberalism which re-uptakes the new sociological critiques of positivist pedagogy in order to reintroduce zones of unquestionable ineffability into the realm of education – we will now change tack and try to set out the philosophical conditions for our question and our task. The conviction that 'education is lacking' has been an essential aspect of all policy from antiquity, yet, as we have been implying, there are many ways in which putative educators have parsed this principle. Here, we ourselves seek to give another inflection, another Idea, to this principle. If we repeat ourselves, it will be because pedagogy itself has demanded it!

Concept and Form

In the *Laws*, Plato stages a conversation that takes education as a central concern. For any possible conception of the just city requires that education be thought through. Not only is it a matter of the city but of philosophy too, whose task is justice: the equal participation of all in the Idea, which is to make it manifest. To make this idea manifest requires that everyone be educated, which in turn requires that education approach everyone justly, assuming their equal capacity for thought – precisely in regards to the thought of the idea. If this idea indeed becomes the thought of the collective, then everyone in the city, no matter the position they come to occupy, will be doing the work of justice – of making this idea manifest. Of course, the very condition of this possibility for Plato is that such a city will itself need to be made manifest. No such city exists, as he says, but it is not impossible. For Plato, philosophy is always necessarily a matter of education and, indeed, at Socrates' death he bequeaths this thinking to all who would pursue philosophy. It is demonstrable that this injunction truly has played itself out in the history of philosophy since.[10]

It is thus from Plato's demand in the *Laws* that this collection takes its cue: 'education should nowhere be despised, for when combined with great virtue, it is an asset of incalculable value. If it ever becomes corrupt, but can be put right again, this is a lifelong task which everyone should undertake to the limit of his strength.'[11] We will speak below about what this corruption amounts to, but in the *Laws* the challenge is issued (and taken up) precisely because education has come to name in the contemporary city only the ways and means of transmitting to the youth a knowledge whose generality masks the particularity of its genesis and ends. Education names an impasse whose content can be summed like this: it is both the knowledge of, and the means whereby, the current knowledge of the city as it is is reproduced as the only possible knowledge of any possible subject. This virtuous circle is exposed as impasse or aporia when the question is asked of this knowledge which education is determined to serve. This question, the simple question of Socrates and that of philosophy hitherto, which asks for the truth of this knowledge, is to break with this instrumental knowledge of education – assuming as it does another knowledge available to it. The full answer requires the matter of inquiry, but the key thing to note is that this question – which is asked of knowledge as such, a knowledge which, as educator, presumes to be the guarantee of all possible knowledge – already marks a point within this knowledge which cannot be of this knowledge itself. Knowledge, as it exists, must already secrete within itself a moment that it itself does not know.

This epistemological cyst (or aporia) is what we can call the point or place of a recommencement. Before we can un-think the knowledge of education that becomes the default form of all established 'states', we need to be able to isolate such a point. Clearly this thinking of education is a *philosophical* task, one, as noted, that has been taken up over and again in every philosophy since Plato, whether explicitly or implicitly, insofar as every philosopher must break at a point with the 'known' knowledge that they confront. This is the orientation of this collection: to intervene upon the knowledge of education current and determinant today; to show the character of its impasse, the knowledge and means of its reproduction, and to mark and set out another orientation to the question *What is Education?* In other words, what this book aims at is to insist that there is in the thinking of education something specific to it which education has taught us to forget.

Today, without any concealment, any hidden curriculum of old, education is formalised in institutions and oriented in its arrangement, curriculum and delivery by the demands and priorities of the 'state': economically, first, and socially and culturally thereafter. Formalised as it is, it is the predominant means of social reproduction, which is as much a 'horizontal' operation as a 'vertical' one. As philosophy has always recognised, this operation of reproduction is not free of antagonism. Antagonism is in fact immanent to the process. Education must transform its subject into one capable of social reproduction – of being in its desires, beliefs and actions in accord with the demands of the current state. However, that a subject capable of being ignorant of such demands must be presumed points to a knowledge of this demand that is not 'naturally' that of this state as such – another knowledge exists, even if it is just in the form of the *ignorance* of the correct forms of social reproduction.

Furthermore, the transformation sought by such education is itself inherently unstable, for it cannot mean only the transformation of ignorance into knowledge in the form of the demands of social reproduction. Transformation, more extensively, can also mean the transformation of these social relations themselves. In this sense, education aims at (the existence of) something beyond or despite or other to the demands of the state for social reproduction. Philosophy as critique and intervention has always aimed at this knowledge of education as transformation of the subject, politically speaking, as collective. Hence the everywhere evident desperation of existing states today to make sure that no such knowledge of transformation remains over in their formalisation of education. This is what is called reform today – the contest in 'innovative' and 'disruptive' ways to make this knowledge (of transformation) unknown.

If we understand that this antagonism is inherent to education, we can also understand that the history of the present form of education is a divided one, in the double sense that there is no linear progress in its concept or practice that today's version realises; rather it is the outcome of a concerted struggle over its constitution and institution. Moreover, and hence it being a site of this struggle, education is always already that which threatens to undo the very knowledge of itself at any given time in its history. That is to say, to be the means of the transformation of this knowledge itself. But to get to this point requires some sort of break.

There is a certain conceit in asking the question *What is Education?* This conceit takes several forms: the question clearly has a metaphysical ring to it, supposing as it does both a singular and universal answer. As such, it goes against the grain of contemporary consensus. Indeed the very form of the question itself supposes that contemporary discourse presents as a consensus and not, finally, as a diversity of competing arguments, theories or practices. The conceit of the question is compounded when we consider again the ubiquity of education: almost everywhere there are primary, secondary and tertiary institutions wherein education is prosecuted, and where these are lacking, there is the demand that there must be such institutions: there are faculties in universities for the study and teaching of education; there are journals and confer-ences the world over committed to all facets of education, theoretical and practical; and government departments to make policy for and of it, and complex bureaucracies to administer its functions; every elec-tion cycle affirms education's utility to the nation, to the economy, to the state; globally, there are both private and public bodies furthering its means and ends by every available technique and in all manner of ways. To ask what it is when it is everywhere deployed, everywhere enacted, everywhere known would seem to show a conceit bordering on a profound, perhaps wilful, ignorance. And, given the diversity of education's appearance, assuming that any answer would take the form of a singular universal appears at best anachronistic and at worst ide-alist. To approach the latter is bad enough, supposing as it does that there exists something like the truth of the thing in question, while the former is symptomatic of a clear failure to adapt to the 'rapids of change' that constitute the contemporaneity of the present, figuring the place of everyone subject to it.

Nevertheless, despite this ubiquity of the knowledge of education, it is also the case that education is everywhere said to be in crisis – at least if we listen to the *same* discourse. Indeed, education is both invoked as the answer to every crisis external to it – the spontaneous answer to every crisis of the economy and every perceived moral, psychological or politi-cal failing – yet education is itself always in crisis. There are crises of funding, of extension, of curriculum, of teaching, of policy, of outcomes, and so on. This discourse of crisis serves the interests of both left liberals and neo-conservatives: the former see the crisis (today) in the shape of neoliberalism, while the latter see it as a creature of left liberalism itself. As such, all repeat – necessarily, even vitally – the fundamental aporia of education itself, as bequeathed to us by Plato. We must have educa-tion; we already know what education is; education is lacking; we must have education . . . The kettle logic, as Sigmund Freud might have put it, is patent.

It is not worth the effort to detail here what is meant by these shifty public terms 'neoliberalism' or 'left liberalism', whose import is nonethe-less peculiarly perspicuous in the literature.[12] The point here is that all putative political positions share an orientation to education as a site of real effects, albeit one to be instrumentalised in the service of the vision of one or the other. In fact, almost all contemporary policy propos-als share something beyond their announced oppositions: a technical conception of education, which is the very aporia identified by Plato. In a certain sense, the very opposition is what inscribes this impasse as the knowledge of education. To speak very broadly, the widest range of critical thinking on education over the past century has fallen on one side or another of this technical conception – the means of decline and renewal. Education is then reduced to being the instrument of this *fort/da* game, rather than something that needs to be rethought with regard to the breaking of this impasse. In short, the impasse is characterised by the fact that all *dominant* positions – notwithstanding that a case could be made for their historical and political complicity *tout court* – still speak as if they *know* what education is.

There remains, then, extant and evident within this incredible ubiquity, signified by this rhetoric of crisis, a lack. Within the knowledge of education, there is the lack of education. Indeed, the entirety of the discourse of education works to fill this lack, which nevertheless keeps on appearing – thus precipitating the necessity of the continuation of the discourse on education. This circle raises the question of this form of the discourse on education or rather this knowledge of education which reproduces its own lack. It raises the question of knowledge itself, the form of knowledge producing its own lack, which it exists to fill. What is its logic? – and, yes, what is its metaphysics? As Gilles Châtelet reminds us, those who eschew metaphysics cannot help but do so on metaphysical grounds, which suggests that the very lack that the contemporary knowledge of education manifests – as its very necessity – might also be what is true of it.[13]

Formulaically: what the knowledge of education does not know, what it produces as its lack and what it must not know given the form of knowledge that it is, is its very truth. What it professes to know most assuredly it does not. Hence the question *What is Education?* is a question that *asks* after the truth of something from out of the ubiquity of its knowledge. The form of the question may be classical, but it is not a classical question, nor even an essentially idealist one. Rather, in the first instance, it is posed as an intervention into an existing discursive scene, exposing its latent metaphysics, its logical modality, with the aim of recommencing that scene in a new way – a way that will not reproduce a repetition of that into which it intervenes. The question supposes or even insists that a new knowledge of the thing itself is not impossible, and that it must belong fundamentally to that thing itself.

The form of the question *What is Education?* is flagrantly Socratic, which is really to say Platonic, but is ultimately to say *philosophical*. It is asked by Socrates in conversation in order to re-open any conversation too captured by circularity, and it reissues a challenge to the discussants to renew the investigation in discursive, enquiring or participatory terms that do not take their cue from the form of knowledge already extant. What Plato is gesturing towards when he deploys this obscure and axiomatic 'statement' *What is X?* – one he knots with Socrates' other great interventionary statements, *I know nothing* and *I am not a teacher* – is the Form of whatever is under inquiry. The interventions seek to provoke or even to force a reanimation of the discussion which has exhausted itself in debate precisely by being too well connected to what circulates as the ubiquitous or ordinary knowledge of the thing or situation as such.

For Plato, a Form, an Idea, is that which is not subject to becoming – to adaptation, innovation, the rapids of change, disruption and so on – and, as such, its definition per se, as opposed to its manifestation, is *not* a matter of inquiry, being as it is always the same or always invariant. In other words, and to invoke a paradox, the Form of established knowledge is the same 'lack', no matter by which means or under what conditions it is made to appear. Thus we can say that definition is what this Form conditions and names. This is why, for Plato's Parmenides, the Forms are the reason all discourse and knowledge is possible.[14] It is not the definition of the object in question that is at stake, but the knowledge or rather the truth of its Form. And it is *this* truth of *this* Form that must be made manifest as the good of the city. There is no other good at which education aims.

As such, our philosophical question, *What is Education?*, which is a question of all philosophy, seeks to illuminate the existence for discourse of that which animates and conditions the variety of its appearances. As we have suggested above, this is what is marked by the discourse on education itself as its constitutive lack, its invariant Form or Idea. What the question asks then is for the demonstration in thought or discourse of the existence of this Form – for the truth of the Form. Is there identifiable, demonstrable and invariant – which means, despite known knowledge, the determinant knowledge of any particular epoch in which education is thought – something of education which is not a contingent feature of the knowledge of an epoch while being at the same time the very condition for it? If there is some invariant of education, then it exists in excess of the knowledge brought to bear as education in any epoch. At this point there is the possibility to start again – without relativism or transcendence – to think what is 'true' of education, and to establish its effect.

In Plato's dialogues, from the first lines of the first dialogue, the *Apology*, to the last section of the last, the *Laws*, the true form of education is at stake whatever the immediate topic of concern.[15] Whether the inquiry concerns justice, being, knowledge or love, it is always considered in terms of transmission and for Plato in terms of transformation – of the individual into the subject of justice or love, and, crucially, as the individual, so the city too. As noted at the beginning of this Introduction, in the *Laws* Plato marks out for us the task of recommencement at the point of a corruption. He invokes this in the context of a discussion on how contemporary considerations of education reduce it to a utility function alone, thus a training in technique in the service of the state or the economy: 'A training directed to acquiring money or a robust physique, or even to some intellectual facility not guided by reason and justice, we should want to call coarse and illiberal, and say that it had no claim whatever to be called education.'[16] Plato concedes that we should not quibble about the name, but begin to attend again to the corruption of the thing itself. Whenever, wherever and by whomever education is announced, it is up to us to inquire as to the form of such an education.

Corruption has at least two senses in Plato, which are again relevant to our present situation and to the aim of this book. The first, intimated in the reduction of education to the logic of utility, is that education is a matter of contemporary and dominant interests: what education *must be*, coincident with its nature, is the means of social reproduction.[17] It must be the discourse and practice of the ways and means whereby the contemporary dominant interests are reproduced in the student as being in their interest. When, for example, Socrates asks Protagoras what the youth Hippocrates will receive from the master in exchange for his money, the master answers 'young man, if you come to me, your gain will be this: the very day you join me, you will go home a better man and the same the next day. Each day you will make progress towards a better state.'[18] Let us note, given that it fits within the remit of our question as an inquiry into the truth of things, that this Protagorean or exemplary sophistic education is in strict accord with its philo-sophistic position, a position which pointedly refuses to account for the being of things on the premise that such things, that they are, cannot be known and, if they cannot be known, then they are not. Protagoras' assertion concerning the gods is further illustrative of his commitment to the ineffable: 'I am unable to know whether they exist or do not exist or what they are like in form; for there are many hindrances to knowledge, the obscurity of the subject and the brevity of human life.'[19]

A virtuous circle of transmission is thereby established as sophistry, wherein interest (that 'necessary' to social reproduction) is the object of reflection proper to any 'educated' subject, and 'to know' is to be properly instructed in an interest in interest. This is thereby the real content and form of all teaching structured by an object impossibility which is beyond transmission itself. For Plato, who makes great play with the term *tokos*, both physical reproduction or 'offspring' *and* interest on a loan, such an exchange of interests was anathema: first, because it guaranteed the false division of the state into classes predicated on particularities that had utility but no truth; secondly, because there is absolutely no equation, as there is in the sophistic promise, between education and money, truth and profit. For Plato, such teachings are predicated on an excessive conceit regarding what constitutes knowledge. The sophists were the teachers of this sort of interest, who made themselves available to the well-off youth of the city as the means of guaranteeing the latter's access to what it had to offer. Hence, the sophists are the agents of the repetition of known knowledge – which is what such an education amounts to. Such an education is only a diversity of techniques such that the dominant interests are reproduced and, in this way, coincidently, each subject, full of potential, is assigned its proper place within this knowledge.

If in Plato's Athens what he all but calls a generalised sophistry pervades – albeit one with *internal* tensions and oppositions of its own and in its own terms producing teachers of brilliance, of renown *and* opprobrium – whose effect was to reproduce the dominant form of social relations, this was not ultimately where the problem of corruption lay.[20] Rather, it was in the very *conceit* of this knowledge: that such knowledge was all there was to know, which is to say, that there must not be any other knowledge. This occlusion is what Plato's Socrates targets: this corruption of knowledge itself as known; that it is the (only) knowledge of all; that there is known (to be) an (unknown) limit beyond which 'man' cannot go.

Clearly, the question *What is X?* targets this very claim – to know what cannot be known – to expose its lack and seek to undo this ubiquitous state of the corruption of knowledge and, more importantly, the education that it affects as its own and as the only education. Once Plato's

Socrates starts to drill down on this question, so to speak, the lack of such knowledge is readily exposed and, as we know, this exposure of 'a hole in known knowledge' is not appreciated: not only by the sophists whom he encounters, but even more so not by the poets, the men of the law courts, the businessmen, the generals or, finally, the majority of his fellow citizens. Socrates is singled out thereby at his trial as the only one in all Athens *who does not educate*.[21] But Plato, by showing or *trying* across the dialogues the inherent corruption of this knowledge itself, is able to turn the charge against Socrates of singular educational corruption upside down (as Callicles notes) such that – since he knows nothing of this knowledge and doesn't teach it – it is he alone who is not corrupt, and thus is the sole figure whose efforts are directed at the ongoing corruption of this corrupt education.[22] Hence the ignorant and non-transmissive form of the intervention *What is Education?* In this sense, the 'lifelong task' that Plato bequeaths to philosophy is this Socratic one – to every time take up the challenge of education at the point of its contemporary impasse.

The Contemporary Impasse

So what is the contemporary impasse? Structurally, we can say that it is the same as that which Plato identifies – indeed historically, which is to say that, since Plato, the same impasse returns over and again in diverse guises. Effectively, it is the impasse of the totalisation of knowledge whose paradoxical character is not as such to know everything but to know what cannot (or must not) be known. Educationally, it is this very form of knowledge that must be transmitted, being all there is; indeed, that education bears upon all there is to know of knowledge is what is ultimately at stake.

Note that it is not that all knowledge is transmitted – after all, individuals only scratch the surface of what is available of knowledge. But what is taught to all and thus, if you like, what makes this all 'subject' in the same way (thus imitating the philosophical conception) is that *there is no knowledge other than this knowledge of all*. The knowledge that knowledge is lacking is what ensures it is knowledge as such. All instrumental treatments of education presume this totalisation of knowledge. One must learn what it is that this knowledge requires to be learned such that it will be remade as this knowledge. So whatever you learn – mathematics, art, a trade, coding, to teach – refers itself back to the knowledge which circulates as such in the city or in the epoch, and of which knowledge is lacking. One practises one's acquired learning or knowledge in the city as it is. Education cannot extend beyond this frame of reference and one's knowledge is a reflection of the knowledge of the time, its *reflexivity*, we might say.

Of course, knowledge is not the same in different epochs. Its content differs relative to the site of its totalisation and the material conditions of the time. For a long period God occupied the place of totalisation to which all forms of transmission were subject, and all subjects – from tentmakers to knights, poets to blacksmiths – were formed in relation to this transmission, oriented to the absolute unknowable God. Today we have what is called a 'knowledge economy' or, less guarded because more assured, a 'cognitive capitalism'. The economy takes the place of God in the structural framework. The virtue, indeed the selling point, is that the greatest diversity of knowledges circulate, are taught and reproduced within this 'market of ideas'. But no matter what, the reflexivity of the knowledge of these knowledges is what is crucial. One practises one's trade in the generalised form of this economy, or *essentially* one does not. As Marx said, this is the chemical power of capital: '[it] turns each of [our] powers into something which in itself it is not – turns it, that is, into its contrary'.[23] It is no coincidence that one of Marx's examples of the 'subjective incapacity' – the incapacity to be otherwise subject – that this inversion convokes is the fellow with the 'vocation' to study but who, without capital, effectively has no such vocation. By contrast, the fellow with no desire to study but the capital to do so effectively has such a vocation. Real powers, the vocation to study, are turned into 'abstract representations', while impotent powers existing in the imagination alone become effective and 'real essential powers and abilities'.[24] In the knowledge economy this is our educational *raison d'état*.

But in this we see again that a certain lack is also reproduced. There can be no knowledge of what guarantees this knowledge; so no knowledge of the market, just as there is no knowledge of God itself. There is, then, in all the knowledges taught and transmitted and reproduced, also the knowledge that what orients all knowledge, what effectively makes it useful, interested and vital for the life of an epoch, is itself unknowable or indeed *ineffable*. In other words, the knowledge of education exceeds education itself as its ineffable foundation or its lack. Thus we have a strange education insofar as it teaches as itself a certain impossibility to know – it teaches that we cannot know or, indeed, at the risk of the subject's very dissolution, that *we must not know*.

Moreover, and with particular concern for the subject – that which any education seeks to produce – when knowledge is structured by a conception of the ineffable, the subject of this knowledge is always mutable, always *potentially* one more thing, flexible and endlessly capable of adaptation to whatever precedes it as its 'real'. Crucially, this means that the subject is never one thing at all, and this becomes the new impossibility built into the subject of knowledge: the impossibility of holding on to something *against* the vicissitudes of knowledge. Structurally speaking, where this knowledge produces its own lack as that which it exists to fill, subjectively speaking it must produce a subject whose only commitment is to the impossibility of commitments *tout court*. Lack and impossibility frame any such education.

This is the 'paradox' of the corruption of education by knowledge. We cannot un-know this knowledge as such, at least not from within that knowledge which insists as guarantee of the very coherence of the diversity of knowledges or techniques. What the Socratic question instantiates here and now, so to speak, is an *other* orientation to this knowledge from *within* it. To think is (to begin) to know nothing of that knowledge – this is the unbearable 'illegal' point that Socrates holds – and from that ignorance what he sets out to do – in inquiry after inquiry – is to make this knowing nothing of that knowledge manifest as what is for all. In a way, Socrates transmits the unknowing of this knowledge – that is the power of *his* corruption – but he does so not in *opposition* to known knowledge as such, for he is not a debater. Rather, as noted, he sets out from the point of its lack, which is to say from the unknown truth of this knowledge of education, which it exposes to be there, in order to expose it to anyone and everyone as what education truly is. The paradoxical means available for this – transformation – means that, by this transformation, an entirely other subject is possible, which is to say that known knowledge, the knowledge of the city or epoch, is no longer currency or, perhaps, is only currency. We could suggest that what passes under the term neoliberalism – a fundamentally and self-consciously pedagogical project – names the combination of this sophistic vision of knowledge in its contemporary form and the 'determination in the last instance' of an economic rationalism.

In these terms we can understand our contemporary situation. On the one side, it is quite plain and simple. What has been called the logic of capital – or now, commonly, neoliberalism – has come to reconstitute all forms of social relation, all forms of the social bond. It is the knowledge of all contemporary knowledges, and what is called education is a key and effective means of this domination. Alain Badiou gives singular force to the paradoxical negativity of this positive constitution: 'the State,' Badiou asserts, 'is not founded upon the social bond, which it would express, but rather upon un-binding, which it prohibits'.[25]

In the twentieth century, in which this logic or this set of relations came to affirm itself as without alternative, as in some sense the good itself, education also came of age, so to speak, insofar as it become fully institutionalised; first across the West (including what used to be called the communist bloc), and slowly but surely across what is called by this West 'the developing world'. The very development of institutionalised education in the developing world is historically, economically and politically tied to the West. One continues to find the formidable nature of this post-colonialism in the policy and curricular prescriptions of bodies like UNESCO and the World Bank and, increasingly, in corporations like Microsoft, Cisco and even BP, who are more and more assuming the role of educational entrepreneurs. Moreover, these same entities, making free use of so-called 'critical pedagogies', have also been heavily involved in 'adjusting' the ex-communist world to the new paradigm (as they are the public *within* the West more generally). The framework here is clearly one of economic utility – primarily technological and managerial – which we don't rule out from the thought of education, unlike the idealist tradition that considers education to exist and to function for its own sake – a position that veils (but is not ignorant of) a whole raft of structural determinations.[26] At this level, then, education is unthinkable as anything but an instrument of a higher knowledge – which we have called 'the knowledge of education' – and clearly this higher knowledge of education is off limits to education itself *at a particular point*, given that such education is constrained by being a particular use of this same knowledge. In other words, it is prohibited that a knowledge exists that is other than that which is a guarantee of this virtuous link between knowledge, subject and state. Known knowledge functions as prohibition.

Education *for* All

The Platonic short-circuit of this coincidence – whereby fundamentally opposed political positions treat education in exactly the same way, thus sharing a predicate beyond their putative opposition – is to link education to its truth, which in Platonic terms is justice. Education must be that of which every subject is capable. In other words, education enacts as itself the capacity of all for justice, and so any knowledge of education that enacts anything less is not an opposing position on what education is, but rather *no* education at all. This is what Callicles, in the *Gorgias*, described as *the world turned upside down*,[27] wherein the education of Socrates, declared by the state to be non-existent, becomes what is education for all. So the education of the market state, which necessarily and admittedly reproduces an in-egalitarian or unjust set of social relations 'for all' – for which equality is *subjectively* impossible – must at the level of our question not be what *education* names. In other words, any form of knowledge predicated upon injustice cannot properly educate, no matter the ubiquity or the variousness of its transmission, and no matter how well instituted it may be. Indeed, such education must remain forever in crisis insofar as it continues to prohibit questions as to its own lack.

The difference we are articulating here can be summed in a formula. On the one side, concerning the different forms of its utility, there is the education *of* all; on the other, that which holds to the intrinsic justice of education, that *there is* no unjust education, there is an education *for* all. In the former sense, all are educated to the ends of social reproduction, *whatever* the organisation of that society. On the other, education insists as what is *for* all despite interest, and thus education is the manifest production in each and every epoch of justice as such. When education is correlated to a higher knowledge, there is the education *of* all in *this* knowledge. When education functions as the very means by which justice is itself manifest as the form of the social relation, we have an education *for* all. In the latter case, justice is assumed as 'here and now', orienting all education and its effects.

Clearly the question *What is Education?* demands that such an education – 'for all' but *not* 'of all' – be thought, that is, demonstrated to exist.[28] This leaves us a task: we need to find in the history of education those invariants that demonstrate its existence. The wager of our question is that such invariants exist. To offer a metaphor of the method: we would examine every epoch of education in its distinction, selecting in each variation manifest traits, procedures, approaches, methods and effects that are the same in each, despite differences of time, place and domination. To isolate these together would be to demonstrate what education is – which is Plato's challenge.

Such an approach, then, aims to short-circuit the false oppositions between distinct social or political positions which treat education as an adjunct of their 'higher knowledge'; which, in other words, tie it inextricably to some form of the state as its means of reproduction. This is not to say that education in the old Soviet bloc, for example, aimed at the same reproduction as that of the capitalist world. Rather, what both share is that education must not operate relative to any other orientation than such reproduction, which is the good of the state. Within the framework given to education to reproduce, education can be the means or driver or reflection of all manner of reforms or innovations, just as it can include within its reproductions all manner of identities – racial, gender, ethnic, class and so on.

The promise of this good is what is for sale today in the extension of the commodity form to education itself. But given this idea of education as social utility, these innovations and reforms can never contest the form of these social relations themselves. Paradoxically, even in the equal admittance into education of all manner of identities, this admittance promising to each the possibility of *individual* mobility across the socioeconomic field (and thus not at all *social* mobility as is often declared)[29] requires that these identities be reproduced as the condition of this possibility. That is to say that education as a utility of a higher knowledge only acts on what is already counted to exist – the raft of identities and differences socially produced *prior* to any education. Such education must remain *representational*, as it assigns these existents to one of any number of pre-established places deemed available to it. This is the double bind of what Jacques Lacan parodically calls the 'service of goods', the crisis of endless reforms progressing towards their supposed ends – but never the end of reform itself.[30]

The Polemic of the Question

Let us sum this up with some polemical force, directed to the present. What Plato's sophists taught for money – very good money in some cases – was the knowledge of the state: better and worse, success and failure, necessary technique. Sophistry sells whatever works to this end, without discrimination as to its good – selling whatever sells – by teaching the youth that the interests of the state are in its interest. In this sense, knowledge and the state are synonymous, implicative. Socrates names the procedure for not knowing this knowledge. Today, more completely than at any other time, education is reduced to being the training ground for good state subjects, as so many policy and curriculum documents, no less than course descriptions, now excitedly attest. The rhetoric of employability, job readiness, adaptation, flexibility, resilience and so on – all of which see the subject in no other terms than that of 'human resources', that great concept of none other than Josef Stalin – permeates and determines the educational discourse of the so-called West and those determined to follow its 'lead'. The educational systems of the latter – ex-Soviet as much as post-colonial – have been humanitarianly intervened-on in the name of the good of education. As noted above, such a good requires, the World Bank tells us:

flexible and nimble institutions and policy frameworks that can adapt to rapid change, and a creative and entrepreneurial private sector that can exploit new opportunities that emerge from that rapid change. Thus creating a society of skilled, flexible and creative people, with opportunities for quality education and life-long learning available to all, and a flexible and appropriate mix of public and private funding.[31]

This is the good the educated West trades on in its interest, repeated in policy documents and faculties of education everywhere without remorse. As Marx noted: 'Whenever it comes across evil it attributes it to its own absence, for, if it is the only good, then it alone can create the good.'[32]

The nineteenth-century dreams of figures like J. K. Shuttleworth[33] – tasked with getting state education off the ground in the UK – for an education that 'promot[es] the diffusion of that knowledge among the working classes which tends beyond anything else to promote the security of property, an appreciation of free trade and the maintenance of public order' are in our age decidedly real and realised.[34] In his excellent if sardonic book, *Rethinking the School: Subjectivity, Bureaucracy, Criticism*, Ian Hunter celebrates Shuttleworth as an unsung hero, bringing to his task 'a non-ideological pragmatism'.[35] Shuttleworth's work as chief pedagogue and saviour of the poor had already caught Marx's attention. Among the pointed critiques, and with a sharper eye for irony than Hunter perhaps, he situated the type: 'the pedagogue takes his place among, and in the service of, the various social reformers, economists, philanthropists, humanitarians, improvers of the conditions of the working class, organisers of charity, members of societies from the prevention of cruelty to animals, temperance fanatics, hole and corner reformers of every imaginable kind'.[36] Each, by these very 'socialist' means (we would say democratic today), seeks only to secure and conserve the continuation of the rule of capital.

Today, UNESCO documents re-present this same non-ideological pragmatism in assigning the moniker 'Low Development Capacity' to countries long ravaged by colonialism and capitalism:[37] a history that UNESCO obscures in its telling, lest it subtract, ironically, from the historical narrative of (subjective) incapacity. This assignation means in effect that these countries qualify for (are now 'ripe for') educational intervention: the model of education being that which makes their country capitalism-ready, in the same way that students today are to be rendered job-ready.

A single example of this global complicity:

UNESCO supports countries in developing strong, holistic and balanced educational systems, and developing the capacities of all stakeholders is essential. We have devised the UNESCO Capacity Development for Education for All programme (CapEFA) for this purpose, pooling funding from different donors to help countries improve the effectiveness of their educational systems. One example of the implementation of this scheme was Côte d'Ivoire, where the challenges included insufficient links between the labour market and training availability, outdated curricula, and lack of quality data.[38]

The problem today is not that neoliberalism is trying to take over education, as so many critical pedagogues, archi-liberals and nineteenth-century-Cardinal-Newman-imitating gentlefolk idealists think (thus maintaining their 'professional' 'critical distance'): the problem today is that *education is now itself neoliberal.* Neoliberalism is the contemporary form of the state. It is the *knowledge of capital.* It provides the norm by which reality is constructed, and by which subjects are created – exactly what the cabal of the Mount Pelerin Society set out for it to be some 70 years ago and which they have achieved: 'a thoroughgoing re-education effort for all parties to alter the tenor and meaning of political life: nothing more, nothing less'.[39] Shuttleworth's dream of free trade for all in public schools is now the everyday knowledge of the school. As Naomi Klein, among others, points out, Chile, après coup and under the pedagogical sway of the Chicago School of Economics,[40] was the contemporary model for living this old dream.[41]

The globalised pedagogy of Mt Pelerin squares with the key idea that animates Emile Durkheim's brilliant study of the history of the school in France: 'that the forms and methods of didactic organization depend on the way in which, in a determined age, the general organization of knowledge is conceived, and above all on how the opening of knowledge towards thought itself is seen. . .'[42] Hence the neoliberal pedagogies which we have embraced and reconciled as the 'knowledge economy': not simply knowledge for sale or reduced like all else to the commodity form, but knowledge as economy itself; economy, the law of the state *qua* household as all-knowing and thus itself unknowable, which, as Agamben shows us, means we are under the administration of angels.[43] What the 'better angels of our nature' occlude, which is their one and only true job, is the opening to thought of this unknowable guarded by some God or other. What Plato demanded as the work of us all, what the current angels of our flexible and flux-able nature occlude, is the thought of education itself.

As noted, Durkheim's observation also includes the contemporary critiques of this form of 'state education'. Thus a further problem remains for thinking education against the market sophistry of today, given that, as we have argued, the great bulk of this critique, emerging out of the 1970s and 1980s – critiques of curriculum, institutional arrangements, the epistemological, psychological and political context and so on – and lately among the enthusiasts of the techno-logo cognoscenti – who provide the edifying site of accusations as to the almost terroristic lack of educational 'innovation' or 'disruption' – shares with the 'knowledge economy' an epistemological predicate: ostensibly that the subjective capacity to know is bound at the limit by some conception of the unknowable or inaccessible or ineffable or unsayable or indeterminate.

We have polemically tracked in this introduction the re-presentation of the sociological critiques of education by contemporary neoliberalism, in order to suggest how such an education must prohibit the thinking of its own lack. This prohibition renders the lack in education ineffable, and thus, in a certain determining sense, a religious matter: 'The solemn and sanctimonious declaration that we can have no knowledge of this or that always foreshadows some obscure devotion to the Master of the unknowable, the God of the religions or his placeholders.'[44] Today education, given over to the nomadic predations of state logic – there is nowhere it cannot go – is the taught knowledge of the lack of education. This is not a paradox but the divided logic of the systemic necessity inscribed in all education today to *not* hold fast. We might call it the *real* hidden curriculum. As Durkheim points out, in the text already cited, with specific reference to education, to what is true for it: 'the recurrent and never fully solvable tension between thinking and knowledge is the rule rather than the exception'.[45] In other words, the thinking of education needs again to be *unbound* from its knowledge and this is why we ask again the question 'what is education?' Our current task is not only to make manifest the lack of and in education, but to establish an orientation that enables us all to continue to inquire as to the consequences of what it means that education must not simply be of all, but for all. This collection is a contribution to this other orientation; that what education is comes once again to exist.

Notes

1. The positivism referred to here, although evoking figures like Auguste Comte and Emile Durkheim, both of whom wrote brilliantly on education (and taught their entire lives), is already a derivation and a reduction of these more extensive conceptions. Educational positivism is something more like a combination of logical positivism's anti-metaphysical or anti-speculative attitude and pragmatism's assertion of evidence by consequence. In other words, there are empirical facts of the matter that we rationally discern and dispose and whose outcomes prove the approach. This attitude to thought and thus to education has returned today in the guise of the assertion that knowledge is itself only 'evidence based'. This comes with the implicit coda that what underpins this new empiricism conceptually speaking is of no matter to the veracity of the assertion and of no consequence in regard to its outcomes. This is what its objectivity thereby amounts to. For a good general overview of 'positivist education', see for example D. C. Phillips, 'After the Wake: Postpositivistic Educational Thought', *Educational Researcher*, 12(5) (1983), pp. 4–12 and M. R. Matthews, 'Reappraising Positivism and Education: The Arguments of Philipp Frank and Herbert Feigl', *Science and Education*, 13(1–2) (2004), pp. 7–39.
2. For an overview on this, see P. Worsley (ed.), *The New Modern Sociology Readings* (London: Penguin, 1991), esp. Part V, pp. 185–228.
3. The following provide the basis of our very general remarks here: P. Bourdieu and J.-C. Passeron, *The Inheritors: French Students and their Relation to Culture*, trans. R. Nice (Chicago: University of Chicago Press, 1979); S. Bowles and H. Gintis, *Schooling in Capitalist America* (New York: Basic Books, 1976); M. Foucault, *Discipline and Punish: The Birth*

of the Prison, trans. Alan Sheridan (New York: Pantheon Books, 1977); P. Freire, *Education: The Practice of Freedom* (London: Writers and Readers Publishing Collective, 1974); H. Giroux and S. Aronowitz, *Education under Siege: The Conservative, Liberal, and Radical Debate over Schooling* (London: Routledge and Kegan Paul, 1986); W. Pinar (ed.), *Curriculum Theorizing: The Reconceptualists* (Berkeley: McCutchan, 1975).

4. The now familiar term 'hidden curriculum' is usually credited to Philip W. Jackson, taken from his important book *Life in Classrooms* (New York: Holt, Rinehart and Winston, 1968).

5. On the extension of this along the lines of a militarised and corporate form, see K. J. Saltman and D. A. Gabbard (eds), *Education as Enforcement: The Militarisation and Corporatisation of Schools* (New York and London: Routledge Falmer, 2003).

6. 'The transitive action of passive nihilism results from the fact that it is always a defeated belief, a belief that has come undone. Alas, the trajectory which, beginning with belief, leads to fatalism by way of passive nihilism has been the trajectory of a considerable part of my generation. The final maxim of this process is "We are right to be satisfied with little" . . . they wish to convey to the young the idea that the essence of discordance consists in the defeat of beliefs, the crisis of ideologies, the crash of Marxism . . .' A. Badiou, *Theory of the Subject*, trans. B. Bosteels (London: Verso, 2011), p. 329. Writing in 1982, Badiou notes that passive nihilism has fatalism ahead of it.

7. See P. Mirowski and D. Plehwe (eds), *The Road from Mont Pèlerin: The Making of the Neoliberal Thought Collective* (Cambridge, MA: Harvard University Press, 2009).

8. Today, for example, a notion like 'life-long learning' (something of a brand name), due entirely to its capture by the contemporary state, works on the premise that at any time any skills one possesses may be rendered useless to the state-economy, and once again the worker becomes a site for a new inscription. Life-long learning, or as Rancière calls it, 'society pedagogicised', can operate thereby as something like an ideological terrorism, whose aim is to realise further the disempowering of workers in all non-privileged sectors. Rancière defines this 'pedagogicisation' as 'the general infantilisation of the individuals that make it up'. Thus, as first and foremost a state function, education functions to disarm those it claims to empower. J. Rancière, *The Ignorant Schoolmaster: Five Lessons in Intellectual Emancipation*, trans. K. Ross (Stanford: Stanford University Press, 1991), pp. 130–1. In similar vein, Ivan Illich notes that

'[w]e permit the state to ascertain the universal educational deficiencies of its citizens and establish one specialised agency to treat them. We thus share in the delusion that we can distinguish between what is necessary for education for others and what is not, just as former generations established laws which defined what was sacred and what was profane.' Ivan Illich, *Deschooling Society* (London: Penguin, 1971), p. 30. The documents put out by education departments are legion, but here is a prime contemporary example that concretises this new phalanx of critical theories and capitalism that forms what we might call the 'neo-liberal sublime'. 'The characteristics,' this document says, 'needed by schools for the emerging information age [are] flexibility; the capacity to problem solve; to adapt to new demands, new markets, new information and new strategic goals. Quality schools will divest themselves of traditional industrial age and bureaucratic restraints to reinvent as dynamic learning organisations in learning communities.' Education Queensland, *Queensland State Education 2010* (Brisbane: Education Queensland, 2000), p. 10. Education NSW, going further, is explicit in stating that those who remain outside a proper state education have a negative effect on Australia. '[The] mores or values' described by Education NSW as intrinsic to its educational system are those which 'contribute to our democracy, have respect for the rights of property, that actively suppor[t] economic development (and the conservation of the environment)'. These along with many others, give 'cohesion, identity and purpose, enabling us to gain our entitlements, and carry out our duties *within* the prevailing political and legal framework'. These will deliver a student who is 'flexible, adaptable, capable of a form of self-analysis that copes with this flexibility' and possesses an 'educability – for retraining across the life-span through a range of media'. The student will be 'capable of designing him/herself a social future', be proficient in 'the *care and maintenance of the self* and practise an 'active citizenship – *within* our democracy'. Education NSW, 'Excellence and Innovation: A consultation with the community of NSW on public education and training' (2004), p. 3, www.det.nsw.edu.au (accessed 6 January 2017).

9. '[C]reating globally competitive knowledge-based economies requires a coherent, proactive strategy that reaches across many different sectors, encompassing areas as diverse as information infrastructure, research and innovation systems, education and life long learning, and government policy and regulatory frameworks. Most importantly, it requires

flexible and nimble institutions and policy frameworks that can adapt to rapid change, and a creative and entrepreneurial private sector that can exploit new opportunities that emerge from that rapid change. Thus creating a society of skilled, flexible and creative people, with opportunities for quality education and life-long learning available to all, and a flexible and appropriate mix public and private funding.' From the same document: 'As in every case of dramatic and sustained economic growth, the reasons for Ireland's boom are complex. However, there is broad consensus that two factors in particular fuelled Irish growth: education and foreign direct investment, the former being a precondition for the latter.' Let's forget that the miracle busted, but let's note how education is positioned here as *the* prerequisite for capitalist exploitation. World Bank, 'Building Knowledge Economies: Opportunities and Challenges for EU Accession Countries', final report of the Knowledge Economy Forum 'Using Knowledge for Development in EU Accession Countries', organised by the World Bank in cooperation with the European Commission, the Organization for Economic Cooperation and Development, the European Bank for Reconstruction and Development, and the European Investment Bank Paris, 19–22 February 2002, May 2002, http://siteresources.worldbank.org/ EXTECAREGTOPKNOECO/Resources/Building_Knowledge_Ec onomies_final_final.pdf (accessed 1 February 2017).

10. For a full elaboration of this premise, see A. J. Bartlett, *Badiou and Plato: An Education by Truths* (Edinburgh: Edinburgh University Press, 2011/ 15).

11. Plato, *Laws*, trans. T. J. Saunders, in *Complete Works*, ed. J. M. Cooper and D. S. Hutchinson (Indianapolis: Hackett, 1997), 644a–b.

12. Probably no one has done more to highlight and combat the neoliberal assault on public education and thereby the very concept of the public itself than Henry Giroux. We by no means wish to denigrate Giroux's work on this, nor that of those many liberal democrats working in this effort. We do, however, want to focus attention on what we see as an un-thought complicity in the metaphysics as it were of both positions, affecting knowledge and thus what is education. An excellent place to begin with Giroux's extensive work is *Neoliberalism's War on Higher Education* (Chicago: Haymarket Books, 2014).

13. See G. Châtelet, *To Live and Think Like Pigs: The Incitement of Envy and Boredom in Market Democracies*, trans. R. Mackay (New York: Urbanomic/ Sequence Press, 2014).

14. See Plato, *Parmenides* 135bc (trans. Mary Louise Gill and Paul Ryan), and *Sophist* 259e–260 (trans. Nicholas P. White), in Cooper and Hutchinson (eds), *Complete Works*.
15. See again Bartlett, *Badiou and Plato: An Education by Truths*.
16. Plato, *Laws* 644a.
17. As Dewey puts them together: 'what nutrition and reproduction are to physiological life, education is to social life'. J. Dewey, *Democracy and Education* (New York: The Free Press, 1966), p. 9. In a recent book, *Undoing the Demos: Neoliberalism's Stealth Revolution* (New York: Zone Books, 2015), Wendy Brown, arguing that neoliberalism has eroded democracy, nevertheless considers education to be the instrument of a properly functioning democracy. Whatever the merits of the argument, and they amount to a contemporary restatement of Dewey's position, it is still the case that education is supposed known; hence its instrumental function as the saving grace of American liberalism. Let us note one thing: Brown makes the claim that the liberal arts education – ubiquitous to American universities post war – that she is defending against the neoliberal assault was instrumental in many of the broadly liberal democratic (and even revolutionary) social movements of the 1960s and 1970s – 'the civil rights movement, feminism, sustained challenges to inequality and to Cold War ideology, and an explosion of other justice minded cultural, artistic, and civic practices' (188). Of course, this may or may not be true for America, but that same education was had by those of the ruling class and the consensual middle classes who actively opposed those movements and who, through neoliberalism, have so far wrung a great victory out of it. Can we really say, *within the terms of this debate*, that these latter have not been 'properly' educated? If so, we need a conception of education that is not shackled to the terms of this debate. Moreover, how would this claim as to the vital democratic utility of a liberal arts education account for the revolutionary masses across the world who actively participated in the real and extensive changing of their world – few of whom were liberally educated? Indeed, how does this account for those American participants who did not receive a 'college education', which was of course, and remains, most people? And this to speak only of the twentieth century! Or would Brown say that democracy or the desire for it or knowledge of it played no part in these movements? If not, how did they come by this knowledge or desire of democracy? To be sure, Brown, as a democrat, is only essentially arguing for the assured existence of

an oppositional framework for a healthy polity, not necessarily for the victory of one side or another, and thus that there is no position extant today to take up one side of this opposition is a clear point of her critique. Of course, as she points out, the irony is that the elite universities who train the ruling class are those alone capable today of continuing this liberal arts tradition – as a sort of veneer or sheen. Although she doesn't mention this, this is actually a repetition (because the social conditions enable it) of the pre-mass education era in which the sons (and later) daughters of the ruling class were sent to be educated in a manner befitting their already assured positions. Thus they were effectively 'cultured'. Of course, this culture or education in turn could then be used (as it is again) as retroactive justification for their right to rule. Being the better educated, it is only proper that they rule for the good of all. Thus, even at this level, education remains an *instrument* of great effect.

18. Plato, *Protagoras* 318a (trans. S. Lombardo and K. Bell), in Cooper and Hutchinson (eds), *Complete Works*.

19. Diogenes Laertius, *Lives of Eminent Philosophers*, trans. R. D. Hicks (London: Heinemann, 1925), 9.41. In his semi-mock recapitulation of Protagoras' ideas in *Theaetetus*, Socrates has Protagoras state that 'In education what we have to do is to change a worse state into a better one . . . the professional teacher does it by use of words'. *Theatetus* 167a (trans. M. J. Levett, rev. M. Burnyeat). He goes on to say that if the teacher can achieve this, he is worthy of his large fees (*Theat.* 167d). Cf. *Apology* 20bc. Citing Apelt citing the Dialexis (an anonymous summary of arguments believed to be based on the lectures of fifth-century sophists), Cornford notes that they really did believe that mastery of eristic discourse gave them the means to pronounce upon any matter from medicine to law to the running of the city and the ordering of men. *Plato's Theory of Knowledge: The Theaetetus and the Sophist*, trans. F. M. Cornford (Mineola, NY: Dover, 2003), p. 191, n. 3.

20. There is a tension between the sophists and the good citizens of Athens, as remarked by Anytus in the *Meno*. However, Plato shows already in that dialogue that Anytus' own knowledge and thereby the arguments he makes share too much with those of the generalised sophistry on offer, and thus the good citizen of Athens who, Anytus claims, any youth can turn to for an education far superior to that offered by sophists is in fact itself sophistic.

21. Plato, *Apology* 25a (trans. G. M. A. Grube), in Cooper and Hutchinson (eds), *Complete Works*.

22. Even a non-Platonist like Althusser acknowledges this in our own time when, in criticising education as the new primary form of the ideological state apparatus, he makes the case for those few teachers who, within this framework, struggle for its undoing. See 'Ideology and the State', in *Lenin and Philosophy and Other Essays*, trans. B. Brewster (New York: Monthly Review Press, 2001), pp. 98–9. It is worth noting that in a proto-Althusserian fashion, Plato claims that if anyone doesn't succumb to the 'present state of society' by means of this educational process, there are fines, punishments and even death for those who fail to achieve the correct qualifications: 'And yet we haven't mentioned the greatest compulsion of all . . . It's what these educators and sophists impose by their actions if their words fail to persuade. Or don't you know that they punish anyone who isn't persuaded, with disenfranchisement, fines, or death.' *Republic*, 492d (trans. G. M. A. Grube, rev. C. D. C. Reeve), in Cooper and Hutchinson (eds), *Complete Works*. A recent Australian education policy document noted that those who 'fail' to be so educated constitute a threat to themselves and to the economic future of the state; see Education Queensland, 'New Basics Technical Paper' (Brisbane: Education Queensland, 2000), pp. 5–11.
23. K. Marx, 'Economic and Philosophical Manuscripts', trans. R. Livingstone and G. Benton, in *Early Writings* (London: Penguin Books, 1975), p. 378.
24. Marx, 'Economic and Philosophical Manuscripts', p. 378.
25. A. Badiou, *Being and Event*, trans. O. Feltham (London: Continuum, 2005), p. 125.
26. A classical idealist position (whose return has accompanied the rise of neoliberalism) on education here would be that of someone like Matthew Arnold as inspector of schools, or that of Cardinal Newman, whose sermons Arnold attended, with his *Idea of a University*.
27. Plato, *Gorgias* 481c (trans. Donald J. Zuel), in Cooper and Hutchinson (eds), *Complete Works*.
28. In his review of several works of the great philosopher/historian R. G. Collingwood, Jonathon Rée notes some terse remarks of Collingwood in his *The New Leviathan*, one being: 'education should be provided on the same basis as medicine – always available when needed, but never forced down anyone's throat; and that the professionalisation of teaching is the enemy of the efficient education of children'. Rée quotes Collingwood: 'What is all this about professionalism, anyhow? Does anyone think that if a man marries he should marry no one but

a whore, or that if sleeping or eating is done it should be entrusted to professional sleepers or skilled prize-winners in eating competitions?' Interestingly, for Collingwood, Rée tells us, this among other contemporary symptoms of the failure of 'classical politics' is down to the failure to 'think dialectically'. See 'Life after Life', *London Review of Books*, 22(2) (January 2000), pp. 9–11.

29. See Brown, *Undoing the Demos*, esp. ch. 6.

30. At a recent and annual conference named 'World Innovation Summit for Education' (WISE), hosted by Qatar, the French Minister for Education argued in perfect relativist fashion that 'education' was, given the constantly and rapidly changing world in which we live, necessarily a site of constant reform (http://www.wise-qatar.org/, accessed 4 January 2017). In short, change – treated as if it were an objective rather than purposive fact – qua reform is the mode by which the state of the situation continues in its current form. Marx had a nice turn of phrase for these gatherings of the 'wise': festivals of 'glorified and ineffective trivialities'. One might also see Romans 1.22.

31. 'Building Knowledge Economies: Opportunities and Challenges for EU Accession Countries', www.worldbank.org/eca/knowledgeeconomy.

32. K. Marx, 'Critical Notes on the King of Prussia', in *Early Writings*, p. 404.

33. First Secretary of the Committee of the Privy Council on Education.

34. J. K. Shuttleworth, 'The Moral and Physical Condition of the Working Classes of Manchester in 1832', in *Four Periods of Public Education* (London: Longman, Green, Longman and Roberts, 1862), pp. 3–84.

35. I. Hunter, *Rethinking the School: Subjectivity, Bureaucracy, Criticism* (Sydney: Allen and Unwin, 1994).

36. K. Marx and F. Engels, *Manifesto of the Communist Party* (Moscow: Progress Publishers, 1986), p. 63. Not coincidently, this diatribe is addressed to 'conservative, or bourgeois socialists'.

37. 'An average income of less than $745 per person per year is considered a measure for inclusion as an LDC. Above $900 average income is not.' UNESCO, *Capacity Development for Education for All: Translating Theory into Practice* (Paris: UNESCO, 2011), p. 26, http://unesdoc.unesco.org/images/0021/002122/212262e.pdf (accessed 4 January 2017).

38. Qian Tang, cited in *World Innovation Summit for Education (WISE), Building the Future of Education*, Doha, 2010, p. 35, http://www.wise-qatar.org/sites/default/files/asset/document/wise_final_report_2010.pdf. Qian Tang is UNESCO Director General for Education and in charge of

the CapEFA project. For the full UNESCO document referred to, see UNESCO, *Capacity Development for Education for All: Translating Theory into Practice*, http://unesdoc.unesco.org/images/0021/002122/212262e. pdf (accessed 4 January 2017). Cf. also A. J. Bartlett, 'Refuse Become Subject: The Educational Ethic of Saint Paul', *Badiou Studies*, 3(1) (2014), pp. 194–216: 'Let us recall that it is to this *refuse* that contemporary pedagogy, local and global, addresses itself as its great virtue. For contemporary global pedagogy, the *refuse* is identified, placed, proscribed *recognised* and recycled in a not dissimilar fashion to what Paul describes albeit according to the dictates of contemporary discourse and pathos. As such, those unreconstructed cases suffering what UNESCO calls Low Development Capacity (LDC), are desperate, ignorant and in need of pedagogical *inclusion*. We could ask of UNESCO, *knowledge* incarnate in terms of contemporary global or encyclopaedic, pedagogy "for all", the question Paul asks the Galatians: "Are you so foolish? Having started with the Spirit, are you now ending with the flesh" (Gal. 3.3)? . . . Pedagogy, in this sense, and it's not a flippant remark, is a recycling venture.'

39. Mirowski and Plehwe, *The Road from Mont Pèlerin*, p. 431.

40. Chicago is also the 'home' of what became known as 'ego-psychology', the psychology that underpins the (cognitive, positive) psychological understanding of the subject that dominates today and orients faculties of education. The link between political neoliberalism and psychological subjectivisation is yet to be explored. Its nexus in education is one of the fundamental productions of our age, and coupled to the relativist paradigm so dominant in 'cultural' and media studies, it produces the symptomatic lived experience that 'there is no alternative'. Jacques Lacan was already well aware of the terms of this nexus in the 1950s, noting its 'Good Housekeeping seal of approval attesting to its suitability to the "American way of life"'. *Ecrits*, trans. B. Fink with H. Fink and R. Grigg (New York: W. W. Norton, 2006), p. 685. See also p. 332.

41. N. Klein, *The Shock Doctrine: The Rise of Disaster Capitalism* (London: Picador, 2008).

42. E. Durkheim, *The Evolution of Educational Thought*, trans. P. Collins (London: Routledge and Kegan Paul, 1977).

43. G. Agamben, *The Kingdom and the Glory: For a Theological Genealogy of Economy and Government*, trans. Lorenzo Chiesa (Stanford: Stanford University Press, 2011).

44. A. Badiou, *Logics of Worlds*, trans. A. Toscano (London: Bloomsbury,

2009), p. 535. Cf. Dobb writing on how Marx's 'philosophical' critique of Hegel is fundamental to the critique of political economy and thus the modus operandi of capitalism: 'Dobb observes [Colletti says] how for some economists abstractions become independent of all reference to realities, and are then hypostatized into "laws" valid for all situations, however heterogeneous and disparate these may be. Subsequently the same economists, trying to extract substance from their "laws", are compelled to bring in "unnoticed", in underhand fashion, whatever particular content their position requires.' Finally, after referring to Marx's early writings, Dobb concludes: 'The examples (Marx) cited were mainly drawn from the concepts of religion and idealist philosophy . . . In the realm of economic thought (where one might at first glance least suspect it) it is not difficult to see a parallel tendency at work. One might think it harmless enough to make abstraction of certain aspects of exchange-relations in order to analyse them in isolation from social relations of production. But what actually occurs is that once this abstraction has been made it is given *an independent existence as though it represented the essence of reality*, instead of one contingent facet of reality. Concepts become hypostatized; the abstraction acquires a fetishistic character, to use Marx's phrase. Here seems to lie the crucial danger of this method and the secret of the confusions which have enmeshed modern economic thought' [emphasis added]. M. Dobb, *Political Economy and Capitalism* (London: Routledge, 1937), pp. 135–6, cited in Lucio Colletti, 'Introduction' to Marx, *Early Writings*, p. 26.
45. Durkheim, *The Evolution of Educational Thought*.

1 Education: Not Impossible[1]

A. J. Bartlett

The dominant currents of contemporary philosophy are too appropriate to the law of the world.

Alain Badiou, *Happiness*[2]

What's at stake now is to know whether we want a humanity of cretins or not. Sometimes it's said that teaching costs too much! Well, how much does a humanity of cretins cost? . . . This is precisely why we need to build devices for the implosion-explosion of cyber-stupidity.

Gilles Châtelet, 'A Martial Art of Metaphor'[3]

What you want is a revolution without revolution.

Robespierre to the opportunists

Something better change!

The Stranglers

Present Prefatory Context

A century of cures to Plato – he who made education and philosophy inextricable – has left us with a twofold impossibility: that of the Idea and that of the subject. Educational theory, especially since the late 1970s, is heavily dependent on the philosophy of this cure and so, without much thought about it, takes up this double deposition. It so happens that this deposition, rooted in the fetish of pure becoming, of flux, is in accord with the demands of the contemporary state form to whose constant innovation there is 'no alternative', and this is why educational theory of this type turns up in policy. All positions agree: no Idea, no subject. That is, no idea which is not already guaranteed to exist and no subject which is not already assigned its place (or displacement). So we have everywhere the discourse of what is what they are not, or in other words, the pedagogy of 'the plausible image'. Philosophically speaking, this proscription is supposed to rule out any surreptitious return to metaphysics and at the level of my concern rules out the fundamental question: what is education? In Plato, truth is at stake, but truths are not a matter of the definition of a thing, but rather the thought demonstration of it, and typically in Plato the demonstration of the existence of that which is deemed by known knowledge to be impossible. Hence the beautiful contention concerning the just city: nowhere visible but not impossible. Precisely in holding out for what is true, rather than what is ruled apparent, Plato tries to think real change – which is to say, change in the very way that change appears to be thought. Any other form of change falls within a clever typology of iteration or repetition, thus making to exist differently what is already seen to exist. The axiom for this is from Ecclesiastes. 'Idea' is Plato's name for this impossibility and as such gives thought its other orientation. Its realisation is a matter of what he allusively calls participation. Participation is his name for the subjectivation of anyone whatsoever as subject. Thus, for Plato, true change is subjective participation in the Idea – that is, to make real what is impossible to the knowledge of the state. Education is therefore the name of this articulation between Idea and subject – it is no-ways else visible. With the rise of internet technologies, a new round of change has been prescribed for education. Yet this rhetoric of change does not constitute a real change in educational rhetoric itself, given that change has been an imperative in discourses on education for over forty years now. New media technology has simply extended and intensified this discursive framework concerning the future of global educational change towards the same end.

Thus and in this context, this essay concerns once again the question of education which, as always, and as Marx almost said, must be prised from the cold dead hands of the 'educators'.

Intervention

The contemporary 'debate' concerning the educational effects or affects of digital technology on education attracts philosophical attention. This is not because philosophy is some instrument of censure or tribunal of value ruling sovereign over all discourse. There are three reasons for this:

1. These debates deploy rhetoric and aver conceptual elaborations that are themselves drawn from philosophy;
2. Insofar as these debates make general claims as to the novelty or inventive aspects of these technologies over and above their technical application and effect, philosophy, ever concerned by the new, by how it comes to be and its consequences, is compelled to take note;
3. Since Plato at least, education and the subject of education have been intrinsic matters for philosophy. Being intrinsic to philosophy means that education is linked, as a matter of course, to truths. The link between truths and subjectivity is what matters, for *truths* orient the subject of education to its situation in a way distinct from that which the *knowledge* of education prescribes. This is the invariant aspect of education, the basis of real change.

What follows is partly intervention, partly analysis. Based on the 'simple' contention that the production of a truth, in a situation, is what education names, this essay argues that 1) educational change must be thought differently from the regimes of change dominant today, and 2) it should be directed specifically against the forms of knowledge these regimes presume to be the knowledge of education. I am thinking here of the collection of educational discourses familiar to everybody today, which range from constructivism to neoliberal reformism, and which regularly make certain claims about educational knowledge, as about how best to harness its effects. The key point is that these regimes, if apparently quite diverse in their presentation, are nonetheless united at the level of their knowledge-operations and subjective effects. The contention is that these regimes, insofar as they condition the contemporary conception of education, produce what I call a *subjective incapacity* – and not, as these regimes necessarily claim, new capacities.

This incapacity can be defined as that form of the subject whose very knowledge of itself as *subject* is the condition of its non-knowledge of its own subjection. Each act of this subject, correlated to the knowledge of the world for which such a subject exists, is an act of the (re)production or, better, the preservation of this incapacity. This incapacity, entirely coterminous with the form of a world for which, as we will see, *modification* is its rule, is the material form of the impossibility of *real* change. The object of analysis for this intervention is the concept of change, which predicates debates over the role of digital technology in education. The analysis will show that this concept of change is inherently un-educative precisely because it is no change at all.

Educational Knowledge and its 'New Media'

Today, there is a major public anxiety over education, prevalent across the globe, whose intensity – both rhetorical and reformist – is ratcheted up at any indication that education might escape the tight rein of established knowledge. Policy documents from Australia, the UK, Europe and the USA are practically unanimous that, as the key feature and facilitator of developments in the 'new knowledge economy', education must be 'constantly' reformed to meet the demands of the 'rapidly changing global economy'.[4] Over the course of the last several decades of global capitalist educational reform, major figures such as Pinar, Bowles and Gintis, Althusser, Bourdieu, Foucault, Giroux and Aranowitz, Illich, and Freire, among many others, have elaborated various critiques of these reforms and their predicates, establishing strong theoretical positions and proposing reforms in turn.[5] Some of these proposals, suitably repurposed, have been registered and even appropriated by governmental policy.[6] A critique of this critique is overdue, if for no other reason than to rescue it from the *inclusive* clutches of the state.[7]

The rapid evolution of new media technology has extended and intensified these already intense debates about the future of global educational change.[8] A recent study notes that in the '[i]nformation age . . . learning itself is the most dramatic medium of [. . .] change',[9] while another asserts that digital technology, in the form of Massive Open Online Courses (MOOCs), will usher in a 'historic transformation' both in the way education is delivered and in the way it is conceived. The 'four V's' of the web – the sheer amount of data out there (volume), offered in so many different modes of delivery (variety), available anytime and anywhere (velocity), and at different levels of data depth, accessible differentially from novice learners to expert researchers (variability) – constitute a 'disruption' of all existing systems of education.[10] Although critics point to the links between the changes wrought by internet technologies to educational engagement and 'participation' and global commercial interests – centred especially on the mining of individuals' data[11] – the backing and involvement of elite educational institutions is, it is said, 'legitimising' these changes, thereby ensuring their impact on the future of education.[12] What these debates suggest is a tension in contemporary discourse on educational change between 'education as change', and thus as an inherently unstable site, and 'changes to education' as the effort to stabilise change itself.[13] This crucial distinction, bearing on our conceptual double – education and subject – will be elaborated further below.

One of the key features revealing this tension is the language used to describe the impact of new technologies and economic priorities on education. Digital technology is said to usher in a 'historic transformation' in not only the way education is delivered but also the way it is conceived, such that there is the potential for 'a fundamentally new paradigm'.[14] Moreover, the 'technological revolution' currently taking place in online education, which, it is said, has the capacity not only to enable information input at a single site to reach anyone on the planet instantly, but allows for the sharing of information, work and data across borders and cultures, is, it is claimed, by virtue of its educational effect, 'a social revolution'.[15] 'New organizations are being created to offer new kinds of degrees, in a manner and at a price that could completely disrupt the enduring college business model.'[16] The discourse of the 'knowledge economy' has already marked this modal complex of policy, economy and technology and is similarly tasked to produce 'flexible', 'adaptable', 'entrepreneurial' and moral subjects: 'lifelong learners, adapting continuously to changed opportunities, work practices, business models and forms of economic and social organization'.[17] Thus in conformity with, rather than in opposition to, this discourse, key figures[18] in digital media and online learning speak constantly of the potential of internet technologies 'to [change] just about everything about how we think about [. . .] education', given that it is now possible to create 'a never-tiring, self-regulating, self-improving system that supports learning through formative on-demand feedback'.[19]

Much of this discourse has been concentrated in discussions of Massive Open Online Courses. 'A MOOC,' one expert claims, 'integrates the connectivity of social networking, the facilitation of an acknowledged expert in a field of study, and a collection of freely accessible online resources.' It is a 'course' that is 'open, participatory, distributed' – life-long networked learning. It is 'not a school or just a course', but an 'event' by which one 'connects and collaborates' – 'engaging in the learning process' but 'in a structured way'. Choice, this expert says, retroactively confirmed via 'participation', is built in. It is a key feature all the way through. And even success is your choice, *just like real life*.[20]

These events of 'rhizomatic community engagement'[21] – 'undefined' by experts but strangely recognisable to 'educators' alone (so it's said here) – are said to be effecting a 'campus tsunami', a 'historic transformation' and an 'education revolution'.[22]

That MOOCs, conceived as an event, are said to build on 'established distance-learning models' while remaining distinct in terms of access and by the forms of participation required to make them work brings to the surface a division well known in contemporary continental philosophy between events and consequences; of thinking at the same time continuity *and* discontinuity. At stake in this is the possibility of the new itself – that is, the advent of something and the *participation* in it required to make it not simply a repetition of the old in the guise of a difference; and, in my reading, of any possible subject not constituted in some way by the 'continuities' of known knowledge. This means that the very *form* of the relation between 'event' and 'consequences' impacts decisively on what one even understands by education. If the MOOC is both event *and* real change at once, ostensibly sufficient in itself to change the 'educational paradigm', we have no subject except as pure emergence. Whether it issues from some (rhizomatic?) conception of unknowable being or from the inexorable logic of the market, no *subjective* participation is required. Rather, one is subject to a rule of unfolding, and thus conformity determines existence. After all, it is a truism that knowledge does not know what it is not. But of course, presenting a continuity as a discontinuity is inherent to 'sophistic wisdom'. If, however (and this is what we will see below), these two – event, participation – are distinct, it is because there exists – or can come to exist – a subject unsupported by whatever discourse of continuity is in effect.

Concomitantly to this sophistic wisdom – and this is an internal debating point, not an opposition to this educational 'event/revolution' – questions concerning the 'educational legitimacy' of MOOCs, the conditions for their possible credentialing, have been 'solved', it is argued, by the coming on board of so-called 'elite institutions' (Harvard, Stanford, UCLA, Edinburgh, Melbourne etc.), which 'are publicly extolling the value and quality potential of online education, and are willing to invest tens of millions of dollars'.[23] Credentialing is key to the capacity of 'partnerships' between entities such as Coursera, Udacity and edX and these institutions to charge fees for these so called 'post-courses' (even if this is not where the money really is).[24]

While 'change' is subscribed to by (almost) all participants in the education-technology debate, for some pre-eminent figures in the world of techno-pedagogy such as Long and Seimans and Butin, and media cheerleaders like Brooks, the potential transformative power of MOOCs is far from being fully exploited. For these thinkers, the 'analytics' (data mining capacity) made available by MOOCs, specifically by the *participants* in these so-called 'post-courses', have been underexploited, and the *educational* potential they possess is being wasted. Analytics means, essentially, that every keystroke, 'tweet, status update, page read online' can be analysed to ensure that every 'learner' is targeted 'with resources relevant to his or her profile, learning goals, and the knowledge domain the learner is attempting to master'. 'The idea is simple yet potentially transformative . . . Continued growth in the amount of data creates an environment in which new or novel approaches are required to understand the patterns of value that exist within the data.'[25] This transformation takes place, of course, under the coincident network rubric of openness, sharing, connectedness, togetherness and community.

The Learner who is Subject, *not* Subject

This discourse of innovation, disruption, transformation and change, rooted in the *learner*, note – in a manner not clearly determined but no doubt ideologically prescient – resonates throughout the blogs, discussion boards, online journals, academic articles, policy documents and book-length research projects devoted to the topic. One commentator sums it like this:

This approach to learning means that learning content is created and distributed in a very different manner. Rather than being composed, organized and packaged, e-learning content is syndicated, much like a blog post or podcast. It is aggregated by students, using their own personal RSS reader or some similar application. From there, it is remixed and repurposed with the student's own individual application in mind, the finished product being fed forward to become fodder for some other student's reading and use.[26]

For Downes, with all the innocence of one unfamiliar with educational history, this means two things: that learning 'is *becoming* a creative activity' (emphasis added) and that the 'venue' is not an 'application' but a platform. What this means, then, is that the notion of the medium is (supposedly) finished – platform and learner are synthesised – and subjectivity, other than, as I'll argue, as *incapacity*, becomes null and void.

This is because this 'self-recursive stream of numbers' effectively renders all creativity, precisely *media*, as inexistent, 'consigned to disappear' as Kittler tellingly remarks, 'into the black-holes and boxes that, as artificial intelligences, are bidding us farewell on their way to nameless high commands'.[27] To be clear, the problem here is the subjective weakness of these 'new' technologies and not their overweening power.

This weakness is precisely expressed in their filial subservience to the prevailing discourses on education, the very 'object' they suppose that they are overcoming. (But note: this is not a mistake.) We constantly re-encounter this structure, whereby declared radicality in fact simply rehearses the most archaic aspects of what it purports to supersede. Boris Groys pointedly articulates this problem against emergence theories in terms of an inability to grasp the key distinction between what is truly new and what is different. 'Difference,' he points out, citing Kierkegaard, 'is recognised as such only because we already have the capability to recognise and identify this difference as difference. So no difference can ever be new – because if it were really new it could not be recognised as difference.'[28]

Certainly, the rhetoric concerning these new technologies is such that we would expect that a real discontinuity or something truly new has been established between what passed as education before – and thus its subjects – and the 'revolution' or 'paradigm shift' now coming to pass.[29] Yet this rhetorical exuberance seems, as in ancient times, to go hand in hand with a casual and inconsistent use of terms and a concomitant conceptual free-for-all. Especially revealing, and a key aspect of the (re) production of this 'subjective incapacity', is the interchangeability and conflation of the terms used to promote the extent of its innovative capacity – change, reform, transformation, revolution, disruption, paradigm shift and so on are used as synonyms and often without reflection on their use.[30] While there is little doubt that 'changes are occurring', it is clearly the case that certain changes may secure existing practices rather than re-*form* them, while certain reforms may serve to strengthen set paradigms; equally, a 'disruption' cannot itself be equated with a revolution. In effect, certain discourses of change may act as limits to rather than an extension of educational change. This is precisely what is meant by modification – as we will see.

Globalisation vs. Universalism

Unguarded assumptions concerning the subject of education abound – in both senses: education as the subject under debate and thus considered as an object, and the subject with which education is concerned. I say *the* subject and not *subjects* because it is the subject which is precisely in question. What implicit, unthought theory of the subject are these debates working with or, more accurately here, what (theory of the) subject are these debates assuming? The continually invoked notion of 'participation' is one example: is the subject the outcome of participation? Is there a subject who participates, or is participation, as in Plato, a subjective or subjectivising process in itself? Or is the subject equated with the individual – conscious, self-reflexive, egoic? Or is there no subject now, only individuals making their way? And of course, this use of participation only raises the question of just what it is one participates in. No doubt 'education' is what one is meant to be participating in, but this again raises the question, if not of 'what it is', then at least of which form of education is at stake. Is it the same form as prior to the digital revolution of all paradigms, or do they have in mind some other education? This applies, by the way, to those on 'both sides' of the claims for this new affective education: those who see it as coincident with the logic of capital, let's call it, and those who see it as emancipatory in some way.[31] In reality, however, at the level of the subject of education – thus what it is *and* what it affects – it appears that little has changed at all. What we certainly have is a new *technique*, but the problem of a new technique – as Plato argued – is that it assumes the knowledge of the thing for which it is a technique. In other words, what type of the subject can technology produce? Is it 'new'? Long and Seimans sum up this 'all change' succinctly.

Something must change. For decades, calls have been made for reform in the efficiency and quality of higher education. Now, with the Internet, mobile technologies, and open education, these calls are gaining a new level of urgency. Compounding this technological and social change, prominent investors and businesspeople are questioning the time and monetary value of higher education.[32]

We note that in each case we have referenced here, the *address* of the claims is always to all. These revolutionary changes issuing from some centre or other will as a matter of course affect everyone insofar as education is a global enterprise. And where such change is resisted – which is always also cast as a sign of barbarity, backwardness or even evil – it will be what education is for them too, one day soon.[33] This is the case, even if the use of terms like 'community' is not without certain conceptual problems (as postcolonialist studies have exemplarily argued), notably to do with modalities of exclusion. Since Marx, that other great thinker of the nexus of technology, knowledge and capital, we know that there are at least two ways in which to think the 'all' addressed by such discourses:[34] in terms of globalisation and in terms of universalism. We can express this for our purposes this way: globalisation is the expression of what can be done with this for all (the subject of the address); universalism is the expression of what this for all can do (as subject).

Transmission, Subjectivity and Transformation

Under this distinction, let us say, then, that there are three fundamental aspects to education, whether globalising or universalist: transmission, subjectivity and transformation. These – the means, form and address of a discourse; the material effect of participation (however understood); the name of the educational effect (again however understood) – one way or another, as we have seen, are recognised by all 'participants' in the debate and by us *who are not*. These will act as the interlinked points by which we proceed to see what truth there is in the claims made for these digital technologies with regard to education. The discourse on MOOCs, as noted, certainly touches on each aspect and in turn conditions the form of their relation specific to it. But what is this change inscribed at the centre of this debate? What can change be in a world where change has established itself as the norm, where the rapidly changing conditions of everyday life are supposed and declaimed as being beyond anyone's control, and where education is nominated not as the facilitator of these changes per se, but as what provides subjects capable of adapting to or being flexible before this *unthinkable* change? Subjects, thus, capable (only?) of reproducing such 'change' as the ground of their subjectivity. These subjects are subject to the absolute unchangeability of the form of change that there is.

In this sense, the much-heralded move from 'application' to 'platform' does not at all challenge this *subjective incapacity* recognised in the 'old ways', but it does 'smooth over' or plane-ify the contradiction that makes any thought of the subject possible. If all is platform or 'plane of consistency' over which content travels indiscriminately, then there is no *point*. We have, no doubt 'violently imposed', what Alain Badiou calls a 'pointless' or 'atonal world':[35] it is clear that atonic worlds are simply worlds which are so ramified and nuanced – or so quiescent and homogeneous – that no instance of what he conceives as the Two, and consequently no figure of decision – a figure pointedly subtracted from the atonality of worlds – is capable of evaluating them. The modern apologia for the 'complexity' of the world, invariably seasoned with praise for the democratic movement, is really nothing but a desire for generalised atony, Badiou contends.[36]

Groys marks something similar when he says that 'innovation has become a ritual'.[37] Referring specifically to internet technologies, he continues that 'all the processes of renewal and innovation etc. have become extra-human, extra-psychological, extra-individual, and are functioning according to the circumvention of individual and collective practices of remembering'. Moreover, '[i]t's just like these [post-modern academic grant] applications in which non-innovation [is] offered as innovation'.[38] In other words, it is the pointless reproduction of pointless worlds, entirely possible because there is nothing not-it to interrupt the flow of 'the conservative succession of instants'. For Badiou, as for Groys, however, the new is, for all this, not impossible; or rather it is the impossibility inscribed at the heart of the platform itself that must be affirmed, held to, and the consequences drawn. Badiou enigmatically says: 'Every human animal can tell itself that it is ruled out that it will encounter always and everywhere atonicity . . .'[39]

This is the double paradox of discourses of change today, to which the technological, for all its intensity and audacity, reveals itself to be only an addition and not at all something new, something subtractive of or withdrawn from the contemporary knowledge of education. On the one hand it belongs to a paradigmatic logic of ends – the *end* of history; the *end* of capitalism and parliamentary democracy as the apex of possible worlds (an end education is tasked to reproduce) – which is to say, there is *now* 'nothing new under the sun' – and, being at the end of history, there is no *history* now of this now not being. And yet, grounded by this *unchangeable* horizon, which is of course, as ever, off limits to thought – inaccessible, ineffable, atavistically infinite or forever 'emergent' – there is nothing but change. If *modularity*[40] is the name of the present void of the technical (educated) subject, *modification* is the transcendental condition of such a world. The cartoon character Homer Simpson provides us with a clear image of this state of the situation when, criticising some new commodity invention as too difficult for him to master, he asks: 'why didn't they just take an existing product and put a clock in it?' One can ask this question, slightly reframed, of the 'reformers' or 'change agents': Have you not just taken an existing product, education, and stuck a (digital) clock in it?

Instrumentalising an Instrumentalisation

Without at all having to leave aside the commodity form of education – which is as intrinsic to this reform debate as it is symptomatic of its ignorance of education – the underlying assumption of this whole reform debate is that it knows already what education is. Paradoxically, in the midst of all this change, education – such as it is known – is unchangeable. That is, what education is is simply taken for granted, and that it might not be or might even exceed in its extension these assumptions is never considered. That there might be something invariable in the Idea of it – making, for example, the education of Plato compatible say with that of Marx or Freud – and thus something resistant always to context or use remains outside the ambit of 'disruption'.

But what will and must in fact continually change within this ambit – and thus *difference* is mistaken for *the new* – is the technique for its manipulation or instrumentalisation relevant to the demands of a logic extrinsic to it. Hence claims such as 'Analytics in education must be transformative, altering existing teaching, learning, and assessment processes, academic work, and administration. When analytics is applied to curricular resources, the traditional view of courses is disrupted.'[41] Thus, if instrumentalised, no matter the technique, it is instrumentalised for something else, for something else beyond education itself. This 'something else', then, must presume to mark the limits of education itself. Which is to say, it takes the form of a known knowledge, a knowledge off limits to education. To put it another way: if there is the knowledge of what must be done to education, there must be the knowledge of what education is that is itself beyond 'education'. This knowledge is the referent then for all educational change or disruption – it is the knowledge education serves, yet doesn't finally know.

But there is another, further twist, since this knowledge of education, which to maintain itself as such must constantly alter its techniques in order to appear as the current knowledge of education, is constrained by an altogether immanent aspect of education: that it is fundamentally about change itself. In other words, the knowledge of education as a technique changes in order that the intrinsic capacity of education for change is made impossible, and from within the debates on education itself. To put it a bit colloquially, the knowledge of education, of what must be done to it – 'constant reform' – which is so ubiquitously on display in debates on education – casual, political, theoretical – is that knowledge whose effect is to limit and finally foreclose from its effect what it is that education can be and consequently can do. This is of course to un-know that knowledge of education itself as knowledge!

The current debates about education are themselves being instrumentalised by the knowledge of education they presume, defer to and support in their efforts to instrumentalise education in support of that knowledge. We have an instrumentalisation of an instrumentalisation. And this doubling takes place in order precisely to forestall, as noted, the transformative effects of education as such, which are known to be troublesome for all states throughout history. Such effects are, in my language, the immanent, invariant truths of any possible concept of education and, for all that, to adopt a notion of Groys, are as such *withdrawn* from the market or the logic of capital, which provides the temporal horizon of our contemporary *state* knowledge. Education is something like a site relative to capitalist knowledge; it *marks* a divested point, an emptiness or excess in the territory of capital that capital cannot nullify nor void, and indeed must and does exploit for the purposes of its own persevering, thus, paradoxically, maintaining within it what is irreducible to it. What is education remains over, and with regard to any 'state knowledge' (capitalism is simply the state of our situation), 'for the purpose of creating something that was meant for eternity and not for time'.[42]

Appropriately, this contradiction, to use some old language, or disjunction, to appropriate some more recent, is not new but part of the history of education itself. Plato elaborates this for us in the struggle against the dominant 'market technique' of his day, sophistry, which already offered the youth or 'learner' the knowledge necessary to know that the interests of the state were in their interest, or to make his individual way in the world *as it is*. This is the mark of an educated subject to this day, even if, following Rancière,[43] we should properly call this *pedagogy*, and reserve the name 'education' for that form which divests itself of this state pedagogy as the mode of its becoming true. That this disjunction, the effect of education's intrinsic withdrawal, is a constant of debates on education should give pause for thought, especially among knowledgeable commentators on education.

Truth/Change

Against this contemporary return and repetition of the sophistic motif, a twofold question must be posed: What is understood by change and what type of subject is conceived, supposed and created with regard to this technological conception of educational change? Of course, these two questions are themselves somewhat supplementary to the question we invoked at the level of the concept: what is education? This question, which cannot be answered with regard to technique *alone*, is always foreclosed in debate precisely because to even pose it supposes a distinct orientation to the *knowledge* of education. In other words it supposes the existence of a point outside knowledge other than on knowledge's terms. I have elaborated a book-length response to the question 'what is education'.[44] It maintains that it is demonstrable: it has a trajectory, consequences and an orientation that can be traced and established as consistent under varying conditions and relative to distinct situations. Thus we can say what it is and hence we can recognise *when* it is not. This cannot be elaborated here.

However, the key to the demonstration is the intrinsic link between education and truths. Alain Badiou observed in 1988, in the manner of Saint-Just, that 'truth is a new word in Europe'.[45] But of course it is always what is at stake in education: that there is something other than known knowledge, that it invests the situation with new forms of transmission and that some subjects form or are transformed on the basis of it. In his 2004 essay on the relation of Art (which produces the truths of the 'art-world') and Philosophy (the discourse of their *composition* with the truths of politics, love and science) Badiou makes the declaration: 'the only education is an education by truths'. He continues: the 'entire insistent problem is that there be truths'.[46] Without them, without their *exceptionality* to the normal course of things – assumptions, laws, beliefs, knowledge as such[47] – education will be only a matter of received or established or dominant opinion; battered this way and that depending on the dictates or determinations of what norms or knowledge prevail outside it, but within the 'class struggle in theory' that is educational reform today.[48] It is this link between education and truths that matters, and does so with regard to what Badiou calls *real* change – as distinct from what he calls 'modifications' or 'facts'.

In the remainder of this chapter I will sketch out in somewhat truncated form Badiou's typology of change within which the claims to change analysed above can be situated. From his earliest work in the 1960s Badiou has been committed to conceptualising the form of *real* change; which is to say, 'can there be something new in the situation'?[49] But of course, as he says, to think the new in the situation we need to think the old. We have done some of that above. In his *Logics of Worlds*, a text from 2005 that builds on his formal reconfiguration of ontology in 1988's *Being and Event*, Badiou sets out a formal, ontologically rigorous typology of change and links it explicitly to a type of subject. It is very useful to any thinking of education for three reasons, which we will take one at a time.

The Truth/Knowledge Couple

Badiou's typology of change refers to a dynamic reconfiguration of the distinction between 'truth' and 'knowledge'. Badiou opens *Logics of Worlds* by wondering what it is we think about our situation today, especially when we are not 'monitoring ourselves' (a suitably pedagogical term).[50] In other words, he asks 'what is our natural belief' – 'in keeping', he says, 'with the rule of an inculcated nature'. He contends that natural belief is condensed in a single statement: 'There are only bodies and languages' (LW 1). This is the axiom of 'democratic materialism', which is for him the name of the knowledge of the world today; the knowledge that fashions us as individuals. Against this, Badiou proposes a counter axiom: 'there are bodies and languages except that there are *truths*' (LW 4). Truths are exceptions to the inculcated, pedagogical rule of democratic materialism and, as such, they are not reducible to or recoupable by knowledge – sensory, experiential, constructivist or linguistic. The modes of change constitutive of the knowledge of 'bodies and languages' are irreducible to the form of change that has done with this knowledge itself. This latter form of change is exceptional to knowledge *tout court*. The key thing to note here is that what I have called education, or rather the change that is properly effective as education, is the latter and not the former. The former are changes to education and not educational change. Changes to education, as noted, are such that 1) it treats it as an object of known knowledge and 2) it works to forestall the real changes that (a non-democratic materialist) education announces and produces as a matter of course. A truth for Badiou is a *generic*, subjective and transformative procedure, while knowledge acts upon truths as a stabilising and reformist force. In other words, truths are dynamic and subjective interventions within situations or worlds of established knowledge, which produce precisely a new orientation to this world whose effect, affected point by point, is to displace this knowledge from within. Truths have to be established in fidelity to an event. They are not what is adequate to or an instance of established knowledge. Hence a true education is oriented to the world with regard to an established break with its knowledge, by what exposes there the site of its lack. A true education invokes its subject.

Knowledge as *encyclopedia*, as Badiou calls it, is predicated precisely on being coincident with the all of the whole. Badiou's ontological formulations show the inconsistency of the latter – the One is not[51] – and the theory of the event, authorised by this rigorous thinking of inconsistency as such, establishes that what is exposed by the event for a situation is this point of inconsistency. In short, there is always within any regime of knowledge its empty point, its void site in strict terms (making it categorically unlike Deleuze!) – around which it organises itself. This 'void' is the 'excess' (unknowable) that any such knowledge guards against and is therefore a *condition* of its knowledge. In other words, knowledge cannot know the void or lack at its heart and must therefore produce as knowledge this non-knowledge. The debates on education that *presume* a knowledge of education and so rely on its currency in knowledge are, then, effectively producing the lack of the truth of education as their knowledge. Knowledge first and foremost produces its own lack of knowledge – for Badiou, this lack can be demonstrated to 'exist' at a site. But that is not the issue per se. Rather, it is the production of this lack as knowledge itself, that is, that this lack must *not be known*, that is the real horizon of this discourse or its genuine excess. For Badiou, while this excess (lacking knowledge) is 'incalculable' and therefore cannot be known as such, it can be decided – in and through the construction of a generic, indiscernible or new configuration or set. In other words, to decide – the mark of the subject, we can say – is absolutely consistent with what ontology formalises.[52]

Truths are not thereby of being itself but are totally contingent on the contingency of an event or the irruption in a situation or world of that which-is-not-being-*qua*-being. But neither is genuine change given to us on the side of appearing, or of the transcendental constitution of being-there, on the side, that is, of worlds. For the appearing of a being in a world (its existence there) is the same thing as its modifications in that world, without any discontinuity and thus any singularity being required for the deployment of these modifications (LW 358). Truths are subjective productions, subtractive of being as of all knowledge. This distinction or coupling between truths and the knowledge which truths interrupt and avoid as a matter of *course* is operative in all forms of discourse, specifically when change or the 'new' is at stake.

Typology

Badiou elaborates a formal typology of change drawn from topos theory, itself a sub-set of category theory. The aim is still to trace the trajectory of a truth in a world but this time in terms of its *appearing* or *being-there*. The sets of relations which affect and determine what it is to appear is what makes up the logic of appearance or 'existence', and topos theory provides a formal account of what Meillassoux calls the 'diverse consistencies revealed to us in experience'.[53] What matters here are the three types of change made thinkable by such an *onto*-logy. These are modifications, facts and *real* change or *singularity*. They are distinguished in terms of their intensity or affect and their relation to the transcendental specific to their world, which is to say, 'established knowledge'. Approximating to the language of the above examples, modifications are akin to reform, facts to disruptions, and real change to transformation or the instance of the new.

For Badiou, any world, in terms of its appearing as such, is transcendentally structured. The transcendental is the 'locus of the relations of identity and difference by means of which multiples make "worlds"'.[54] This is a relation of order of a specific sort insofar as what appears does so in terms of intensity and intensity is a matter of relation – the relation of one multiple to another. What appears most intensely in a specific world determines the intensity of appearing of the other multiples marked to exist in that world. A world is structured in terms of a maximal intensity of appearing or existence, and a minimum. 'The intensities of objects and relations are measured according to a singular temporal transcendental, which objectivates in their appearing multiplicities . . .' (LW 359). In a world, for example, where knowledge provides the transcendental rule, those deemed knowledgeable will appear more intensely

50   A. J. Bartlett

than the unknowledgeable or 'uneducated'. This is a reductive example but accurate enough, especially when we think about how this 'distinction' is wielded to exact the right to privilege. Most objects relative to a world, Badiou says, appear somewhere in the middle.

It is impossible to flesh out the entire nuance, let alone all the technical apparatus of this onto-logic. If we understand that to appear in a world is to appear for the transcendental of a world, thus relative to the knowledge of the sets of relations organised vis-à-vis the order of intensity, then what we need to know is simply that 'the appearing of a being in a world is the same thing as its modifications in that world, without any discontinuity and thus any singularity being required for the deployment of these modifications' (LW 358) – in a world stabilised by an established knowledge, one in which any point of difference, such that its difference cannot be marked by that knowledge, is always already the operation of a modification. To *be there* with some degree of intensity above the minimum (which is to inexist for a world (which is not to not be)) is to exist as and to consist in being modified.

[T]his logical identity of a world is the transcendental indexing of a multiplicity – an object – as well as the deployment of its relations to other multiplicities which appear in that world. There is no reason to suppose that we are dealing with a fixed universe of objects and relations, from which we would have to separate out modifications. Rather, we are dealing with modifications themselves . . . (LW 358)

In other words, modification, as the 'rule-governed appearing' of difference as such, is the norm of a world and is not *change*. Change is something more than mere modification and something distinct from a fact. However, while modifications are coincident with the transcendental, a fact and a *singularity* (real change) have in common what Badiou calls a 'site'. In short, a site marks the limit point within a world or situation of established knowledge. Beneath the site, so to speak, there is nothing: it marks the point of *inexistence* or an abnormality inadmissible to the logic of the state. It is present but not represented; its parts are un-*knowable*. A fact, then, is a site, Badiou says, 'whose intensity of existence is not maximal' (LW 372). It is not *evental*. It does not carry in its becoming the disruptive force necessary to effect a change in the logic of that world itself. While a fact is not of the law as such, it cannot alter this law either. A fact points at change but is not itself real change. A fact is recoverable for a world.

Badiou admits into the schema a distinction in singularity between weak and strong. A weak singularity is an evental site such that it does not produce consequences. In other words, it cannot make a minimal existence pass into a maximal as can an event or strong singularity. A strong singularity – which is an event – is 'a site whose intensity of existence is maximal' (LW 372). *Every world admits an element properly inexistent to it.* This properly inexistent will be an element of a site. If there is an event, it is the eruption of this properly inexistent or that which exists minimally for that world, such that what happens becomes the index of its happening: hence 'singularity'. The minimally appearing element of that world comes to appear maximally – which, given that the site has no known or presented elements, is patently illegal (un-knowable). So an appearing minimal of a site, of a sudden appears maximally. What the event signifies is the non-impossibility of a change in that order – in the 'unbroken phrasing of the world' – as Badiou says. However, this is not enough: the *world* is not changed except that an exception has been marked; that an exception is not impossible. But maximality is *consequential.* In the world as it goes, there is a maximal appearing and this gives the world its rule – the order to its appearing – and thus when the minimal becomes maximal, the possibility exists that the entirety of the transcendental order be changed – nothing becomes everything. So if 'nothing' or rather the *trace* of the event (events as such appear to disappear) comes to occupy this place, or in other words to present itself as the new point of orientation for the conjunction of a topos (or world) – a new form of collection – all relations are up for grabs. This trace, Badiou says, is the 'eternal' existence of the inexistent, the outline or statement, in the world, of the disappeared event. Education, we can say, is this trace: manifest in the object body constructed by a subject point by point; an orientation, a trajectory, a materiality, a transformation, addressed to all. 'There is no stronger transcendental consequence than the one which makes what did not exist in a world appear within it' (LW 376). The event gives to the subject the chance of an *other* orientation than that deemed to exist. 'The event is neither past nor future. It presents us with the present' (LW 384).

Educating Subject

These modes of change are elaborated with a theory of the subject linked generically to both truths and transformation – that is to say, participation. In this way education is linked to truths or what is new, beyond what is already known, and thus intrinsically to change and not extrinsically, as for reform movements and technical 'innovators'. The three types of the subject derived then are the reactionary, obscurantist and faithful. The key is that each subjective type is also linked for a particular world to a singular *event* of that world. Subjects, then, are *reactionary* to, *occlusive* of or *faithful* to an event. These figures of the subject are the appearance of three forms of subjectivation, relative to the 'new body in the world' that an event makes possible. That of the reactionary is of an 'indifference: to act as though nothing has taken place or, more exactly, to be convinced that, were the event not to have occurred, things would be basically the same'. It 'quashes what is new within the soft power of conservation'. The subjectivisation of the occlusive 'is hostility: to consider the new body as a malevolent foreign irruption that must be destroyed. In this hatred of the new, of all that is "modern" and different from tradition, we recognize obscurantism.'[55] Thus the obscurantist changes or intensifies its forms of rhetoric or, if in a position to do so, its repressive capacities in order to make sure there is no fundamental change, while the reactive subject adapts to the world in terms of its ordinary modifications since 'there is no alternative'. Conceptions of education correlated to either of these forms of subjectivisation cannot be considered educational precisely because they refuse to think the impossibility of their worlds and so presuppose a knowledge of the limits of knowledge as such – which cannot itself be known. Moreover, these two forms, often presented to us in the form of an opposition – the terms of the 'debate' – effectively exhaust the logic of our contemporary world and thereby, as I have intimated above, the logic of educational discourses. This exhaustion, peopled by 'self-deluding nomads' and voguish 'gardeners of the creative', is that which Gilles Châtelet memorably diagnoses as the desire 'to live and think like pigs'.[56] Which, in speaking to the present of democratic materialism, I take also as alluding to some mockery of Protagoras by Socrates in the *Theaetetus* (161c).

Real change is the upheaval in a world of the very logic that holds it together, that provides its consistency, and is at the same time the procedure by which a new truth of that world is set out for it, point by point and by which a new body or subjective formation for that world is constructed – one that draws on the equal capacity of all inhabitants of that world to 'not know its knowledge'. In other words, the faithful subject is marked by its 'incorporation within the [new] body, enthusiasm for what is new, and active fidelity to that happening that locally disrupted the laws of the world through its advent'.[57] Somewhat enigmatically, fidelity marks that:

a truth process is the construction of a new body that appears gradually in the world as all the multiples having an authentic affinity with a primordial statement are drawn together around the latter. And as the primordial statement is the trace of an event's power, we can also say that a body of truth results from the incorporation within the consequences of an event of everything, within the world, that has been maximally impacted by its power.[58]

Here is the crux. Badiou, in a Platonic gesture, establishes via a universalisation of non-inclusion the not-impossible belonging of all to the new truth of their world. Real change is correlated not to the management of innovation, the mastery of technique, but to the non-knowledge of this same world, exposed in the event, whose consequences are manifest as a new truth of and for this world, and are drawn by the subject, who will have been, each and every time, what is *education*.

One More Effort Please . . . to Recommence

Technology is always much weaker than its advocates seem to believe. In truth, this weakness is concentrated in this belief. In 1795, when the French Revolution had, much like today, gone over to the side of restoration, the Marquis de Sade wrote a tract exhorting his fellow countrymen: 'Frenchmen, one more effort please if you would become Republicans'. Sade offered a new radicality to what it invariantly is to 'become Republican', to follow this 'desire' right to the end. Without this, he declared, the real 'murderers and thieves', the state and the wealthy, would keep on getting away with it. The rhetoric of the MOOC (condensing the wider 'thrill to technique'), of its educational capacity, despite the animate desire of its most wide-eyed proponents, only delivers this new technique over to the hands of those in a position to continue to get away with determining for all what education is, and thus even more critically what it is not and must not be. Despite what such technological innovations can do, what possibilities they suppose, MOOCs and their like will remain inscribed in the vicious, expansive circle of capitalist or state logic, replicating and repeating, modifying over and again the subjective incapacity that this logic demands. Moreover, they will reproduce it anew. The weakness of technology, shackled to this logic, is that it never actually does what is claimed, that its subjectivisation is actually of a bastard kind: it engenders what it does not want and wants what it cannot engender. And thus it is difficult to see these changes, or innovations or disruptions, as reproducing anything but what Plato calls in the *Laws*, speaking explicitly about technique, a 'queer sort of education' and thus a queer sort of subject.

Beneath all the fanfare of its arrival, its result – the intensification of the procedures of the pedagogy that already exists – commands only new rounds of cynicism, fatalism, defeatism: in the last instance, and at best, an emergent, ecstatic nihilism – a queer celebration that this is all there is – supported by a hybrid humanist-vitalism – this is the proper end of life for beings like us – which is destined merely to repeat, with difference to be sure but without the very possibility of the truly new: thus, no Idea; consequently, no subject; and finally, then, no education. Such is why the rhetoric of the MOOC is so fervent, so desperate, so hollow, so contemporary: but the symptom, nevertheless, everywhere animate, of a real desire *for* education, which demands to be taken up. If the greatest efforts of technique return us yet again and with greater intensity to what there is, then what is *there*? What can be done? What is there is the trace of a truth, the force of the subject, the demand that we truly recommence to be educated.

Notes

1. A version of this essay was published previously as 'Innovations in Incapacity: Education, Technique, Subject', *Digital Culture and Education*, 5 (March 2013), pp. 2–17.
2. A. Badiou, *Happiness*, trans. A. J. Bartlett and J. Clemens (London: Bloomsbury, 2017).
3. G. Châtelet, 'A Martial Art of Metaphor: Two Interviews with Gilles Châtelet', https://www.urbanomic.com/document/gilles-chatelet-mental-ecology/ (accessed 6 January 2017).
4. These three are merely indicative. The latter two in particular are what we might call the global template: at once iterations and reiterations. D. Gonski, *Review of Funding for Schooling: Final Report, 2011* (Department of Education, Employment and Workplace Relations, 2012); World Innovation Summit for Education (2011), retrieved from http://www. wise-qatar.org/ (accessed 7 January 2017); World Bank, 'Building

Knowledge Economies: Opportunities and Challenges for EU Accession Countries', final report of the Knowledge Economy Forum 'Using Knowledge for Development in EU Accession Countries', organised by the World Bank in cooperation with the European Commission, the Organization for Economic Cooperation and Development, the European Bank for Reconstruction and Development, and the European Investment Bank Paris, 19–22 February 2002, May 2002, http://siteresources.worldbank.org/EXTECAREGTOPKNOECO/ Resources/Building_Knowledge_Economies_final_final.pdf (accessed 1 February 2017).

5. Again, an indicative list. See note 3 in the Introduction to this volume.

6. Education Queensland, *Queensland State Education 2010* (Brisbane: Education Queensland, 2000), p. 10; UNESCO, *Capacity Development for Education for All: Translating Theory into Practice* (Paris: UNESCO, 2011), http://unesdoc.unesco.org/images/0021/002122/212262e. pdf (accessed 5 January 2017); World Bank, 'Building Knowledge Economies: Opportunities and Challenges for EU Accession'.

7. Such a critique would note, however, that its *representation* there, in state policy, raises the question of some conceptual complicity underpinning its oppositional elaboration. This is a task for another time. Cf. Châtelet, who does not hold back on this complicity: 'It has never really been a question of "respect for the Other," of Democracy, of Rights, etc.; never has cyber-bourgeoisie pedantry been so giddy with categories and false concepts dressed-up with capital letters . . . And never, meanwhile, has real power – the power to create the field of the possible – been so concentrated in the hands of such a tiny minority: Central Banks, private and totally inaccessible, ultra-confidential information networks, companies that have nothing to do with any election, entirely in the grip of operators capturing financial flows that rival those of a state . . .' Châtelet, 'A Martial Art of Metaphor'.

8. E. Bulut, 'Labour and Totality in Participatory Digital Capitalism', in C. McCarthy, H. Greenhalgh-Spencer and R. Mejia (eds), *New Times: Making Sense of Critical/Cultural Theory in a Digital Age* (New York: Peter Lang, 2011). pp. 51–69; D. Jorgensen, 'The Digital, the Virtual and the Naming of Knowledge', *The Fibreculture Journal*, 10 (2007); T. Scholz, 'Why Does Digital Labour Matter Now?', in T. Scholz (ed.), *Digital Labour: The Internet as Playground and Factory* (New York: Routledge, 2013), pp. 1–10.

9. C. N. Davidson and D. T. Goldberg, *The Future of Learning Institutions in a Digital Age* (Cambridge, MA: MIT Press, 2009).

10. D. W. Butin, 'What MIT Should Have Done', *eLearn Magazine* (29 June 2012), http://elearnmag.acm.org/featured.cfm?aid=2263018 (accessed 7 January 2017). Butin cites K. Carey: 'the monopoly has begun to crumble. New organizations are being created to offer new kinds of degrees, in a manner and at a price that could completely disrupt the enduring college business model.'

11. Scholz, 'Why Does Digital Labour Matter Now?'.

12. P. Hill, 'Online Educational Delivery Models: A Descriptive View', *Educausereview* (November 2012), http://er.educause.edu/articles/2012/11/online-educational-delivery-models--a-descriptive-view (accessed 1 February 2017).

13. P. D. Long and G. Seimans, 'Penetrating the Fog: Analytics in Learning and Education', *Educausereview* (September 2011), http://er.educause.edu/articles/2011/9/penetrating-the-fog-analytics-in-learning-and-education (accessed 1 February 2017); M. A. Peters, 'Afterword: Manifesto for Education in the Age of Cognitive Capitalism', in C. McCarthy, H. Greehalgh-Spencer and R. Mejia (eds), *New Times: Making Sense of Critical/Cultural Theory in a Digital Age* (New York: Peter Lang, 2011), pp. 349–60; G. Roche, 'Thoughts from a MOOC Pioneer', *Academic Technology Blog*, http://at.blogs.wm.edu/thoughts-from-a-mooc-pioneer/ (accessed 7 January 2017).

14. Butin, 'What MIT Should Have Done'.

15. S. Downes, 'E-Learning 2.0', *eLearn Magazine* (October 2005), http://elearnmag.acm.org/featured.cfm?aid= 1104968 (accessed 6 January 2017).

16. Butin, 'What MIT Should Have Done'.

17. For distinct treatments of this, compare A. J. Bartlett, *Badiou and Plato: An Education by Truths* (Edinburgh: Edinburgh University Press, 2011/15), with Queensland Department of Education and Training, 'New Basics Project' (2010); UNESCO, *Capacity Development for Education for All* (2011); World Bank, 'Building Knowledge Economies: Opportunities and Challenges for EU Accession'.

18. Or perhaps I should say 'players', given how much ink is wasted on the desultory notion of 'play' in this area.

19. Butin, 'What MIT Should Have Done'; Long and Seimans, 'Penetrating the Fog', p. 32. While it is clear the notion of revolution is overwrought, even hysterical, in this context, it is important to note that it has a class basis of the kind Marx and Engels allude to in the *Communist Manifesto* – 'The bourgeoisie, historically, has played a most revolution-

ary part' (Karl Marx and Friedrich Engels, *The Manifesto of the Communist Party* [Moscow: Progress Publishers, 1986], p. 48); or that Gramsci, in the *Prison Notebooks*, marks when he says that under the bourgeoisie 'the state has become an educator' (Antonio Gramsci, *Selections from the Prison Notebooks*, trans. Quentin Hoare and Geoffrey Nowell-Smith [New York: International Publishers, 1971], p. 260); Jacques Rancière, in *The Ignorant Schoolmaster: Five Lessons in Intellectual Emancipation*, trans. K. Ross (Stanford: Stanford University Press, 1991), pp. 130–1, calls this rule of knowledge that designates the sites of non-knowledge the pedagogicisation of society.

20. D. Cormier, 'What is a MOOC?' (2010), http://www.youtube.com/watch?v=eW3gMGqcZQc (accessed 6 January 2017).

21. D. Cormier, 'Rhizomatic Education: Community as Curriculum', *Innovate Online* 4(5), http://davecormier.com/edblog/2008/06/03/rhizomatic-education-community-as-curriculum/ (accessed 1 February 2017). Cf. Châtelet: 'Remember that, in the 20s, it was Franco-Belgian imperialism that invented the concept of nomad-work, which consisted in "de-sedentarizing" certain peasants for seasonal work. After all, isn't slavery a nomadism?' Châtelet, 'A Martial Art of Metaphor'.

22. D. Brooks, 'The Campus Tsunami', *New York Times*, 3 May 2012, http://www.nytimes.com/2012/05/04/opinion/brooks-the-campus-tsunami.html (accessed 6 January 2017); M. Boxall, 'MOOCs: A Massive Opportunity for Higher Education, or Digital Hype?', *Guardian Professional*, 8 August 2012.

23. Hill, 'Online Educational Delivery Models'.

24. The real money is in the data mining that can be carried out on all 'users' – previously called students.

25. Long and Seimans, 'Penetrating the Fog', p. 32. Of course, the increased capacity for data mining is also the golden egg many 'investors' are ultimately after. That it comes in the guise of a virtue – education – makes it all the sweeter, given that there is nothing better than to hide one's bushel under a light.

26. Downes, 'E-Learning 2.0'.

27. F. Kittler, *Gramophone, Film, Typewriter*, trans. G. Winthrop-Young and M. Wutz (Stanford: Stanford University Press, 1999), p. xxxix.

28. B. Groys, 'On the New', # *Artnodes* (2002), https://www.uoc.edu/artnodes/espai/eng/art/groys1002/groys1002.html (accessed 1 February 2017).

29. While some advocates acknowledge the privacy implications, they

are certainly not considered to be overarching. The nexus of capital, knowledge and surveillance is finding a new avatar. There are many books and articles now dealing with the question of 'digital labour', but the key qualifier here is the notion of education, which is the trump card for the business investors. Under the cover of 'learning' almost anything is possible – as it once was under the cover of God.

30. Boxall, 'MOOCs: A Massive Opportunity for Higher Education, or Digital Hype?'; Butin, 'What MIT Should Have Done'; Long and Seimans, 'Penetrating the Fog'; T. L. Friedman, 'Come the Revolution', *New York Times*, 15 May 2012, http://www.nytimes.com/2012/05/16/opinion/friedman-come-the-revolution.html?_r=3& (accessed 6 January 2017).

31. In the words of one commentator: 'A fully-automated, massively-networked, natural language processing, data-driven, feedback-friendly, learning analytics system.' See Butin, 'What MIT Should Have Done'.

32. Long and Seimans, 'Penetrating the Fog', p. 32.

33. See my 'Refuse Become Subject: The Educational Ethic of Saint Paul', *Badiou Studies*, 3(1) (2014), pp. 194–216, for a discussion of how UNESCO situates what it calls Low Development Countries as 'backward', in this sense picking up the long history of colonialism – if, now, presenting it with the human or ethical face of the pedagogue!

34. Cf. Thesis 3 of Marx's 'Theses on Feuerbach': 'The materialist doctrine concerning the changing of circumstances and upbringing forgets that circumstances are changed by men and that it is essential to educate the educator himself. This doctrine must, therefore, divide society into two parts, one of which is superior to society. The coincidence of the changing of circumstances and of human activity or self-changing can be conceived and rationally understood only as *revolutionary practice*.' Here Marx clearly distinguishes between the globalisation thesis – that the world is changing and we must adapt – and the universalist thesis – that change is always already a matter of the subject. And indeed in these theses Marx is clearly arguing for a fully materialist – not simply techno-mechanist-adaptationist – theory of the subject. And let's note here that the famous Thesis 11 invokes the need to think real change and not, as Marx notes, merely interpret it or, as with our globalists, propose a subject as in reaction to it. And of course, it is the case that this reactive subject *is* an idealist construct, which the techno-mechanist materialist simply accepts – especially when it rejects the necessity for the subject – the better to forge the reality in which the forgetting of

the possibility of real change is standard knowledge. Thus what can be done to vs. what can be done!

35. A. Badiou, *Logics of Worlds*, trans. A. Toscano (London: Continuum, 2007), p. 510.

36. Badiou, *Logics of Worlds*, p. 420.

37. B. Groys, '. . . Our Fate as a Living Corpse . . . : An Interview with Boris Groys', *Theory Culture Society*, 28(69) (2011), http://theoryculturesociety. blogspot.com.au/2011/06/interview-with-boris-groys.html   (accessed 6 January 2017).

38. 'For example, if you want to obtain funding for a scientific or artistic grant application, you will, of course, have to explain what the new results of this application will be even if you are thinking in a post-modern fashion. I have read a great many applications of this kind. They all were, or are, postmodern, and they all claim in their texts that there is nothing new. But in the rationale for why they should receive money, it suddenly transpires that they have absolutely revolutionary, new insights. We are living in this situation in which we want to be innovative not because we are driven by creative insights and energies, but because we are carrying out the rituals of innovation, which are repetitive in themselves.' Groys, 'Our Fate . . .'

39. Badiou, *Logics of Worlds*, pp. 509–14.

40. A. Nash, 'Affect and the Medium of Digital Data', *The Fibreculture Journal*, 21 (2013).

41. Long and Seimans, 'Penetrating the Fog', p. 38.

42. Groys, 'On the New'.

43. See Rancière, *The Ignorant Schoolmaster*.

44. Bartlett, *Badiou and Plato: An Education by Truths*.

45. '[W]e are contemporaries of a new departure in the doctrine of truth, following the dissolution of its relation of organic connection to knowledge. It is noticeable, after the fact, that to this day veracity, as I call it, has reigned without quarter: however strange it may seem, it is quite appropriate to say that truth is a new word in Europe (and elsewhere).' A. Badiou, *Being and Event*, trans. O. Feltham (London: Continuum, 2005), p. 3. Cf. Lacan: in referring to the *truth* of Freud's discovery and consequently of how *truth* carries a universal address and that, despite what one might claim, there is no one not 'personally concerned by truth', Lacan says: 'It must seem rather odd that I should be flinging this word in your faces – a word of almost ill repute, a word banished from polite society.' J. Lacan, *Ecrits*, trans.

B. Fink, H. Fink and R. Grigg (New York: W. W. Norton, 2005), p. 338.

46. A. Badiou, 'Art and Philosophy', in *Handbook of Inaestehtics*, trans. A. Toscano (Stanford: Stanford University Press, 2004), pp. 13–15.

47. Badiou, *Logics of Worlds*, p. 1.

48. After Rancière's thoroughgoing critique of Althusser, which is indeed a lesson, we use this term with some circumspection. More accurately, the education debates referred to here are internecine insofar as most participants share a concept of education and, as mostly academics, a 'class' position – whether related to 'cultural capital' or otherwise. That the effects of the debate, registered in schools and universities, overwhelmingly maintain class positions is clear despite protestations (legitimations) of wanting to effect the contrary. The much-vaunted notion of social mobility through education is exemplary. What is referred to here can only be individual mobility within society as it is, and certainly not class mobility such that society is changed. An individual may 'ascend' out of the working class into the heaven of the bourgeoisie, but the working class as such must not rise.

49. See A. Badiou, 'Can Change Be Thought', in *Alain Badiou: Philosophy and its Conditions*, ed. G. Riera (New York: SUNY Press, 2005), pp. 237–61.

50. Badiou, *Logics of Worlds*, p. 1. Subsequent references will be abbreviated to LW and cited in the text.

51. Badiou, *Being and Event*.

52. For this concept of the generic or the new, Badiou draws on the work in transfinite set theory of mathematician Paul Cohen. That a *generic* set, one not bound in its construction to any existing predicates, can be shown to exist serves as the formal model of how a truth can be thought entirely distinct from knowledge. As generic, a truth is 'for all' insofar as there is nothing to prevent 'anyone' being connected to it. Indeed, it is that fact that everyone shares the capacity to *not* be known by the 'state' – represented by it or included in it (or counted as one-part by the power-set) – that is the basis for some new truth of a world. *Forcing*, the 'law of the subject', is intrinsically related to this set and is another of Cohen's terms. Forcing is the operation by which this generic set or new truth (everything being a 'multiple') comes to be in or for a world. Coming from the 'nothing' that is there, this new collection of elements forces the situation to change on the basis of its capacity to demonstrate or to manifest its being there as a part of that world – precisely 'where and when' no such part could be known. See Badiou, *Being and Event*, Part VII.

53. Q. Meillassoux, 'History and Event in Alain Badiou', trans. T. Nail, *Parrhesia* (2011), p. 12.

54. A. Badiou, *Second Manifesto for Philosophy*, trans. L. Burchill (London: Polity, 2011), p. 175.

55. Badiou, *Second Manifesto for Philosophy*, pp. 91–2

56. G. Châtelet, *To Live and Think Like Pigs: The Incitement of Envy and Boredom in Market Democracies*, trans. R. Mackay (New York: Urbanomic/Sequence Press, 2014). Cf. 'Paradoxically, the system at one and the same time aims to uniformize, and to accelerate inequalities tremendously. The market makes a claim to rationality, and a nice festive equilibrium. A whole fringe of the middle classes have even taken up the slogans of '68. This is what I call festive mercantilism, the society of the cellphone, where you can call yourself a nomad even while you remain trussed up in your ego, in your own house, and keeping among your own.' Châtelet, 'A Martial Art of Metaphor'.

57. Badiou, *Second Manifesto for Philosophy*, p. 91.

58. Badiou, *Second Manifesto for Philosophy*, p. 90.

2 Education and the Enclosure of Knowledge in the Global University

Silvia Federici

It can hardly be disputed that a pillar of the globalisation of the world economy has been the transformation that has taken place in the field of education, an international phenomenon that clearly signals a historic restructuring of class relations. At the centre of this process has been the *corporatisation of the university*, in the double sense that universities have been increasingly funded by corporations and, regardless of whether they are public or private, that they now work according to the logic of the market and profit-making. We have also seen the development of the 'global university'. This refers to the development of educational institutions, primarily in the United States, but also in Australia and the United Kingdom, that not only seek to recruit an international student body but also operate internationally, reshaping the educational programmes of universities abroad, in the process setting the standards for education worldwide. The driving force, however, for the reform of academic life has been the *abolition of free public schooling* which had been a key element of the social contract between capital and labour in the post-war period, presumably as the guarantor (for capital) of rising labour productivity, political stability and upward mobility for the working class. In many ways, the end of free education has been a pillar of the reform of the universities both as a source of monetary accumulation and as a means to intensify the disciplinary character of schooling. But equally damaging has been the digitisation of the classroom with the rise of 'online education', and the increasing replacement of the teacher with the computer.[1]

In this chapter, I discuss these developments, examining the main factors that have motivated them, starting with the shift in class relations that has taken place since the mid-1970s which has given the capitalist class greater control over the life of educational institutions at all levels. I believe such preliminary discussion is important, because without an understanding of the politics driving the life of academic institutions today, attempts to redefine pedagogical goals are bound to remain frustrated or to merely provide safety valves in programmes otherwise dominated by political and economic considerations. I thus examine the effects of the commercialisation of academia on education, arguing that it has resulted in an 'enclosure of knowledge', since education is increasingly out of reach for many young people or else is acquired at the cost of massive indebtedness, and its content has been impoverished and degraded. Instead of being appreciated for its contribution to individual and social improvement, education has become something to be bought and sold and a contributor to social inequality. We have also witnessed a standardisation of cultural paradigms, because the dominance of Anglophone educational institutions that have the power to intervene in the setting of educational programmes internationally poses serious constraints to the knowledge that can be produced, at least in institutional settings.

I use the concept of *enclosure* to conceptualise these changes in order to highlight their continuity with other forms of 'expropriation' that the globalisation of the world economy has generated. 'Enclosure' is the concept that Karl Marx used in his famous discussion of 'Primitive Accumulation' in *Capital*, Vol. 1, to describe the expulsion of the peasantry from the land in sixteenth-century England, which – he argued – was the primary condition for the rise of capitalism. In Marx's account,[2] the 'enclosure' of what had formerly been communally held land was the foundation of capitalist development because only with the separation of the peasantry from the land could the formation of a waged proletariat become possible. I suggest, however, that 'enclosure' can also be used to conceptualise the processes by which knowledge is presently privatised and commercialised, such as I describe in the discussion that follows. The term 'enclosure' has historically designated the fencing-off of communally held land so that the former users would be forbidden access to it. In reference to knowledge, then, its use may seem an inappropriate metaphorical extension. Yet by evoking the 'separation of the producers from the means of production', which was the premise for the development of capitalism, 'enclosure' helps us place the changes occurring in the educational field in a historical perspective and highlights the consequences for millions of young people of losing the possibility of acquiring a formal education or not acquiring a knowledge that corresponds to their needs. 'Enclosure' also reminds us that *knowledge too is a commons*, produced through multiple collective creations and exchanges, and its privatisation therefore can only be an arbitrary and violent act.

Enclosures have always been met by resistance and the enclosure of knowledge is no exception. Thus, in my discussion, I look at the struggles that students and other social movements are making on campuses across the world against the 'edu-factory' and in favour of the construction of non-commodified forms of knowledge. In addition to the literature produced on the topic and my own experience as a teacher, I rely on my work as a member of two organisations that have sought to spread information concerning the neoliberal reform of higher education and students' and teachers' struggles against it. These are the US-based Committee for Academic Freedom in Africa which from 1990 to 2003 raised support for the struggles of African students against the dismantling of public education, and the Edu-factory network, which starting in 2007 has organised a broad international exchange of experiences on the effects of the ongoing commercialisation of knowledge.

Studying 'Under the Link':[3] The Enclosure of Knowledge in Structurally Adjusted Africa

In Africa in the early 1980s, one could already see the outlines of a policy that in the following decades was extended to every part of the world, including the United States. The disinvestment in African public education appeared initially as a consequence of the 'debt crisis' and the austerity programme that the World Bank and IMF imposed on African countries in the name of economic recovery. It was soon clear, however, that debt was a tool that international agencies were using to impose structural reforms on Africa's political economies, and that the cuts in government spending for education had a political as well as an economic dimension, as they were often justified by pointing to the excessive social expectations that the post-independence expansion of the university system had generated among the new generation.

Be this as it may, under the pressure of debt repayment, by the early 1990s African governments were de-funding every aspect of academic life: infrastructure maintenance, library budgets, teachers' wages and the wages of non-academic staff. Student allowances too (for food, transport, books) were eliminated. Consequently, within a short time African university campuses began to look like battlefields as everywhere new buildings stood unfinished, and the cuts were met with strong resistance from students, eliciting in turn a brutal repression.[4] Student organisations were driven underground, campuses were shut down for long periods, scores of students were arrested, and the massacre of more than thirty on 5 May 1986, while they were peacefully protesting on the campus of Ahmadu Bello University in the northern Nigerian town of Zaria, clearly staged for the benefit of arriving IMF officers, sent a signal that austerity was irreversible and that blood would be spilled in the face of any opposition.[5] Meanwhile, payments to teachers and staff were delayed and soon it became difficult to make a living teaching in Africa, so that those who could began to migrate.

The end of government investment in public education was the first step in the commercialisation of African universities. The next was the development of 'dependent education', for once public funds were cut, every institution had to find independent forms of self-financing or go under. In part this was achieved through the introduction of 'user fees', as demanded by the World Bank. But academic institutions also began to host courses and research programmes financed by international NGOs or by the World Bank and to establish links with universities abroad that provided curricula, books and other pedagogical materials.

As a result, over time African campuses have witnessed the development of a two-tier system of education. On one side there are the remnants of the previous publicly supported education system, with no funds, no resources, no pedagogical tools, none of the infrastructural amenities that make studying possible and with an unpaid faculty that reduces its teaching to a minimum as a result of the need to find other sources of income to keep body and soul together. On the other side, African universities have been hosting well-financed programmes provided by foreign 'donors', boasting air-conditioned class rooms, functioning toilets, computers and up-to-date publications, all provided by NGOs and the World Bank, which are clearly taking advantage of their monetary clout to dictate what Africans should be taught.

With 'dependent education', a shift has also taken place in the orientation of university curricula, away from the humanities and in favour of business accounting and courses aimed at grooming a generation of technocrats sensitive to the needs of foreign investors. This is what the World Bank has called 'Africa Capacity Building'.[6] Critics have labelled it 'studying under the link' to denounce the loss of control over the means by which academic knowledge is produced.

In search of commercial proficiency, African universities have also undergone a balkanisation process, as a class differentiation has come into place depending on different departments' money-making capacity. Institutions and departments with the 'link' call the shots, while the others follow along. What this implies has been described by the Ugandan scholar/activist Mahmood Mamdani, in *Scholars in the Market Place*. Mamdani has shown that, under the pressure of 'solvency', each department has begun to function as a self-subsistent unit, with its own budget and its own money-making ventures, leading to a fragmentation of academic life. Things have gone so far that the more affluent departments have attempted to break away and organise themselves as independent units, not wishing to contribute the money they are making to the rest of the university.[7] But even if this has not succeeded, commercialisation has spelled the end of the university as a unitary project. Mamdani has also denounced the development of 'turf wars', as departments seek to teach the most profitable courses, regardless of their academic specialisation and expertise.[8] Under these conditions, teaching and research have taken a back seat. Busy searching for funds, teachers pretend to teach and students pretend to study, often organising a division of labour among themselves, so that those who attend certain courses take the exams for others as well, in the certain knowledge that their frequently absent teachers will not notice.

Why has there been such a massive attack on educational systems that for the most part were only beginning to emerge from a colonial past in which they only served the children of the colonisers and a restricted group of aboriginal people groomed for indirect rule? And why has education been so severely undermined at a time when knowledge is held to be the primary means of production? Most important, what can be done, beside resisting the politics of cuts and profit-making? What alternative pedagogical programmes can be instituted?

The Political Roots of the Worldwide Commercialisation of Education

If we look at the restructuring of education solely from an African viewpoint, we have to conclude that publicly funded higher education was gutted in Africa because of the new international division of labour that has emerged from the globalisation of the world economy. Africans have not been expected to be producers of knowledge, but have been destined to be producers of raw materials and cheap labour for the international market, as in the colonial period. This is what a representative of the World Bank explicitly admitted in a meeting of African vice-chancellors, held in Harare in 1986, where he proclaimed that Africans had no need of universities! Not surprisingly there has been little concern in international circles about the massive brain drain which the dismantling of public education in Africa has caused, and the fact that yesterday's students and teachers are today's migrants, risking their lives crossing the Sahara, and making their passage to Europe on overcrowded boats through the Mediterranean, where it is calculated that more than 15,000 have drowned during the last decade.

Further support for this theory is the fact that the disabling of the African educational system has favoured the exploitation of African wealth by transnational corporations (TNCs). As George Caffentzis has shown, the collapse of African universities has had three major effects: it has enabled TNCs and international financial agencies to present themselves as the centres best equipped to preserve the wealth of the continent in all its forms (agricultural, genetic, cultural); it has weakened the ability of African countries to develop, on the basis of local knowledge, cheaper products than those marketed by the TNCs; and it has made available to them a rich pool of cheap intellectual labour and research facilities in Africa's higher learning institutions.[9] In sum, there is no doubt that the disabling of African universities has stemmed from a re-colonisation drive, which has also thwarted (as we have seen) the expectations of the new generation of Africans who, coming of age in the post-independence period, by the 1970s were demanding a new world order based on a more just distribution of wealth.

If, however, we broaden our scope to include Europe and the US, we realise that something else has been at stake, for the same developments that began in Africa in the early 1980s, apparently in response to the 'debt crisis', have since then unfolded in every other part of the world. What we are witnessing, then, is best described as a change in capital's relation to the reproduction of the workforce that takes specific regional forms but has long-term objectives that are at once economic and political.

From a strict economic viewpoint, education is undergoing the same 'financialisation' process[10] that all public services (healthcare, pensions etc.) have undergone as part of the neoliberalisation of the world economy, which aims to cheapen the cost of labour production and turn every aspect of our reproduction into a point of capital accumulation. According to autonomist Marxists, this restructuring of the educational system is also an effect of the central function that knowledge and 'cognitive labour' have acquired in the organisation of work in the present phase of capitalist development.[11]

There is, however, a political dimension to this transformation. De-funding public education, forcing students to pay for services that once were supported by the state, and placing universities under the guardianship of international financial institutions has first of all been a disciplinary strategy, forged in response to the student movements of the 1960s and 1970s, when campuses worldwide played a major role in the struggle against war, colonial domination and the authoritarian character of education. This was certainly the case with the de-funding of African universities, which by the 1980s were educating a generation of students who were striving to free themselves from the vestiges of colonialism, who read Frantz Fanon, and who organised support for the anti-apartheid struggle in South Africa. In the US as well, disciplining the campuses and, through them, the future workforce has been a major objective of the corporatisation of academic life.

The Corporatisation of the University in the US: 'For Profit Education' and the 'Digital Diploma Mills'

Promoted in the 1950s as a means to gain technological superiority in the race with the Soviet Union for dominance of space, mass education in the US by the 1970s was deemed by politicians to be a Himalayan miscalculation. Far from producing obedient citizens and more productive workers, investment in the colleges produced the Berkeley revolt, and the free speech and anti-war movements. Not surprisingly, even before the official inauguration of Reaganomics, state and federal subsidies to schools were reduced and, in state after state, 'open admission' was eliminated, forcing students to devote a larger part of their academic time to acquiring the funds to enable them to study. Not only have tuition fees been introduced, they have increased at such a pace (three times the rate of inflation) that college education has become unaffordable for the majority at the very time that it is promoted as the only avenue to a living wage. Thus, short of possessing considerable means, for US students studying 'comes with tears', as they can expect to leave university with an average debt of 30,000 dollars, which, given the state of youth employment, will hang around their neck like an albatross for many years after their courses have ended.[12]

Certainly, putting a price tag on education is congenial to the neo-liberal idea that citizens should pay for social services and that higher education is an individual and not a social good.[13] But tuition and debt are also powerful control mechanisms. Williams speaks of a 'pedagogy of debt', arguing that (like testing in high school) the disciplinary element of debt is 'central to the aims of higher education'; it is what students are expected to learn, which is that education is not an entitlement, that paying back one's debts is a priority and must govern career choices, that the market is the social 'prime mover' and, above all, that life must be prudently calculated, for any misstep (like missing a payment) can plunge us into ruin.[14] And the ideology is working. Such is the crisis that debt is producing in students' lives that 'indentured servitude to the banks' is a now a popular concept that is increasingly used on US campuses to describe student status. Meanwhile, six million have already defaulted on their payments, raising the spectre of another financial crisis.

Debt is not the only mechanism that has been deployed to discipline students. While ever more costly, education has been steadily degraded and so has the work of the providers. Fifty per cent of the teaching staff on US campuses today – from 'for profit' universities to the elite Ivy League – are graduate students, and 'online' education, in which interaction between students and teachers is minimised, is constantly gaining ground.[15] The content of courses is also being reduced to serve narrow economic goals. College after college are merging departments and eliminating courses believed to have low economic utility, such as courses on the arts, literature and philosophy, which are clearly to be reserved for the elite. Teachers too are expected to be business-like and to bring money directly to the universities, by applying for government-sponsored or other types of grants and engaging in activities that give lustre to the institution. Teaching and even publishing are no longer sufficient. What matters now is knowing how to write a grant application or appearing on a TV show or being frequently quoted in refereed journals and books. Constant evaluation and ranking, measuring how each teacher and institution approximates the goal, further degrade academic life, submitting decision-making on knowledge to be produced to quantitative criteria.

As education is reclassified as a consumer good, a change is also taking place in the personnel running the universities. In US academia this is the time of the administrators, whose number and salaries keep growing, and the company men. CEOs are becoming presidents of academic institutions – exemplary is the recent appointment as president of the University of Southern Maine of a CEO of the Maine Power Company – or participate in the construction of curricula, and they are allowed to hold events on campuses which students are encouraged to attend, even though they have no academic value. Conforming to this trend, campus space too has been reorganised by the market, with student unions being replaced by Pizza Hut, Domino's or similar commercial ventures, and luxury dorms being built on select campuses to provide well-to-do students with all the amenities they desire. In educational 'hot spots' such as New York, entire new buildings are being constructed to project a sense of economic and cultural power and to turn universities into hubs to attract students from across the world.

The Rise of the Global University

Anticipating a more general conclusion, we can say that through these developments, capital is taking into its hands the task of selecting, training and disciplining not only the present students but the future workers. As already emphasised, this is an international trend, but it is not a uniform one. Like the global economy, global education too has a pyramidal structure, as prestigious North American and European universities build campuses abroad, especially in affluent countries, and restructure the educational systems of countries that have been economically 'adjusted', reshaping programmes, curricula and examination procedures, establishing computer networks and so forth. In this way, North American universities, together with universities in the UK, France and elsewhere in the west and international NGOs, are becoming the gatekeepers for education and knowledge production across the world, setting the standards for what should be considered pedagogically valuable on a global level. The same universities also recruit a multinational, multicultural student body, presumably to forge the future managers of the global economy, and pipe courses into the colleges of impoverished/indebted 'third world' countries, taking advantage of the fact that in the aftermath of adjustment their educational systems have been degraded and made dependent on external experts and aid.

Through the rise of the global university, then, a *centralisation of knowledge production is being carried out* that is congenial to the globalisation of capital accumulation and the formation of a global proletariat. This means that the same countries and institutions that control the world economy also set the rules, the canons, the ideological paradigms for education and culture on a global level, so that despite the seeming drive towards multi-culturalisation, knowledge in reality is becoming more homogenised and more controlled to reflect the interests of the world powers. Few 'peripheral' teachers, for instance, can afford today to concentrate their research work on their regions' or localities' concerns, as the need to have their work published in Anglophone refereed journals in order to get a job or be promoted prompts them to select topics of interest to Anglophone academic audiences. Thus, while we are told that we have access to 'globally produced knowledge', the knowledge that we actually gain is spoken in the same tongue, as from South Korea to Abu Dhabi, developing scholars must follow the same handbook of rules and publish in the same refereed journals if they wish to see their work recognised, if not appreciated. Occurring in a field of unequal power relations, the 'knowledge exchange' is thus a top-down process, an imposition of cultural and pedagogical standards amounting to a form of cultural imperialism.

From Public Education to the Production of Knowledge Commons

As dismal as the academic landscape appears in much of the world, it would be a mistake to assume that corporate interests rule the campuses unchallenged. Struggles against the structural adjustment of education have surged on African campuses since the 1980s, with students linking with unemployed youth, unions and other grassroots social forces.[16] Resistance has also been mounting on North American and Latin American campuses. In the US students have been fighting on several fronts, at times coordinating their activities with those of Canadian students, recognising that they have the same problems.[17] They have fought against recruitment on campuses by the military and the CIA, which escalated after 9/11 and the war against Iraq. They have also been active in the anti-globalisation movement, urging universities to disinvest from their World Bank Bonds and opposing the presence in universities of items produced under sweatshop conditions. Graduate students – the bulk of the academic labour force – have fought for the right to unionise. In the wake of the Occupy movement, however, the main form of resistance has been the struggle against tuition fees and student loan debt which, constantly growing, reached the staggering figure of 1.3 trillion dollars in April 2016, and is increasing at $2,726 per second.[18]

A strategy that students have used in the past to dramatise the consequences of their debt was the construction on campuses of 'tent cities' in which they would live to demonstrate the impact of debt on their lives and the need to move away from universities that are becoming purely financial operations. Since then, the anti-debt movement has diversified its goals and tactics. Some organisations have taken a reformist approach, aiming simply to slow down the pace of tuition increases or win the right for indebted students to declare bankruptcy. But others, like the New York and California based Strike Debt, have declared student debt illegitimate and are aiming to create a mass debt-refusal movement.[19]

Strike Debt aims not only to win a cancellation of all debt, a 'debt jubilee' as it were, but, more importantly, to establish that under no circumstance should education and knowledge be turned into commodities. According to this principle, activists on and off campuses have also striven to create *knowledge commons*, that is, spaces where knowledge can be produced and accessed without any price-tag attached and where learning is through self-education. Models have not been missing. The free universities created in the 1960s and the alternative pedagogies that have been produced by radical movements (Marxists, anarchists, pragmatist) have offered important examples.[20] A particularly interesting model has come from the programme instituted in Italian factories in the 1970s under the name of the '150 Ore' – that is, the 150 paid hours of study on factory time that metal-mechanic workers won in 1974.[21] Staffed mostly by radical teachers, the courses that the programme generated were models of self-instruction and collective cooperation in the production of knowledge, as in most cases workers decided to select as their topic of study the factory system in which they worked and the modalities of their own exploitation. A different model of self-education is that proposed by Freirian pedagogy,[22] which also takes the understanding of one's oppression as the starting point for an analysis of social and historical structures.

A precondition, however, for the success of these efforts is *a change in the material conditions of education.* For if the drive towards the commercialisation of academic life is not reversed, not only will alternative educational models fail, but their partial implementation could have a mystifying effect, promoting versions of cultural pluralism. Moreover, it is only in the course of the struggle to free education and knowledge production from the logic of profit that new pedagogical models can be created. In this context, a lesson that we have learned is that students and teachers by themselves cannot change the educational process. What is needed is a broad coalition of forces bringing together all those who are, or should be, interested in reconstructing education as a common good. The call for such collective reconstruction is far more than an expedient to build power from below and shift power relations. The struggle to define education as a common good is central to workers and capital relations at all levels. Student debt, for instance, is a wage-cut, no less than all the free labour that under the guise of 'internship' students are now forced to provide as a condition for future employment. Most important, the key question we are confronting is how to ensure that education ceases to be an instrument of social hierarchy and exclusion and becomes instead an instrument of economic and social liberation.

Along these lines, as Gigi Roggero, a founder of the international Edu-factory network, recently pointed out, the first step is to refuse the logic of 'meritocracy' which today reigns in the academic world, creating divisions among students and making the failures of the academic institutions appear as individual failures.[23] It is also crucial to demonstrate that – to paraphrase the title of an important student conference held in 2009 on the campus of the University of Minnesota – 'beneath the university is the common'. That is, what appears as a public good is in reality a commonwealth created by years of labour and struggle by many who will never be present on the ground of the campuses. Starting from this realisation we can further articulate what direction the construction of alternatives to the commercialisation of education must take. For the purpose of free, non-commercial education will be to reverse the process that has so far guided the creation of universities and the knowledge produced by them. It will mean freeing knowledge production from the selective mechanisms that define our schools: grading, ranking, testing, whose purpose is to determine who will be condemned to purely manual labour and who will be given a chance to acquire knowledge not limited to the acquisition of technical task-oriented information. It will also mean expanding our conception of who is a producer of knowledge, acknowledging, for instance, that the workers who every day reproduce the life of academic institutions have much to contribute to the decision-making concerning the educational models to be adopted, often exceeding, owing to their life experiences, the wisdom of the experts. Expanding our radical imagination and paving the way to the 'liberated' educational models that we must create, we can begin a struggle not only to refuse the cost of knowledge production, but to demand group exams, collective grading,[24] assemblies of all school workers, and schools without walls, open to the needs and desires of the communities that support them and free from business and military presences and projects. To achieve this goal, 'ignorant schoolmasters'[25] are not enough. More important is to redefine who 'educates the educators'.[26]

Notes

1. On this topic, see David F. Noble, *Digital Diploma Mills: The Automation of Higher Education* (New York: Monthly Review Press, 2001).
2. Karl Marx, *Capital* (London: Penguin, 1976), Vol. 1, chapter 26.
3. I take this title from an article by Karim Hirji, which powerfully describes the creation of dependent education in Tanzania. See Karim F. Hirji, 'Academic Pursuits under the LINK', in C. B. Mwaria, S. Federici and J. McLaren (eds), *African Visions* (Westport, CT: Praeger, 2000), pp. 67–84.
4. On the 'structural adjustment' of African universities, see G. Caffentzis, 'The World Bank and Education in Africa', S. Federici, 'The Recolonization of African Education' and 'The New African Student Movement', and S. Federici and G. Caffentzis, 'Chronology of African University Students' Struggles', in S. Federici, G. Caffentzis and O. Alidou (eds), *A Thousand Flowers: Social Struggles against Structural Adjustment in African Universities* (Trenton; Asmara: Africa World Press, 2000), pp. 3–18, 19–24, 87–112, 115–50.
5. Scores of students were also massacred, in retaliation for a peaceful demonstration, at the University of Lumumbashi in the DRC (then Zaire) on 11 May 1990.
6. See G. Caffentzis, 'The World Bank's Africa Capacity Building Initiative', in Federici, Caffentzis and Alidou (eds), *A Thousand Flowers*, pp. 69–82.
7. Mahmood Mamdani, *Scholars in the Market Place: The Dilemmas of*

Neo Liberal Reform at Makerere University, 1989–2005 (Kampala: Fountain Publishers, 2007), pp. 175–87.

8. Mamdani, *Scholars in the Market Place*, pp. 119ff.

9. G. Caffentzis, 'The International Intellectual Property Regime and the Enclosure of African Knowledge', in Mwaria, Federici and McLaren (eds), *African Visions*, pp. 7–14.

10. I refer here to the process whereby increasingly people have to pay for the same services that were once subsidised, in many countries, by the state – health, education, transport – and must do so by becoming indebted to the banks through the credit system.

11. See C. Vercellone, 'From Formal Subsumption to General Intellect: Elements for a Marxist Reading to the Thesis of Cognitive Capitalism', *Historical Materialism*, 15 (2007), pp. 13–36. For a critique of Vercellone's position, see G. Caffentzis, 'A Critique of Cognitive Capitalism', in M. A. Peters and E. Bulut (eds), *Cognitive Capitalism, Education and Digital Labor* (New York: Peter Lang, 2011), pp. 23–56.

12. On the impact of debt on student lives, see Strike Debt, *The Debt Resisters' Operation Manual* (Oakland and New York: PM Press and Common Notions, 2014).

13. Jeffrey Williams, 'The Pedagogy of Debt', in The Edu-factory Collective (ed.), *Towards A Global Autonomous University. Cognitive Labor, the Production of Knowledge and Exodus from the Education Factory* (New York: Autonomedia, 2009), pp. 89–96 (p. 91).

14. Williams, 'The Pedagogy of Debt', pp. 91–6.

15. See Noble, *Digital Diploma Mills*, chapters 4 and 5.

16. Inspired by them, in the early 1990s a groups of scholars/activists, of whom I was one, mostly composed of former teachers on African campuses, formed the Committee for Academic Freedom in Africa (CAFA), which during the following ten years, from 1991 to 2004, informed people in North America about the new African student movement. A compendium of the bulletins that we periodically produced is now collected in the volume already cited: *A Thousand Flowers, Social Struggles against Structural Adjustment in African Universities*. Archive material acquired through CAFA's activism is also available at May Day Rooms in London, including correspondence with African students and teaching staff organisations, World Bank reports on education in Africa, and material produced by student and teachers' organisations. See http:// maydayrooms.org/ (accessed 6 January 2017).

17. A good source of information on students' struggles in the United States

is Campus Activism (see www.campusactivism.org, accessed 6 January 2017). This is a website that introduces the Democratizing Education Network (DEN), a broad coalition of student groups based in the US and Canada. The following is the Charter that DEN has adopted which reflects what a broad spectrum of students in the US are demanding:

- Full public funding for public higher education
- Free access to higher education and the abolition of tuition
- Affirmative action to end institutionalised racism and sexism
- Full recognition of the rights of students and workers to organise
- Democratic self-government of higher education
- Service to the public welfare not to corporate profits
- Free speech and academic freedom
- Debt forgiveness of student loans
- Civic education for a democratic society
- Education not war
- Schools not jails

18. See http://www.marketwatch.com/story/every-second-americans-get -buried-under-another-3055-in-student-loan-debt-2015-06-10 (access-ed 6 January 2017) and http://collegedebt.com/ (accessed 6 January 2017).

19. On Strike Debt, see *The Debt Resisters' Operations Manual*, and the Strike Debt website: www.strikedebt.org (accessed 6 January 2017).

20. See, for example, R. H. Haworth (ed.), *Anarchist Pedagogies. Collective Actions, Theories and Critical Reflections on Education* (Oakland: PM Press, 2012).

21. On the experience of the '150 Hours', see P. Causarano, 'Lavorare, studiare, lottare: fonti sull'esperienza delle "150 ore" negli anno '70', http://www.historied.net/portal/index.php?option=com_content&view=article&id=9&Itemid=13 (accessed 22 April 2015).

22. P. Freire, *Pedagogy of the Oppressed* (London: Bloomsbury, 2000).

23. G. Roggero, presentation on 'Cognitive Labor, Cognitive Capitalism and the Transformation of the University in an Enterprise', Cornell University, Ithaca NY, 13 November 2014.

24. Collective grading as well as 'group exams' were gains of the Italian student movement of the 1960s.

25. The reference is to Jacques Rancière's *The Ignorant Schoolmaster: Five Lessons in Intellectual Emancipation*, trans. K. Ross (Stanford: Stanford University Press, 1991), otherwise an extremely powerful and inspiring indictment of the authoritarianism that pervades our educational models.

26. That the 'educator herself needs educating' is the challenge posed by Karl Marx (1845) in his 'Third Thesis on Feuerbach'. See 'Theses on Feuerbach', in *Marx, Engels, Lenin: On Historical Materialism* (Moscow: Progress Publishers, 1972), pp. 11–12.

3 Knowledge Enclosure and University Education: Notes from 'Post-restructured' Bangladesh

Mushahid Hussain

The neoliberalisation of university education, in terms of the extensive marketisation that has accompanied the withdrawal of state provision, has been the subject of much recent discussion and criticism. Such concerns are especially pronounced in the so-called developing world, where questions of education in general, and university or higher education in particular, are intrinsically tied to issues of material self-determination for the vast majority of the world's population in their struggle against capitalist exploitation in the context of neoliberal economic restructuring.[1] Consequently, these discussions provide an opportune juncture for re-examining what is meant by 'education' in the contemporary era. How, for instance, do we envisage education beyond the production, dissemination and use of knowledge, and contextualise its modalities within contemporary sociopolitical, economic and historical processes? It is through this broad concern that I approach the re-examining of education in light of the critical conceptual framework found within the 'new enclosures' literature. I draw on the case of university education in contemporary Bangladesh and how the meaning of such education and its practices have in the past (as well as in the present) undergone transformations in and through processes of enclosure. The theoretical development of 'enclosure' as a conceptual notion can, of course, be traced back to Marx's well-known discussions on primitive accumulation in part eight of the first volume of *Capital*.[2]

The core proposition in Marx regarding enclosures involves the process of primitive accumulation which 'is nothing else than the historical process of divorcing the producer from the means of production'.[3] This proposition was developed by Marx in the context of land enclosures, the primary means of production in the agrarian England of the sixteenth and seventeenth centuries, and how it violently changed the social relations between the dominant and subordinate classes, paving the way for capitalist relations to take root. There has been much theoretical debate on the status of Marx's notion of primitive accumulation and the enclosures, a complete account of which is outside the scope of this chapter.[4] It suffices for my purposes to note that the new enclosures perspective is theoretically premised on the understanding of primitive accumulation as not only a precondition for capitalist accumulation, but a continuously unfolding process which is integral and contemporaneous to the latter, especially in the context of mitigating its crises.[5] Such an approach retains consistency with Marx's theory of the capitalist mode of production based on alienated labour, in which the separation of such labour from the means of production is taken to progressively higher degrees as capitalist development takes place. For instance, as Marx notes in his *Theories of Surplus Value*:

Thus primitive accumulation, as I have already shown, means nothing but the separation of labour and the worker from the conditions of labour, which confront him as independent forces. The course of history shows that this separation is a factor in social development. Once capital exists, the capitalist mode of production itself evolves in such a way that it maintains and reproduces this separation on a constantly increasing scale until the historical reversal takes place.[6]

The new enclosures perspective builds on this to clarify the substantive theoretical difference between accumulation and primitive accumulation as one of specific modalities through which the fundamental condition of alienated labour is produced and reproduced historically. The tremendous advantage of such a reconceptualisation lies in its opening up of the notion of enclosure to the critical rethinking of alienated labour in a wide range of historical and sociopolitical contexts as well as production processes, including that of knowledge production within the 'neoliberalising' university space. Putting these together, I argue here for a conceptual framework that envisages capitalist development as a contested process requiring the reproduction of alienated labour located within subordinate positions, where the objective requirements of capitalist production and reproduction combine with the historically contingent outcomes of struggles to construct both the facilitating and inhibiting conditions for processes of continuous enclosure in particular spatio-temporal settings.

Rethinking processes of enclosure in this manner as a facet of conflicting interests and struggles within and integral to capitalist accumulation is a conceptual watershed in terms of envisaging anti-systemic movements. Of the many instances of new forms of enclosures taking place around us today, the university seems an unlikely focus, but it is nevertheless an important arena in which this process is unfolding. Conceptually, the modern university can be seen as the *outcome* of the process of enclosure, especially in the colonial context. The requirement of the colonial state to enclose knowledge and use it for purposes of domination had in fact led to the establishment of such institutions in non-settler colonies, where it was intricately associated with both political and civil society and formed a cornerstone of state power. A question, however, arises immediately: how can the university be undergoing enclosure if it is already the outcome of earlier enclosures and thereby an integral part of the state machinery? Drawing on the particular conceptualisation of the processes of enclosure noted above, it is clear that the enclosure of knowledge within and through the modern university is neither discrete nor self-terminating, but continuous.[7] In other words, an enclosure that institutionalises knowledge to sustain the existence and expansion of capitalist relations simultaneously invokes, as we will see, continuous antagonisms and opposition to the processes that bring such relations into being, and thus renders such enclosure 'incomplete' in all instances. Moreover, the degree to which such enclosure approximates 'completion' is determined by the contextual and historical specificities of the case, and thus ultimately indicates the relative strength of class positions in the particular context of the struggle.

I attempt to analyse such relative class positions, the actual and potential processes of knowledge enclosure they facilitate, and their impact on university education by theoretically deploying the Gramscian notion of civil society in examining the historical role of the university in Bangladesh, tracing briefly its transformations from the colonial to the neoliberal era.[8] I argue that the neoliberal assault on the civil society space, limiting the articulation of subordinate interests and the subsequent struggles to realise them, has initiated a process of knowledge enclosure by radically extending the commodity logic in the sphere of university education in unprecedented ways. Moreover, the current context of the privatisation of university education is seen not only as an intensification of the knowledge enclosure process, but also as an important empirical reference point for highlighting how multiple forms of enclosure operate in conjunction to sustain capitalist relations premised on alienated labour.

The case of Bangladesh is particularly useful for two reasons, one substantive and the other methodological. The substantive reason is that Bangladesh is one of the classic cases of neoliberal economic restructuring of the 1980s, and in many ways is a pioneer of university privatisation in the Global South, where the first such university came into being in the late 1980s. The methodological reason is that my employment as a lecturer at a private university in Dhaka allows me to draw on both my own everyday experiences, and those of others whom I have managed to interview, in examining these processes in some detail at the micro-level. The institution I was with, being representative of private university practices in Bangladesh, serves as a subject of relatively detailed scrutiny. I conclude by laying out some of the possible conditions and modalities through which the processes of knowledge enclosure in and through university education can be struggled against and overcome.

From the Colonial to the Public University

The official establishment of the first modern university in Dhaka in 1921 can be understood in the context of the then existing political society and processes of colonial enclosure. The colonial state broadly saw knowledge among the local population in the colonies through two interrelated perspectives. The first was the lens of how such knowledge could be moulded to serve the interests of commerce (and thereby administration), including both commodity exports and subsequently core industrial manufactures imports.[9] The second involved concern with the sufficiency of such knowledge for the minimum material sustenance needs of the exploited peasantry in the context of maximising return on coerced cash-crop production for export.[10] Indigenous productive and reproductive knowledge thus had to survive in the sphere of subsistence under the constant threat of being subsumed by the accumulation objectives of the colonial state. Such knowledge was required to be strictly 'monitored and regulated' by the state administrative apparatus in order to reduce the potential for material autonomy, and thus create exploitable dependencies among the peasantry through both economic and extra-economic means. From this perspective, the colonial university can be seen as an institution which appropriates indigenous knowledge selectively on the basis of interests conducive to capital accumulation, churning out administrators, cartographers and scientists in the service of empire. It simultaneously restricts access to, as well as determines the legitimacy of, such knowledge in order to undermine the class power of actual producers in the colony.

At a lower level of generality, however, the existence of the university can be seen to have been brought about by intra-class power struggles within political society. In the case of the first such university in Dhaka, the institution was the outcome of a tripartite power tussle between the colonial state and the Hindu and Muslim elites in the immediate aftermath of the first partition of Bengal in 1905 and its subsequent annulment in 1911.[11] Risking a vulgar compression of history, the modern university system in Bangladesh can be traced back to the British colonial politics of Hindu–Muslim 'divide and rule', a facet of which manifested itself in the disfavoured position of the Muslim elite in administrative power sharing with the colonial government. One of the 'remedies' in the view of this educated elite in Bengal was the establishment of a modern university within its geographical constituency, which could potentially train more Muslims for positions of colonial power. Consequently, it was envisaged as a strategic political shift in the dependence of the Muslim elite on institutions in and around the Hindu-majority regions of Calcutta. Both regional and communal tensions among elites, fuelled to a great extent by colonial policies, along with the willingness of these elites to share subordinate positions of power, were important aspects in the exercise of colonial hegemony through political society. The university thus began as an integral part of the state by virtue of its genesis within political society, whose dominant objective of state-administered surplus extraction required a particular type of knowledge enclosure that could potentially be facilitated through such an institution.

By directly controlling the production and appropriation of knowledge as well as its access and legitimation through the colonial university at the apex, the colonial state therefore initiated a formidable process of enclosure. However, the understanding of this process of colonial enclosure through the prism of elite politics and the state remains incomplete. For Gramsci, the state is constituted by both political and civil society, and it is the latter to which we must turn for a more complete explication. Civil society is relatively more intractable than, as well as closely interrelated with, the political in terms of covert manifestations of inter- and intra-class antagonisms. Simply put, civil society operates at the level of discourse and knowledge, and is primarily involved in shaping consent to the structural domination of capital. In other words, it generates and sustains capitalist hegemony: the corollary, however, also emerges simultaneously, whereby the processes of generating such consent also render the space contentious.[12] However, such 'hegemony' itself is determined in the last instance by transformations in the economic apparatuses of society at the level of material production and exchange, whose perpetual systemic mutations require continuous adjustments that are facilitated, Gramsci argues, through the 'educative and the formative role of the State'.[13] The relevant question then is: how does such hegemony, which is formed and sustained at the level of the collective, achieve individual compliance through consensual means? It is precisely in answering this question that the notion of civil society acquires crucial importance for Gramsci, where his explication of its role within the state apparatus in obtaining 'hegemonic consent' is definitive of what the modern education system seeks to achieve: 'the latter [domain of civil society]', he argues, 'operates without "sanctions" or compulsory "obligations", but nevertheless exerts a collective pressure and obtains objective results in the form of an evolution of customs, ways of thinking and acting, morality, etc.'[14]

This 'evolution', in other words, is an adjustment necessity mandated by the continuous mutations of material circumstances in sustaining processes of capitalist accumulation, of which the contemporary neoliberal phase is a particular juncture, with its own spatio-temporal specifications defined by the clear dominance of the logic of finance capital. The processes of adjustment, of which education is an integral facilitator, are diverse yet 'homogenising', given that they are outcomes of contestations both for and against subordinate interests under the influence of similar hegemonic discourses disseminated through transforming educational apparatuses. Knowledge, insofar as it lies outside hegemonic discourse at a particular historical juncture, is thus required to be 'enclosed' within the logic of accumulation processes in order to mitigate actual and potential antagonistic impulses emanating from subordinate positions. However, such enclosure itself constitutes, and is constituted by, contested processes that are intrinsically intertwined with changes in material circumstances accompanying shifts in the dominant capitalist logic for sustained accumulation. Hence, the colonial university must be envisaged as generating and enclosing knowledge within an imperial project that defines the spatial dynamics of surplus accruals, where absolute and subsequently relative extraction determines the establishment of material conditions in particular temporal junctures, which consequently set the parameters for subordinate struggles. Substantiating this would, of course, require the contextual mapping of historical processes in concrete cases, examining the modalities through which struggles in the domain of civil society are carried out. Such an approach is akin to the one Gramsci takes when he emphasises the necessity for 'an accurate reconnaissance of each individual country'.[15]

Defining the university as an institutional apparatus which encloses knowledge consequently makes it a pivotal part of civil society engaged in the production and circulation of hegemonic discourse. However, this is where an important dialectical tension must be pointed out. Gramsci's critical insight regarding the ineffectiveness of direct assault on state institutions (and thereby capital) derives from his understanding of civil society, whose tenacious creation of hegemonic consent must first be dismantled through a difficult process of contestation, or 'war of position', before capitalism's antagonistic tendencies can even be perceived as such.[16]

The colonial university, as the site of knowledge production and appropriation under 'state-mediated' capitalist relations, becomes vulnerable in terms of potential manifestations of contradictory class interests only under conditions of entrenched struggles in the sphere of civil society. This, in turn, attains the possibility of actualisation when the interests of intellectual actors in the 'education sector' are both sharply defined and conflictingly aligned towards subordinate and dominant positions, respectively. Consequently, the actions of such actors acquire a higher probability of conscious engagement in contestations over undermining and preserving the prevalent hegemony, a situation that shapes as well as being shaped by periods of profound transition or turmoil in political and civil society.[17] In this case, the transition from the colonial to the public university under nationalist movements is the carrying out of, among other struggles, contestations across civil society in delegitimising the hegemonic consent to imperialism. It can thus be perceived as an important structural rupture whereby the local capitalist class asserts its sovereignty over its imperial counterpart through effective compromise with the subordinate classes.

This transition to the public, 'national' university is thus the outcome of *intra-class* conflict, of which the institution itself is an important arena as far as the struggle in civil society is concerned. But this conflict required the domestic ruling classes not only to muster their own strength, but also to gain the support of the masses of the dominated classes upon whose shoulders they necessarily had to stand. As a result, after independence from direct imperialism, the new nationalist state was compelled to accommodate the interests of these subordinate classes to a certain extent across both political and civil society, as a consequence of recognising the latter's disruptive power vis-à-vis its authority. Consequently, the university too began to accommodate these 'subordinate interests', marking the initiation of an intensified *inter-class* struggle within civil society through what was essentially a partial roll-back of knowledge enclosure. Access to the university became more broad-based as it began to include the subordinate classes through affirmative policy measures, and knowledge production within the institutional space increasingly began to be concerned with social improvement. Interestingly, this transition reveals how both intra- and inter-class struggles in the spheres of political and civil society affect the processes of knowledge enclosure in conjunction. It is clear that such enclosure is not 'undone' in any sense as an outcome of such struggles, but that there is a qualitative shift at its apex, the modern university, whose composition is affected to the extent that it intensifies the potentiality for contestation against the state and its constitutive ruling interests.

Historical evidence in this context goes a long way towards validating this last statement. During the second (direct) colonial period from 1947 to 1971, before the creation of the Bangladeshi state, the public university became the central arena of struggle in the sphere of civil and political society. It was the students and teachers of Dhaka University who were instrumental in initiating the 1952 Language Movement, and who continued to play a crucial role over the next two decades in struggling for what ultimately became a linguistically and ethnically defined statehood.[18] The university was where capitalist hegemony under the West Pakistani military regime(s) faced its first radical opposition.

Since processes of enclosure, including that of knowledge, are necessary for the creation of proletarian and/or subordinate conditions under capitalism, struggles in the realms of both political and civil society against dominant capitalist interests are also resistances against such processes. As we have already established, enclosures are not merely anachronistic preconditions for facilitating capitalist accumulation processes and mitigating their crises, but are both intrinsic to and indispensable for the perpetuation of such processes. The public university, therefore, by virtue of its being at the epicentre of such contestation in post-1947 East Bengal (Pakistan), gradually became an institutional space that was predominantly antagonistic towards the very processes (of enclosure) that had brought it into existence. Of course, the class composition in this struggle was far more nuanced, and resembled closely the positions and interests of the ruling elite, as in the years preceding independence from British colonial rule in 1947, albeit with different actors this time. However, subsequent class compromises as mentioned above allowed for greater articulation of subordinate interests within the university that partially transformed the decolonisation struggle within it to give it a relatively more inter-class character, and thereby gave fresh impetus to struggles against the enclosure of knowledge.

The Private University in the Neoliberal Era

The neoliberal transition in Bangladesh was operationalised by the multilateral agencies-led structural adjustment programmes, with their gamut of policy turns, including the withdrawal of state welfare measures, market liberalisation, public disinvestment, privatisation and the 'NGO-isation' of social movements through the strategic channelling of foreign aid. Its effects began to be felt on the university system by the late 1980s in a context where the public university sphere had been subsumed by the political situation through the wanton violence characteristic of over a decade of right-wing military dictatorship and degenerating democratic politics. At the root of such violence in the university was not only the assault on concessions attained by the subordinate classes after 1971, but also an attempt to initiate a process of rapid proletarianisation of the latter with the aim of creating a pool of cheap labour. Neoliberal economic reintegration required such labour for the production of commodities for the world market, as well as to meet the needs of rising world demand for low-cost manual labour in non-tradeable sectors, such as, for instance, in the wake of construction-led booms in the Middle East and Southeast Asia since the 1980s. The university system was therefore required to adjust according to these changing conditions, brought about by global economic restructuring, at the forefront of which was the logic of the commodity form institutionalised and implemented by multilateral agencies through structural adjustment programmes that emerged out of the so-called 'Washington Consensus'.

As noted, the decolonisation process which intensified at the turn of the twentieth century and culminated in the creation of independent nation-states in South Asia was the outcome of substantive class compromise. Mobilisation of the subordinate classes by political and intellectual elites during the anti-imperialist struggle was conditional upon their recognition of the demands of the former as legitimate. At a very general level, such demands were articulated by the subordinate classes in terms of conditions that would improve their own material circumstances. These elites therefore, after assuming state power in the newly formed nation-states, were responsive to such subordinate interests and demands, as they recognised both the disruptive and stabilising potential of the latter classes for either undermining or consolidating their hold on power. Consequently, the word 'socialism' found its way into the constitutional preambles of these states, and substantial plans were laid out for increasing the general level of productivity and implementing social welfare programmes and affirmative action measures. Mass education at all levels through the public sector featured prominently in this early phase of decolonisation, and was considered indispensable for facilitating the primary objective of rapidly increasing local productivity through industrialisation and capitalist modernisation. While the larger political scenario in East Bengal (Pakistan) between 1947 and 1971 was complicated by the fact that it remained an ethnically defined colonial outpost within a decolonising national political economy, there was nevertheless a secular trend in terms of expanding access to education at all levels, for which the public university remained a crucial site for intensifying this crucial component of the decolonisation process.

Access to education, including at the university level, was not mediated through the market until the neoliberal turn in the 1980s. It was, and continues to a large extent to be, facilitated by the state as part of its objective of ushering in capitalist modernity while simultaneously mitigating the resultant antagonisms through social and educational policies, with their potential for reining in political and economic instability. Therefore, the enclosure of knowledge in general, and barriers to access in particular, cannot be understood in terms of purchasing power in the market, since the education system in the post-colonial period was, and largely remains, overwhelmingly public and free. What is perhaps required is the contextualisation of changes in the university education system within broader sociopolitical and economic contexts, a task to which I now turn.

Re-contextualisation

The contemporary scenario characterised by the neoliberal turn, as Caffentzis aptly put it, seeks the 'totalization of the commodity form'.[19] In the case of the private university in the neoliberal era, it attempts to achieve such 'totalization' through two simultaneous processes. Not only does it commodify tertiary education in the name of 'efficiency', but at the same time it shifts the focus of such education from facilitating 'relatively autonomous' capitalist development cognisant of local conditions for maintaining sociopolitical stability and economic improvement to reintegration into global circuits of production and finance, accompanied by a changing global division of labour characterised by heightened volatility. At a more fundamental level, the pedagogical content of tertiary education and the processes of knowledge generation that determine such content can be examined historically under three periodic demarcations in the Bangladeshi context. First, the colonial era was marked by intensified processes of enclosure, where the knowledge generated by and disseminated through higher education served broadly to operationalise the administrative apparatuses of extraction within what could perhaps be termed the 'classical imperialist phase of global capitalist expansion'.[20] Access was primarily based on certain specific meritocratic criteria determined by the political objectives of imperial governance and actualised only for individuals from particular class positions along existing social and economic divisions.[21]

In the second period, decolonisation presented a radical rupture insofar as it partially incorporated the material interests of the subordinate classes, permitted potentially widespread access, and thereby generated greater potential for conflict in the realm of both civil and political society.[22] Hence, the establishment of universal public education in the post-colonial era in what is now Bangladesh was part of a decolonising process that is not in any sense immediately inconsistent with capitalist development, nor does it initiate processes of knowledge generation that are free from the constraints, contradictions and crises of capitalism. However, by envisaging decolonisation as an ongoing process, we are able to gauge the extent to which it presented and continues to present actual and potential *possibilities* for radical rupture through struggle. In other words, the public education system in general and the public university in particular, by actually and potentially enabling subordinate classes to participate and articulate their interests, assist these subjects in rolling back the enclosure of knowledge to the extent that such knowledge serves to improve their social and economic circumstances. Moreover, one cannot rule out the higher probability of the radicalisation of education brought about on account of such participation and articulation, insofar as the subordinate classes, being at the receiving end of systemic oppression, are more likely to critique such oppression and bring to the fore through their struggles the tensions and crises under capitalism.[23]

In the third or contemporary demarcation, it is argued that the commodification of higher education through the private university is a consequence of more fundamental systemic capitalist crises, which the neoliberal turn seeks to ameliorate. By subjugating education to the commodity logic at a level that is perhaps relatively crucial for knowledge generation, the private university effectively attempts to exorcise such education of its critical leanings, borne out of struggles to make it more responsive to subordinate interests. Let us expand on this briefly through the following steps. First, valorising education in the same way as every other commodity requires as a precondition that the knowledge it disseminates should epistemologically embody the totalisation of the commodity form logic. Alternately, by virtue of its increasing subjugation to market forces, university education is deemed useful *only* to the extent that it furthers processes of labour formation and the simultaneous maintenance of reserve labour according to the requirements of capitalist expansion under neoliberalism, an outcome that necessarily requires the epistemological embodiment of the commodity logic within knowledge itself. Secondly, this directly perpetuates a fundamental transformation whereby the 'educative role of the state', as Gramsci puts it, has decreasing relevance in a context where 'neoliberal knowledge' itself reinforces education as an exchange value for individual subjects that may or may not be realised in the labour market. The third step follows, in which, by integrating higher education into circuits of accumulation and depriving it of any use value for individual subjects, capital's increasing imposition of mechanisms of market control in the education sector appears relatively more effective than state mediation for the above purposes. By opening up spaces for contestation, the state, especially in contexts where post-colonial political societies emerge as democratic polities through substantive subordinate struggles and subsequent class compromises, becomes increasingly problematic for capital, including the mediation of its interests in and through the education sector. The very fact that a number of major movements in post-1947 East Bengal (contemporary Bangladesh) that articulated and embodied subordinate interests originated and were subsequently sustained by students and teachers in public universities indicates how the educational apparatus in civil society can generate subjects antagonistic to the capitalist logic, and potentially open up spaces for anti-systemic contestation.

The 1952 Language Movement, which resulted in an intensification of the decolonisation process and presented a genuine possibility for radical systemic rupture, was clearly one such instance in the Bangladeshi case. At the same time, however, we also observe how such spaces, on account of their embeddedness within larger political economic transformations, are also vulnerable to the extent that they are part of a civil society that constantly seeks to reassert hegemonic consent to systemic perpetuation. Hence, they often become ambiguous spaces where processes of knowledge generation themselves are fundamentally at stake. Since the 1980s, such processes have increasingly been assaulted by the logic of the commodity form as discussed above, primarily as a response to systemic crises, of which decolonisation was (and still is) an important element. This counter-tendency appears to have been very successful in Bangladesh, where over the past three decades the public university has increasingly begun to resemble its colonial counterpart from half a century earlier with regard to the nature and direction of contestations within it, in the sense that such contestations appear to have a diminished inter-class component. It thus shifted again to a space predominantly figuring intra-class conflict, only this time the opposing factions were mobilised by elites who mustered a rare consensus on one thing, even if to varying degrees – that of the 'neoliberal agenda' broadly defined.

The ensuing political turmoil at the public universities greatly undermined the credibility of these institutions in the sphere of civil society, weakening the gains made against the enclosure of knowledge during the post-colonial era prior to the 1980s. In fact, with neoliberal restructuring, subordinate class positions were aggressively attacked within the university system, thereby intensifying this process of enclosure. This intensification reached a new level with the passing of the Private Universities Act by the newly elected democratic government in 1992.

Class power dynamics and resistance in political and civil society had made the public university, as a central institutional component of the state, both accessible to, and amenable towards, the interests of the subordinate classes to a great extent. This began to be severely undermined with the establishment of the private university, which is not a competing institutional space vis-à-vis the public, but a phenomenon that changes the very nature of the university system in a number of important ways.

First, by mediating access to the university through market relations, it ushers in the unprecedented dominance of the capitalist class in political and civil society insofar as this institutional space remains an integral part of both. Secondly, the private university is an important cornerstone for the neoliberal agenda, where its rate of expansion dwarfs that of the public university in accordance with the agenda's focus on public disinvestment.[24] Thirdly, a two-way intensification of the enclosure process is initiated by the state in permitting the public university to degenerate under increasing budgetary constraints, infrastructural stagnation, political violence and bureaucratic corruption, while its private counterpart is actively promoted through a regime of loosely regulated licensing. Fourthly, such intensification occurs in conjunction with the escalation of other forms of enclosure in ways that often reinforce each another. As capital pours in to capture the surpluses from this 'industry', knowledge increasingly becomes a marketable commodity, profitability in the education sector becomes a driving concern, and goals of social justice and equity recede to the background.[25]

Working Out the Processes of 'Knowledge Enclosure'

The manner in which the private university operates requires some detailed explication in order to grasp the full extent to which the process of enclosure has been intensified. In this section, I will mostly draw on my own experiences as a lecturer in one of these institutions over the course of a year. Unless stated otherwise, I will address practices generally, since they are more or less representative of practices in all private universities.[26] To begin with, the private university in Bangladesh is a business venture, usually modelled like a top-heavy corporate enterprise with a bureaucratic organisational structure. Students are paying clients as well as end products, teachers and administrators are the labour force, and the difference between revenue and expenditure (largely labour costs) is the extractable surplus or profit which goes to the investor.[27] The teaching part of the labour force, by virtue of its engagement in intellectual work, is an important tool for capitalist domination in the sphere of civil society. As private universities become increasingly large employers of university teachers, while neoliberal policy chokes public universities, this labouring class is often compelled to produce intellectual work consistent with the needs of the former for the sake of their jobs. More often than not, such work reinforces capitalist hegemony in its neoliberal manifestation. Furthermore, the decline of the public university in conjunction with the rise of the private means that an important space for subordinate classes to contest state power has diminished, thrusting both teachers and students from these classes directly into accentuating exploitative relations. As a result, the difference between dissent and complicity for this labouring class is often a question of material survival. Of course, such a scenario can only apply to any significant extent in contexts where enclosures in their varied material forms are simultaneously taking place, and thereby expanding the scope and social pervasiveness of market relations.

The violent and disruptive precedents set by student politics in the public university over the last three decades which resulted from some of the grievances that we briefly examined earlier continues to provide an important impetus for depoliticising student bodies in the private university. The naïve aspiration for education that is attuned to an ever-expanding labour market or lucrative entrepreneurial opportunities, as facilitated by neoliberal discourse, has been a powerful ideological component in actualising this depoliticising process among students. For faculty, the extremely precarious nature of employment has contributed largely to rapid depoliticisation. Furthermore, bureaucratic, patron–client style practices in hiring and promotion, the constant threat of unemployment and a competitive and increasingly saturated labour market with its consequent conditions of low pay have rendered the faculty extremely vulnerable. Increasingly, teachers from reputable public universities neglect their duties in their home institutions and lecture part-time in private universities. Such practices become attractive to teachers in a context where public universities face budgetary cuts and are thus unable to raise pay in line with growing inflation. It is also conducive to the profiteering objectives of private universities as they do not have to pay full-time salaries. The resultant effect on the quality of teaching, as teachers hop every day from one university to the next, battling through daily traffic and pollution in cities such as Dhaka and Chittagong, is perhaps not too difficult to imagine.

Furthermore, the research engagements of most academics in the university today involve ad hoc, project-based consultancy work that is often directly funded and thus 'guided' by international agencies such as the World Bank. Involvement in such consultancy work is a measure of faculty success within the university, and is an important criterion for promotion. Such work inevitably advances the neoliberal agenda where concerns are neither geared towards the subordinate classes' interests nor towards goals of social well-being.

Political organising and the expression of dissent by students and faculty have been effectively curtailed to a great extent by the very conditions of work themselves. Control mechanisms in the private university increasingly resemble those in a Taylorist factory. A number of so-called 'managerial strategies' are deployed in this context. For example, faculty are required to stay on campus for eight hours at least in many private universities, conducting, for most of the time, a range of meaningless bureaucratic tasks that 'keep them busy'. Teachers' unions are explicitly discouraged, classes are often monitored, and 'informers' stalk campuses to detect and report subversive activities to the administration. The airing of grievances has become individualised, and must follow the 'proper' administrative channels if teachers wish to keep their jobs. Students are also strongly discouraged from forming political organisations and are required to bring up grievances in a similar way. The lack of state regulatory oversight in the operation of private universities has meant that these campuses often run according to the whims of their capitalist promoters. One of the more egregious outcomes in this regard is the attack on Bengali culture and Bangladesh's proud history of emancipatory student movements. The curricula have been varyingly redesigned along North American disciplinary models with complete disregard for local requirements. Often a degree from a North American or West European university is explicitly required in applying for faculty positions. The largest department by far in almost all private universities is the business administration department, which, besides training particular types of labour for the direct use of capital, is also the biggest revenue earner for universities, and therefore, as per the logic of profiteering, influences university policies disproportionately.[28] What is even more alarming is that public universities under neoliberal structural adjustment have embarked along a similar path and operate more and more like these institutions.

With the intensification of university enclosure and the rapid proliferation of market relations in the education sphere, a number of alarming practices have emerged. One of the more sinister of these is the emergence of privately owned and operated 'academic coaching service centres' across the country, which provide supplemental income to university teachers. These are institutions that offer academic assistance to students after college hours, and they have had numerous perverse impacts on the university system. First, as a lucrative source of income, such institutions discourage faculty from expressing dissent at work, as well as enabling them to tolerate poor conditions and woefully inadequate salaries. Secondly, the quality of classroom teaching is often wilfully diminished as a strategy to motivate students to pay extra money for one of these individual 'coaching' sessions. Dubious practices, such as the purchasing of examination question papers, attract students to these centres as well, and prevent them from complaining about the poor lectures in school and university classrooms. Such developments plague not just tertiary or university education, but the education system in general, right from the primary level.

The problem is more acute in the case of public educational institutions where pay is often lower than in the private sphere, and most teachers have to survive almost solely on these supplemental incomes. While it might seem that the greater economic autonomy achieved by teachers through such practices would be likely to embolden their resistance against the enclosure of knowledge in the university, this is not so in reality. Teachers are reliant on their employment at the university to create good reputations in order to attract students to their private sessions, and thus they cannot afford to lose their jobs as a result of dissent. Furthermore, most teachers feel that the bureaucratic tussles and the threat of job loss are not worth the time and effort, which can be better utilised for economic gain in the private sessions.[29] Therefore, it is a context where the neoliberal ideals of market individualism and economic gain increasingly reign over cognitive labour at the cost of oppositional thinking in the struggle for social improvement.

Moreover, the institution I was involved with serves as a suitable example in visualising how the intensification of knowledge enclosure, like processes of enclosure in general, does not occur in isolation. Privatisation and the spread of capitalist market relations involve a direct assault on every form of erstwhile commons, which are inherently antithetical to the proliferation of such relations.[30] In Bangladesh, the enclosure of rivers, which from time immemorial have been treated as commons, is one of the more alarming developments. Large swathes of rivers across the country have been turned into private property. In the city of Dhaka where both land scarcity and speculation have driven up the price of land tremendously, its major rivers, Turag and Buriganga, as well as other low-lying water channels, are being filled with sand to be sold in the real estate market by private 'entrepreneurs', or are being appropriated by various local as well as central state institutions, again for the purpose of profiteering in the 'patronage-driven' land market sector.[31] Apart from the environmental devastation, these enclosures are related to the enclosure of knowledge in interesting ways.

My university is a case in point. This private university is located on a street named Embankment Road, so called by virtue of its being adjacent to a river embankment. Ironically, however, its buildings stand on an embankment where the river is supposed to flow! It was erected on 'land reclaimed from the river' – which is an oft-heard euphemism for unscrupulous river-filling, especially when such land is distributed directly by the state.[32] Two other private universities and a large hospital project developed by a multinational charity group also have 'land' on that same stretch. Students can look out of the windows of almost any of the classrooms and see the river being filled in all around them. They can see the poles that demarcate the river boundaries, and how those poles now stand in the middle of land, while the once magnificent, life-giving river recedes into an insignificant drain of human waste.[33] Such enclosures have been normalised from their point of view: land-grabbing and river-filling are the natural order of things for many of the younger generation who have not lived through a time that was otherwise. It is thus not only transformations in the curricula and the organisational setup within the university, but in the very environment around these students which make them oblivious to how they might apply their education for social well-being. The process of knowledge enclosure is thus intensified to what is perhaps an unprecedented extent, in conjunction with other forms of enclosure that squander the very basis of sustenance for private gain.

Intensification and Resistance

This conceptual framing of university education as integral to the contested apparatuses of civil society allows us to envisage the privatisation of the university space as an intensification of the process of knowledge enclosure, insofar as it constitutes an assault in the sphere of civil society against subordinate positions. In other words, if such education is not simply conceptualised as processes involved in the production and dissemination of knowledge, but also as historically evolving practices which articulate and contest conflicting class interests in civil society, then the gradual proliferation of market relations in the mediation of such processes simultaneously indicates a process of enclosure which transforms the spaces for contestation therein. The transformation itself is riddled with conflicts, which gives some support to the argument that market forces can only go so far in subjugating social relations and that resistance against such subjugation is increasingly likely after a certain point.[34]

Everyday experiences confirm the proliferation of such resistance. A particularly severe conflict from the many such incidents that occurred during my stint as a private university teacher in Dhaka can serve as a case in point here. In this particular case, students took to the streets and blocked roads around the campus for many hours in protest against an arbitrary change in the registration rules which would require many to stay an extra semester, resulting in more expense and delayed graduation. The profit motive behind the decision was clearly seen by the protesting students as unjustified, and rightly deduced to be an outcome of the commodity logic that mediated their relation to the institution; thus it was successfully protested against. In informal settings, faculty often discussed such negative practices and their poor work conditions, which appeared to most as insurmountable problems given the 'business model' logic of private university education, whose unyielding profiteering engines they seemed to be incessantly oiling. Nevertheless, there have been cases of collective protest against wrongful dismissals of lecturers, as well as demands for pay rises and appropriate changes in the curricula in the university where I worked; moreover, my research indicates that such incidents are becoming increasingly common across private universities in Dhaka. Protest and the articulation of dissatisfaction are relatively more visible in the public universities which are much more politicised and thereby still retain a modicum of public accountability and outrage, despite the dominance of neoliberal hegemonic interests. Students protesting against fee hikes, struggles over the reclaiming of hostel accommodation from political goons, teachers' strikes for better salaries and work conditions, teacher-student protests against the misuse of funds, corrupt practices of appointment and promotion, and so on, are in the news media almost every other week and are indeed too numerous to be recounted here. The important point is that we are beginning to witness what can perhaps be termed a peculiar 'politics of resentment and dissatisfaction' which seems to characterise contemporary struggles within the Bangladeshi university. This politics increasingly appears to articulate itself in opposition to the dictates of market forces and their consequent outcomes, which undermine the expression and realisation of subordinate interests.

However, it is also clear that such a politics on most occasions is merely a response that seeks to ameliorate the symptoms arising out of the enclosure of knowledge within university education, and is not a radical questioning of the hegemonic consent to neoliberalism in civil society. In order therefore to trace the possibilities for such a radical questioning in the sphere of university education, I have briefly examined how the conditions that have historically undermined market encroachment in and through the production and dissemination of knowledge came into being and operated in the post-colonial era prior to the 1980s. As we have already seen, the post-colonial state in its implementation of objectives within the decolonisation process had, as an integral and complex strategic component of this process, conceded to subordinate pressures in establishing the public university, where education gradually acquired a contested dimension that proved conducive to furthering struggles in the realm of civil society. Hence, the transition from the colonial to the public university was characterised by a range of processes, conditions and events whose outcome, to crudely summarise, allowed for the articulation of subordinate interests in terms of enabling their struggle for substantive concessions towards material and social improvement. This is a (rather stylised) historical instance that explicates a 'reversal' in the enclosure of knowledge, and by virtue of that indicates retrospectively the existence of an education that was thoroughly antithetical to neoliberal reasoning, even while it remained accommodating to the logic of capitalist development in general. However, the immanent antagonism that explains the subsequent vulnerability of the university space to neoliberal assault in the contemporary era becomes clear once we conceptualise such a 'politics of resentment', drawing on Gramsci's crucial insights as alluded to earlier. With characteristic attention to detail, Gramsci, following Marx, renders problematic the Hegelian conception of the 'ethical state' with its dual basis for furthering dominant interests – these include the education and the legal systems, the former as a positive and the latter as a repressive or negative modality of reinforcement.[35] He notes, however, that in actuality there exist a 'multitude of other so-called private initiatives and activities [which] tend to the same end – initiatives and activities which form the apparatus of the political and cultural hegemony of the ruling classes'.[36] These 'private' spheres thus essentially seek to acquire hegemonic consent through civil society, which Gramsci conceptualises as having an inherent tendency to subsume the 'armor of coercion' into regulated society, where 'it is possible to imagine the coercive element of the state withering away by degrees, as ever more conspicuous elements of regulated society (or ethical state or civil society) make their appearance'.[37] Consistent with his call for historical and contextual 'reconnaissance', we extend these conceptual insights to this case of the decolonisation process by arguing that in order to identify instances against the enclosure of knowledge, it is crucial to map the nature and direction of specific struggles and contestations between dominant and subordinate interests in the realm of *both* civil and political society.

As a component of the civil society apparatus, university education serves as a concrete site for such mapping and brings to prominence the immanent antagonism that we have been trying to clarify, which takes the form of a question as to why the post-colonial university space appears to have succumbed to the neoliberal logic, despite being a space for radical contestation in the past. We argue that by retaining consistency with capitalist developmental processes, the knowledge generated and disseminated through university education in the post-colonial period succumbed to neoliberal appropriation precisely on account of the tendency that Gramsci points out, where the hegemonic consent to dominant interests in civil society persistently resists actual and potential subordinate challenges through such 'private initiatives'. Consequently, any space that the post-colonial state opens up for accommodating the struggle for subordinate interests is increasingly likely to yield to hegemonic dominance if it remains within the sociopolitical and economic domain of world capitalism. An increasing likelihood of appropriation is itself triggered to a large extent by responses to crises resulting from the actualisation of these struggles. Such responses enclose knowledge insofar as they facilitate the eschewing of education as a contested terrain, mutually constituted by struggles for subordinate interests. The neoliberalisation of university education through privatisation is thus a specific modality through which this contemporary knowledge enclosure is effected.

It would consequently appear that the public university as a state institution cannot muster a radical challenge to neoliberal hegemony and its enclosure of knowledge, which, besides presupposing the private, is also subject to neoliberal encroachment that effectively undermines its role as a space for the articulation of subordinate struggles in civil society. This is, however, only partly true on account of the fact that the university space within civil society is a rather ambiguous one, consisting of a terrain that can perhaps only be mapped through historical processes that go beyond concerns with education alone. It is with such an understanding that we can begin to explore the university as 'commons', and thereby arrive at possible conditions for reclaiming its potential for the articulation and realisation of subordinate interests.

The University as Commons

The university as commons can be broadly envisaged as a self-governing institutional space operating to further the interests of the community in which it is embedded, as opposed to a sphere subordinated to the interests of capital accumulation and the mitigation of its crises, defined and circumscribed variously by the state and the market. At its most fundamental level, the 'commoning' of university education would require a reconfiguration of the social relations under which knowledge is produced and disseminated within the university space. Since the modern university is a civil society apparatus within capitalist hegemony, seeking such a reconfiguration would amount to an assault on capitalist social relations in general. Such a conceptualisation of the university as commons might therefore sound at best outrageous, or else simply naïve and utopian. My task here is to lay out some of the preliminary conditions that have either already emerged or are likely to emerge in the near future; once these are laid out, I hope that the above suggestion will appear neither outrageous nor naïve, but a possible and necessary alternative that restores to education its emancipatory potential. I begin by conceptualising briefly the notion of the commons in its evolution in critical theoretical discourse and practice.

For Marx, the commons is, of course, not simply the diametric opposite of private property enclosed through the process of primitive accumulation, but a set of relations which define social production, reproduction and exchange as against such definition in terms of the capital relation.[38] Based on such a conceptualisation to varying degrees, recent discourses on the commons have ranged from theorising the notion on the basis of principles of communal sharing (Bollier and Helfrich), management of common property resources through the public–private confluence (Ostrom), and the 'metropolitan production and exchange in common of non-excludables' including social and intellectual practices, cultures and languages (Hardt and Negri), to the prefiguration of an alternate mode resting on collective solidarity (Federici and Caffentzis, Linebaugh) and reproduction outside the sphere of market and state control (Zibechi).[39]

In the context of the 'commoning' of education in general and that of university education in particular, the most significant conceptual advances can be found in the works of Silvia Federici and George Caffentzis, whose notion of the commons is premised as 'autonomous spaces from which to reclaim control over the conditions of our reproduction, and as bases from which to counter the processes of enclosure ... [that] should enable us to gain more power with regard to capital and the state and embryonically prefigure a new mode of production, no longer built on a competitive principle, but on the principle of collective solidarity'.[40] However, the strength of their approach lies not in the normative formulation of such premises, but in their strategic identification of struggles through the spatio-temporal contextualisation of these premises, enabling the location of critical questions regarding knowledge production and education. This approach facilitates what is indeed the Gramscian 'reconnaissance' for an entrenched 'war of position' in the sphere of civil society, which is necessary for envisaging and initiating a radical rupture against the capitalist subsumption of knowledge generation and dissemination.

In their essay 'Notes on the Edu-factory and Cognitive Capitalism', Federici and Caffentzis point out precisely the crucial role that knowledge plays today in both facilitating and contesting the economic restructuring of capitalist production and exchange, where its potential as a 'crisis variable' results in its identification as the object of enclosure via 'privatisation, commodification and expropriation through intellectual property regimes'.[41] What we have identified in our study of the university in contemporary Bangladesh since the colonial era is that such expropriation and enclosure acquires varying degrees of intensification along a temporal dimension based on sociopolitical and economic changes, which consequently makes the university space a site of contestation that paradoxically shifts between hegemonic and antisystemic tendencies at different junctures. This is perhaps on account of the nature of knowledge itself, whose social construction has to be located within processes of conformation and rupture in political and civil society: if the objective conditions of capitalist perpetuation run up against knowledge which is contrary to their logic, there is likely to be friction whose outcome would then be contingent on the relative strengths of the opposing forces at play. Therefore, our approach here does not make what would perhaps be a futile attempt to identify the existence of knowledge 'outside' hegemonic dominance, but instead examines the more interesting processes of how interactions between historical, sociopolitical and economic changes may affect the stability of such dominance and produce a radical 'outside'.

Adapting the commons perspective, which internalises potentially radical struggles within processes of continuous enclosure, allows us to identify the conflicting tensions between class forces as the most likely modality through which the enclosure of knowledge can be simultaneously facilitated and resisted. Consequently, it enables us to redefine resistance to the enclosure of knowledge as a sphere of education that furthers spaces for contestation in civil society, and thereby generates the possibility of articulating and realising subordinate interests in a way that eschews a mode of production, reproduction and exchange based on capitalistic competition in favour of alternatives based on communal solidarity. Hence, I focus on the importance of envisaging a 'struggle for' as much as a 'struggle against', where the former is not a naïve search for some predefined and packaged 'radical anti-systemic education', but is rather an active learning process constituted by the identification, adaption, combination and deployment of potentially radical tendencies generated within the numerous manifestations of the latter across spatial and temporal contexts. As a result, we historically identify in the Bangladeshi case the antagonism between processes of knowledge enclosure and struggles against the discontent that they foster, which finds expression in the contemporary context as a 'politics of resentment' that spontaneously opposes the education regime within the university space. Mobilisation around such a politics can perhaps facilitate the generation of the aforementioned learning process through a 'struggle against' that is subsequently likely to establish the necessity of a 'struggle for', drawing simultaneously on present manifestations of cumulative processes such as decolonisation, as well as numerous historical struggles for subordinate interests across varied spatio-temporal contexts.

Hence, the task of envisaging a 'struggle for' becomes less overwhelming when we recognise the role of historical processes, and how contesting agencies are defined through countless everyday struggles against hegemonic dominance. It is in this context that the struggles of students and teachers against practices in private universities, and for the reclamation of public universities, become important resistances against the reappropriation of enclosed knowledge.[42] These struggles are steps in the process of 'commoning' university education as long as they seek improvement in the circumstances of the many against the interests of the few.

As an important part of civil society, the university is a terrain which is inherently contested in terms of being in favour of, and opposed to, capitalist hegemony. The neoliberal assault appears to have tipped the scales against anti-hegemonic tendencies, particularly in the post-colonial context from the 1980s onwards, but it continues in the process to generate discontent among the many which simultaneously provides opportune junctures, as we have argued, in mapping the conditions for mobilising processes of radical contestation and reconstruction. Normatively, such reconstruction is envisaged as the transformation of university education as the commons, and it is perhaps appropriate to conclude by examining what such a university space might look like.

The university as commons is an institution that does not become an isolated space but retains the positive characteristics of the modern university in terms of making use of the synergies of collaboration in research, the exchange of ideas, and building strong bonds between communities and ecologies across the planet. The sought-for change is in terms of the relationship that the university has with society. Such a change would necessarily involve the construction of a symbiotic relationship in which knowledge serves the purpose of social equality as opposed to inequality and unjust exclusion. The university as commons is thus envisaged as a space that would seek fundamentally to transform knowledge in terms of 'power to' rather than 'power over' individual subjects in society. Knowledge production and dissemination in such a context ceases to be the output of alienated labour, integrated into circuits of accumulation for the sake of accumulation. Rather, it becomes part of a totality enabling social advancement while being truly emancipated from utilitarian constraints, resting finally on intellectual motives that value the grandeur of ideas, the thrill of discovery and the challenge of critique. It is perhaps the very real attainability of such alternatives within and through the university as a contested space which is anathema to the perpetuation of capital, thereby making the enclosure of knowledge an objective necessity within its structural logic, which is consequently carried out with increasing vehemence.

While struggles to challenge the legitimacy of state policies in favour of capitalist interests and the privatisation of university education constitute an important step towards the commoning of knowledge, the main thrust of our argument indicates that the struggle to build the commons per se cannot be isolated in this sphere alone. There is an important recognition among advocates for the commons that such self-governing institutions in isolated spheres of activity and geographical locality make little sense. For how can struggles against processes of knowledge enclosure in and through the university space be sustained if the very land which gives such space its concrete spatial dimension is not under the collective control of the struggling subjects? In the last instance, therefore, capitalism must be understood as a set of interconnected processes, relations and practices that can appropriate isolated communal relations which might hinder the expansion of capitalist market relations. This recognition is absolutely crucial if the conditions for anti-systemic struggle are to be conceived, mapped and mobilised with any degree of precision and resoluteness.

At the same time, such struggles and the alternatives that they seek to construct cannot be preconceived projections of future institutions and practices, but might perhaps be envisaged as outcomes of learning processes as struggles proceed. The conceptual and practical cognisance of enclosures and how they function as continuous processes that limit social self-determination in production, reproduction and exchange can assist in such learning, and thereby reduce the probability of succumbing to such enclosures while enhancing the sustainability of hard-fought gains on the part of the subordinate classes. The commons, as Peter Linebaugh puts it, is therefore 'best understood as a verb'.[43] While the struggle for the public remains relevant, only a struggle to build the commons in this sense can form a sustained basis for organising the kind of collective action that is most likely to overcome the processes of knowledge enclosure in and through university education.

Notes

1. This is perhaps why multilateral agencies like the United Nations and the World Bank are often so keen on formulating higher education policy,

carrying out advocacy and implementing programmes for 'appropriately' conditioning through education subject predispositions that are broadly consistent with the transforming global conditions for capitalist development and accumulation processes. The World Bank, for instance, continues to aggressively pursue its neoliberal agenda through the frequent inclusion of conditionalities vis-à-vis the education sector for developmental loans, a trend which began with the mid-1980s structural adjustment programmes in many Asian, African and Latin American countries. Cf. World Bank, *Higher Education in Developing Countries: Peril and Promise* (Washington, DC: Task Force on Higher Education and Society, 2000), http://siteresources.worldbank.org/EDUCATION/Resources/278200-1099079877269/547664-1099079956815/peril_promise_en.pdf (accessed 7 January 2017). A number of United Nations agencies such as UNESCO, UNICEF and the Department of Economic and Social Affairs have a range of programmes that advocate a similar neoliberal agenda or seek palliative responses to crises fostered by it, formulated in their characteristically technocratic, apolitical manner, and variously termed as, for instance, the 'Education for All Agenda', 'Capacity Development Program', 'Higher Education Sustainability Initiative' or the 'Global Education First Initiative'. See UNESCO, *Capacity Development for Education for All: Translating Theory into Practice* (Paris: UNESCO, 2011), http://unesdoc.unesco.org/images/0021/002122/212262e.pdf (accessed 4 January 2017); *Education Transforms Lives*, Education for All Global Monitoring Report (2013), http://unesdoc.unesco.org/images/0022/002231/223115E.pdf (accessed 7 January 2017); *Sustainable Development Begins with Education: How Education Can Contribute to the Proposed Post-2015 Goals*, Education for All Global Monitoring Report (2015), http://unesdoc.unesco.org/images/0023/002305/230508e.pdf (accessed 1 February 2017); and UNESCO, *Pricing the Right to Education: The Cost of Reaching New Targets by 2030*, Policy Paper 18, Education for All Global Monitoring Report (2015), unesdoc.unesco.org/images/0023/002321/232197E.pdf (accessed 1 February 2017). A critical examination of some of the most pressing issues in this regard can be found, for instance, in the newsletters published by the Committee for Academic Freedom in Africa in the 1980s and 1990s (also see the volume compiled from some of these studies, entitled *A Thousand Flowers: Social Struggles against Structural Adjustment in African Universities*, ed. Silvia Federici, George Caffentzis and Ousseina Alidou [Trenton; Asmara: Africa World Press, 2000]).

2. The use of the adjective 'primitive' in English has been the subject of some disagreement on both theoretical and epistemological grounds, and alternative translations from the German have variously preferred the use of 'original' or 'primary'. I use this particular adjective simply for convenience's sake, given that it has found more prevalent usage over the years – any substantive questioning of it would, of course, lead to a different discussion altogether.

3. K. Marx, *Capital, Volume I*, trans. Samuel Moore and Edward Aveling (Moscow: Progress Publishers, 1976), pp. 874–5.

4. For a concise summary of some of the prominent discussions and debates in this regard, see, for example, M. De Angelis, 'Marx and Primitive Accumulation: The Continuous Character of Capital's Enclosures', *The Commoner*, 2 (2001), pp. 1–22.

5. Variations along these lines in the reconceptualisation of Marx's notion of primitive accumulation as continuous processes of enclosure can be found, for example, in M. De Angelis, 'Separating the Doing and the Deed: Capital and the Continuous Character of Enclosures', *Historical Materialism*, 12(2) (2004), pp. 57–87; S. Federici and G. Caffentzis, 'Commons against and beyond Capitalism', *Community Development Journal*, 49(1) (2014), pp. 92–105; S. Federici, *Caliban and the Witch* (New York: Autonomedia, 2004); S. Federici, 'The Debt Crisis, Africa and the New Enclosures', *The Commoner*, 2 (1992), pp. 1–13; P. Linebaugh, *Stop, Thief! The Commons, Enclosures, and Resistance* (Oakland: PM Press, 2014); Midnight Notes Collective, 'Introduction to the New Enclosures', *Midnight Notes*, 10 (1990), pp. 1–9.

6. K. Marx, *Theories of Surplus Value* (Moscow: Progress Publishers, 1969), p. 970.

7. A more specific rendition in this regard in terms of the neoliberalisation of education can be found in S. Federici, 'Education and the Enclosure of Knowledge in the Global University', *ACME: An international e-journal for critical geographies*, 8(3) (2009), p. 455, http://ojs.unbc.ca/index.php/acme/article/view/843 (accessed 2 February 2017). For Federici, the 'enclosure of knowledge' occurs where education is evaluated in terms of profitability and not in terms of its significance for social improvement; such processes of enclosure can be clearly discerned in the modern university, especially in the context of newly emerging private universities in the Global South.

8. A profound dialectical insight in Marx, and following him, Gramsci, is that both the highest development of the means for establishing the

conditions for alienated labour under capitalism as well the means to undermine the same finds its expression in and through the realm of civil society. Given its contested nature in this sense, the theoretical conceptualisation of civil society fits well with the reconceptualised notion of primitive accumulation as both a precondition and a continuous process conditioning capitalist accumulation. This also helps to underscore the point that the modalities distinguishing primitive from capitalist accumulation in the traditional, sequentially interpreted sense of their interpretation does not rest on objectively defined economic laws or subjectively construed extra-economic means, but rather on the historically contingent outcomes of struggles. Further clarification in this regard will be provided later in the discussion on the complex links between civil society, education and enclosure.

 9. A nuanced account of the link between the interests of British commerce and the changing education policy of the imperial Raj in the Indian subcontinent can be found in S. Seth, *Subject Lessons: The Western Education of Colonial India* (Durham, NC: Duke University Press, 2007).

10. It would be incorrect to say that the colonial state was directly concerned with the material subsistence of the peasantry, but since the latter were the primary producers of valuable export commodities, their survival was clearly of consequence for capitalist accumulation through unequal exchange. The colonial state thus perhaps had some interest in checking excessive oppression by the local tax agents and ensuring that land tenure and taxation systems did not disrupt subsistence agriculture. Such a perspective, however, is debated. See, for instance, B. Chaudhuri, 'Agrarian Relations: Eastern India', in Tapan Raychaudhuri and Irfan Habib (eds), *The Cambridge Economic History of India* (Cambridge: Cambridge University Press, 1983), 2, pp. 86–176.

11. Arguably, one of the most detailed sources on the history of the first modern university in Dhaka during the British colonial period is the book by Sadar Fazlul Karim in Bengali, *Dhaka BIshshobiddaloy O Purbo Bongio Shomaj: Oddhapok Abdur Razzaker Alapcharita (Dhaka University and Society in East Bengal: Interviews with Professor Abdur Razzaq)* (Dhaka: Dhaka University Press, 1984). This is a detailed account of the university's history and role in society by the Bengali political theorist Abdur Razzaq, corroborated with Karim's own historical research and commentaries. This section draws largely on this account of the history of Dhaka University.

12. Gramsci develops this notion of hegemony specifically in the context of

his theory of the state, where the latter comprises of both political and civil society: 'For it should be remarked that the general notion of state includes elements which need to be referred back to the notion of civil society (in the sense that one might say that state = political society + civil society, in other words hegemony protected by the armour of coercion).' A. Gramsci, *Selections from the Prison Notebooks*, trans. Q Hoare and G. Nowell-Smith (New York: International Publishers, 1971), pp. 262–3 [Q6§88]). In other words, the notion of 'civil society' in Gramsci eschews the liberal conceptualisation, by which such a space not only accommodates articulations against state power, but also reinforces it, thus making 'civil society' an inherently contested sphere. This is captured through his notion of hegemony, which can be understood in terms of how it creates 'subversive' subjectivities (in the sphere of civil and political society) among the proletarian or subordinate classes so as to obscure exploitative capitalist relations of production and reproduction, and thereby facilitate capitalist reinforcement through state power. At the same time, however, by providing a space for the articulation of subordinate interests against such state power, possibilities for fostering anti-hegemonic struggles are also facilitated within its domain.

13. Gramsci, *Selections from the Prison Notebooks*, p. 242 [Q13§7]. Perhaps the clearest theoretical systematisation following this line of Gramscian thought regarding the state, education and civil society can be found in Louis Althusser's discussions on the 'ideological state apparatuses' in the context of how relations of material production are reproduced. Althusser notes: 'To my knowledge, Gramsci is the only one who went any distance in the road I am taking. He had the "remarkable" idea that the State could not be reduced to the (Repressive) State Apparatus, but included, as he put it, a certain number of institutions from "civil society": the Church, the schools, the trade unions, etc.' L. Althusser, 'Ideology and Ideological State Apparatus', in *Lenin and Philosophy and Other Essays*, trans. Ben Brewster (New York: Monthly Review Press, 1971), p. 143.

14. Gramsci, *Selections from the Prison Notebooks*, p. 242 [Q13§7].

15. Gramsci makes this particular point in his critique of Lenin's strategy for the direct assault on state power in the context of liberal democracies, where apparatuses of civil society have to be engaged in a prolonged struggle if such an assault is to have any hope of dismantling capitalist hegemony. He argued: 'In the East the state was everything, civil society was primordial and gelatinous; in the West, there was a

proper relation between state and civil society, and when the state trembled a sturdy structure of civil society was at once revealed. The state was only an outer ditch, behind which there stood a powerful system of fortresses and earthworks: more or less numerous from one state to the next, it goes without saying – but this precisely necessitated an accurate reconnaissance of each individual country.' *Selections from the Prison Notebooks*, pp. 236–8 [Q7§16]). I argue for extending this line of reasoning in the context of the colonial university as an emerging apparatus of civil society in the 'East', which increasingly began to define such delineations of power as Gramsci mentions by the turn of the twentieth century.

16. Gramsci draws such a conclusion: cf. *Selections from the Prison Notebooks*, pp. 236–8 (Q7§16).

17. Cf. Gramsci's distinction between organic and traditional intellectuals. Gramsci seems to suggest that such positions become increasingly well-defined *during transitory periods of struggle for establishing hegemonic domination*: his own argument is formulated in the context of the transition from the feudal to the capitalist mode in Europe. See *Selections from the Prison Notebooks*, pp. 5–16 [Q12§1]). By generalising the notion of 'traditional' intellectuals, I argue that they occupy an anachronistic position insofar as they exist and espouse the interests of classes that are increasingly being subjected to processes of subordination within a hegemonic setup defined by the organic intellectuals of the dominant class. In this understanding, struggles in civil society in general, and in the education sector in particular, are played out by actors who are likely to be positioned in a manner similar to that of such 'traditional' and organic intellectuals, where their conflicting stances cannot be abstracted from changes in both inter- and intra-class positions within the sociopolitical and economic context in which they act.

18. See A. F. Salahuddin Ahmed's *Bengali Nationalism and the Emergence of Bangladesh* (Bengal: International Centre for Bengal Studies, 1994), for an account of the 1952 Language Movement, its genesis in the university, and its subsequent challenge to the West Pakistani regime.

19. G. Caffentzis, 'On the Notion of a Crisis of Social Reproduction: A Theoretical Review', in *Letters of Blood and Fire: Work, Machines, and the Crisis of Capitalism* (Oakland: PM Press, 2013), p. 260.

20. There are, of course, contesting theoretical arguments regarding what the essential characteristic of imperialism was at this juncture. While Lenin rightly pointed out that it was a phase characterised by the

dominance of finance capital and the monopolisation of industry under its hegemonic grip, the notion of primitive accumulation remained for him a historical precondition for capitalist relations. See V. I. Lenin, *Imperialism, the Highest Phase of Capitalism, with an Introduction by Prabhat Patnaik* (Delhi: Leftword Books, 2007). Consequently, his argument does not capture the intricacies of anti-imperialist struggles in the colonies, where radical subjects were forged out of very different contexts than the one he envisages. On the other hand, R. Luxemburg in *The Accumulation of Capital* (London: Routledge, 1963), maintained that relations outside the capitalist mode were a necessity for realising surplus value under capitalism, the conditions of which were maintained by imperial exploits. Primitive accumulation therefore acquires in her explication an objective status outside class contestations, and is the outcome of one-sided violence and political repression which again fails to explain anti-imperialist struggles. My argument, based on the new enclosures perspective, combined with the Gramscian notion of civil society and the contestations within it, perhaps permits a more nuanced inquiry into envisaging anti-imperialist contestations as struggles internal to processes of primitive accumulation, taking into consideration the intricacies in the tripartite state–capital–subordinate relation. However, developing this further is beyond our purpose here – the digression is initiated to briefly contextualise our specific argument within the broader theoretical tradition that explicates colonialism under the capitalist mode. Cf. D. Harvey, *The New Imperialism* (Oxford: Oxford University Press, 2003).

21. For instance, the class position of individuals in Hindu society was (and is) largely determined through complex interactions with the caste system, which traditionally defined occupational choices, property relations and access to formal education and literacy, among other things. This system was not substantively affected by imperial laws and policies, which found ways to circumvent it, coexist with it and occasionally confront it on a contingent basis. In this context, it can be stated generally that the socioeconomic circumstances of the upper castes were more favourable towards their obtaining subordinate positions of power within the imperial administration through university education than those of the lower castes – this had little to do with the market mediation of such access. Bhimrao Ambedkar, one of the foremost intellectuals and activists of the early twentieth-century decolonisation movement, recognised the intersection of oppressions behind the facade of meritocratic

access and formal equality espoused by the education system under capitalist imperialism, and thereby struggled against the reformists for its radical dismantling along with the casteist divisions that it often helped retain. A socialist revolution was for him an obvious precondition for such a dismantling, for as long as knowledge remained an instrument of capital, it would continue to mobilise oppressive systems and practices (like the caste system) to further its own self-expansion. One of his more polemical and terse arguments along these lines can be found in his well-known undelivered lecture published under the title *The Annihilation of Caste* (1936). The socioeconomic divisions in Muslim society were arguably more or less analogous, whereby hereditary occupational structures were just as rarely breached, and social mobility and class positions remained circumscribed in similar ways, even with the formal dismantling of the caste system.

22. It is, however, pertinent to note the use of the word 'partial' here, since it crucially denotes that decolonisation is not simply characterised as a series of events but rather as a cumulative process whose particular outcomes at any spatio-temporal juncture are contingent on subordinate struggles. The nature and direction of such struggles are determined by present sociopolitical and economic contests in conjunction with the extent of 'gains retained and accumulated' from their past instances. The interpretation of 'gains' here is construed in the widest possible sense, from actual material concessions to the formative processes of collective consciousness and the application of past strategic formulations in contesting for subordinate interests.

23. Marx argues in *Capital* that capitalist production, by turning the labourer into a 'crippled monstrosity', undermines its own dynamism. Since productive forces under capitalism mutate incessantly, it requires a labour force that is capable of adapting continuously, which is less likely to be achieved if the labourer is allowed to degenerate into such a state that his intellectual capacity is severely undermined. The bourgeois education system is therefore attuned to this need, whereby subordinate classes are allowed to participate and maintain a degree of critical intellectual capacity that fosters amenability to adaptation. Herein lies Marx's insight regarding a well-known contradiction: while education of the subordinate classes is necessary to solve the problem of adaptability as productive forces develop, it simultaneously exposes these classes to processes of knowledge generation and use which, by encouraging their awareness of their own exploitation and oppression, could in turn be

deployed in struggles against capital itself, affecting the relations under which it is produced and reproduced (Marx, *Capital, Volume I*, pp. 235–6, 280). I use 'classes' here in the plural since it can be credibly argued that this insight would apply both to large segments of the peasantry and to other petty producers and traders, especially in the context of a major part of the post-colonial world under neoliberal hegemony.

24. While data for accurate comparison are scarce, a confirming inference can be made in this regard from both primary and secondary sources. One indication of the financial 'squeezing' of public universities could be derived from a comparison of teacher–student ratios from recent data made available by the Bangladesh Bureau of Educational Information and Statistics. Computing the teacher–student ratio from these data reveal that the ratio has fallen by around 47 per cent between 2008 and 2013 in public universities. In the same period, this ratio increased by around 45 per cent in the case of private universities. Furthermore, a study on the privatisation of higher education for the International Institute for Education Planning under UNESCO provides some con-firmatory evidence in this regard. See M. Alam, M. S. Haque and S. F. Siddique, *Private Higher Education in Bangladesh*, ed. N. V. Varghese (Bangladesh: International Institute for Educational Planning, 2007).

25. Alam et al.'s 2007 study points out that the rate of profit in this sector could well be over 40 per cent (*Private Higher Education in Bangladesh*, p. 11), generated mostly through tuition fees from students. In the case of my erstwhile university, such profitability was also bolstered through the exploitation of legal loopholes. For example, faculty salaries were paid in cash through a 'cooperative society', the most likely reason being for the purposes of tax exemptions and avoidance, thus generat-ing higher surplus for the private promoter.

26. Informal conversations and semi-structured interviews with faculty members and administrators over the course of a year from a number of private universities across Dhaka, as well as my own experiences as a lecturer, enable me to make this assertion. These include universities that have significant number of enrolled students and sizeable faculty bodies. This clarification is made in light of the fly-by-night 'degree-sellers', a number of which continue to operate across the country (see, for example, a recent notice from the University Grants Commission mentioning universities with court cases against them for dubious prac-tices and gross legal violations, http://www.thedailystar.net/no-rules-left-to-be-broken-35426 [accessed 1 February 2017]).

27. Many private universities continue to operate out of rented apartments and shopping complex offices in order to minimise infrastructural costs. The Private University Act of 2010, however, mandates the construction of campuses within a stipulated time after establishment.

28. Even a cursory look at the numbers of students and faculty in business administration departments across some of the largest private universities, such as North South, BRAC, Independent, East West, IUBAT and Asian, reveals the disproportionate size of these departments. Much of it has to do with the changing nature of the labour market as a result of economic restructuring. Increasing numbers of managerial and sales positions are being created for export-oriented industries, in addition to those that result from the proliferation of consumerism facilitated by the growth of local and multinational manufacturers of consumer goods. Better employment prospects are reported for private university graduates (Alam et al., *Private Higher Education in Bangladesh*), which, given the disproportionate share of business administration majors, is not surprising in the context of this restructured economy and its rising demand for a 'managerial' and 'service' workforce. Cf. S. Federici's chapter in this volume.

29. These findings are primarily based on informal conversations and semi-structured interviews with a number of faculty members from the private university I worked for, as well as from three private universities and a public university in Dhaka.

30. See, for example, P. Linebaugh's 'Some Principles of the Commons', in *Stop, Thief!*, pp. 24–6.

31. Reports of land-grabbing and river-filling in the daily news are far too numerous to be cited here. For recent scholarly works on land-grabbing in the Bangladeshi context, see S. Feldman and C. Geisler, 'Land Expropriation and Displacement in Bangladesh', *Journal of Peasant Studies*, 39(3–4) (2012), pp. 971–93. For studies on the extent of the river and canal encroachments in and around Dhaka, as well as the alarming conditions of urban space, see A. Ishtiaque, M. S. Mahmud and M. H. Rafi, 'Encroachment of Canals of Dhaka City, Bangladesh: An Investigative Approach', *GeoScape*, 8(2) (2014), pp. 48–64, and K. N. H. Haque, 'The Political Economy of Urban Space: Land and Real Estate in Dhaka City' (2012), https://www.academia.edu/2079563/The_Political_Economy_of_Urban_Space_in_Dhaka_City_Accumulation_by_Dispossession (accessed 7 January 2017).

32. I learned this from the capitalist promoter of the university (who was

also its vice-chancellor and chair of its Board of Governors) during one of our conversations, when I asked him how he got hold of the property. He was visibly uncomfortable with the question, and said that the land actually belonged to the municipal authorities and that he was neither responsible for, nor worried about, how it came to being.

33. These poles were erected to demarcate the boundaries of the river after the Bangladesh Environmental Lawyers Association won a public interest litigation in the Dhaka High Court in 2009 in favour of dredging the major rivers in Dhaka and removing illegal establishments from their banks. The implementation of this ruling has thus far been dilatory. See, for example, http://www.thedailystar.net/hc-orders-ignored-20885 (accessed 7 January 2017).

34. I refer here to K. Polyani's argument regarding what he calls the 'double movement' (*The Great Transformation* [New York: Rinehart, 1944]), whereby once market relations subsume the very substance of society (in his conceptual framing such subsumption takes place when land, labour and money are completely commodified), processes of de-commodification become increasingly likely to set in as a result of resistance to commodification. Some of the better known problems with this line of reasoning include what can broadly be defined as the 'agency problem' and the 'specification problem'. See, for example, F. Block and M. R. Somers, 'Beyond the Economistic Fallacy: The Holistic Social Science of Karl Polanyi', in Theda Scokpol (ed.), *Vision and Method in Historical Sociology* (Cambridge: Cambridge University Press, 1984), pp. 47–84, and B. J. Silver and G. Arrighi, 'Polanyi's "Double Movement": The Belle Époques of British and US Hegemony Compared', *Politics and Society*, 31(2) (2003), pp. 325–55. Nevertheless, the concept of the double movement seems to have some theoretical and empirical currency, especially under neoliberal conditions which appear to be undermining the very basis of capitalist production and reproduction.

35. Gramsci, *Selections from the Prison Notebooks*, pp. 258–9 (Q8§179).

36. Gramsci, *Selections from the Prison Notebooks*, pp. 258–9 (Q8§179).

37. Gramsci, *Selections from the Prison Notebooks*, pp. 262–3 (Q6§88).

38. This is derived from Marx's critique of classical political economy of the Lockean variety, whereby the commons is *not* the socialisation of production, reproduction and exchange by the association of individual property owners and producers through a perfectly competitive market, but is understood in terms of collective labour producing value

on the basis of 'an association of free men, working with the means of production held in common, and expending their many different forms of labour-power in full self-awareness as one single labour force'; Marx cited in D. Harvey, 'The Future of the Commons', *Radical History Review*, 109 (2011), p. 105. The neoliberal espousal of the commodity logic, which seeks to turn alienated labour into 'human capital embodied in the entrepreneurial capacities of the masses', is yet another attempt to obfuscate capitalist exploitation that rests precisely on the extension of this Lockean argument discredited by Marx. For a more detailed explication along these lines, see Harvey, 'The Future of the Commons'. For an important discussion on how this liberal conceptualisation of the 'commons through the market' has been appropriated by the neoliberal agenda of multilateral agencies such the World Bank, see Federici and Caffentzis, 'Commons against and beyond Capitalism', especially the section on 'Co-opting the Commons'.

39. D. Bollier and S. Helfrich (eds), *The Wealth of the Commons: A World beyond Market and State* (Amherst, MA: Levellers Press, 2012); E. Ostrom, *Governing the Commons: The Evolution of Institutions for Collective Action* (Cambridge: Cambridge University Press, 1990); M. Hardt and A. Negri, *Commonwealth* (Cambridge, MA: Harvard University Press, 2009); Federici and Caffentzis, 'Commons against and beyond Capitalism'; Linebaugh, 'Some Principles of the Commons', in *Stop, Thief!*.

40. Federici and Caffentzis, 'Commons against and beyond Capitalism', p. 100.

41. S. Federici and G. Caffentzis, 'Notes on the Edu-Factory and Cognitive Capitalism', *The Commoner*, 12 (2007), pp. 63–70.

42. As Federici and Caffentzis argue, however, it is important that struggles over the 'public' reinforce struggles for the commons and vice versa, while keeping this important distinction in mind. Since the 'public' represents the products of our past labour, it must be reappropriated alongside with struggles to build the commons. See 'Commons against and beyond Capitalism', p. 114.

43. Linebaugh, *Stop, Thief!*, p. 24.

4 Beyond the Human State: Bergson, Education and the Art of Life

Keith Ansell-Pearson

Let us have done with great systems embracing all the possible, and sometimes even the impossible! Let us be content with the real . . .

Henri Bergson

Education is the guidance of the individual towards a comprehension of the art of life . . . Each individual embodies an adventure of existence. The art of life is the guidance of this adventure.

A. N. Whitehead

In his corpus Bergson is deeply engaged with the question of philosophy's relation to the art of living, as well as with the reformation of education. Bergson insists that he has no wish to elaborate a programme of education; rather, he restricts himself to indicating certain habits of mind that he considers unfortunate and that schooling all too often encourages in fact, while repudiating in principle. In this chapter I aim to show the relevance of Bergson's thinking on intelligence and intuition for a philosophy of education, and here there are two key insights: first, that education needs to resist the substitution of concepts for things, and, secondly, that it needs to advance the idea that there is not only the *socialisation of the truth*.[1] Bergson's philosophy of education consists in showing that philosophy should be an empiricism in as much as it is focused on realities, and here it has an intimate connection with a schooling in the art of living. He is inspired, for example, by the ambition of taking philosophy out of the school, as he puts it, including the disputes between the different schools of philosophy, and bringing it into more intimate contact with life (CM 126). Indeed, if we follow the contours of 'intuitive life' with its special kind of knowledge, then the promise is opened up of bringing an end to 'inert states' and 'dead things': 'nothing but the mobility of which the stability of life is made' (CM 127). Such knowledge will do two things: it will enrich philosophical speculation – we see for the sake of seeing and for the enrichment an enlarged perception offers us – and it will nourish and illuminate everyday life (it will enhance our power to act and live, for example). In order to restore our contact with life it is necessary to conquer the deadening world of habit: 'For the world into which our senses and consciousness habitually introduce us is no more than the shadow of itself: and it is as cold as death' (CM 128). In his essay on 'Good Sense and Classical Studies', Bergson contends that the stubborn clinging to habits (raised to the status of laws of life) is to repudiate change and allow one's vision to be distracted away from the movement that is the condition of life.[2]

Bergson makes a crucial distinction between the provinces of science and philosophy, with the former concerned with well-being, and at most pleasure, and the latter holding out the promise of delivering us over to joy. Bergson does not wish to denigrate the importance of the convenient life, the life of well-being, but it is clear that he sees a superior reality in the joyful existence since it is here that we encounter creative life, including the creation of self by self. It is this set of concerns, centred around Bergson's attempt to revitalise philosophy's investment in the art of life, that I wish to explore. The task is to galvanise perception, to extend perception, and to effect a conversion of attention. The method for doing this is intuition, and the overriding aim is to become accustomed to seeing all things *sub specie durationis*: in this way, what is dead comes back to life, life acquires depth, and we come into account with the original impetus of life that serves to encourage us to create new things. In short, a Bergsonian-inspired philosophy of education restores to the human the vital impetus that lies at the origins of things. The task of education is to become a master in the art of living, and this is something perhaps unique to philosophy.

In what follows I first outline Bergson's fundamental conception of philosophy as the discipline that takes us beyond the human state or condition. I then turn to his specific method, namely intuition, and seek to illuminate this in two sections. In the fourth section I explicitly address Bergson on education. In my conclusion I suggest that Bergsonian thinking on education promotes a style of living beyond the logic of capital.

Philosophy

Bergson conceives philosophy as the discipline that 'raises us above the human condition' (*la philosophie nous aura élevés au-dessus de la condition humaine*') (CM 50) and makes the effort to 'surpass' (*dépasser*) the human condition (CM 193). In *Creative Evolution* Bergson conceives philosophy as 'an effort to dissolve again into the whole'. Moreover: 'Intelligence reabsorbed into its principle, may thus live back again in its genesis'.[3] Such a method of thinking has to work against the most inveterate habits of the mind and consists in an interchange of insights that correct and add to each other. For Bergson, such an enterprise ends by expanding the humanity within us and even allowing humanity to surpass itself by reinserting itself in the whole (CE 124). This is accomplished through philosophy, for it is philosophy that provides us with the means (methods) for reversing the normal directions of the mind (instrumental, utilitarian), so upsetting its habits. In spite of what one might think, for Bergson this makes philosophy's task a modest one.[4] The key insight is the following one: if we suppose that philosophy is an affair of perception,[5] then it cannot simply be a matter of correcting perception but only of extending it. There is nothing at fault with the human condition, and its fundamental errors and habits do not require correction. Rather, the task is to extend the human present, which is the aspect of time in which the human necessarily dwells, a necessity to be explained through the dictates of evolution such as adaptation. Deleuze writes on this: 'The human condition is the maximum of duration concentrated in the present, but there is no co-exclusivity to being, that is to say that there is not only the present'.[6]

Why should we feel motivated by this endeavour to think beyond our human state? Deleuze provides the essential insight that is required here: we find ourselves born or thrown into a world that is ready-made and that we have not made our own. This world always goes in the direction of the 'relaxed aspect' of duration, Deleuze argues.[7] It is on account of the fact that the human condition is one of relaxation that we have such difficulty in understanding the meaning of creation – precisely the notion that proves essential for artistic invention, for new modes of ethical being, and for philosophical reflection, and that lies, of course, at the heart of Bergson's project.

In his writings Bergson advances several conceptions of philosophy, of what it is and of its chief tasks. Sometimes he will stress its capacity to enable us to see: philosophy exists to extend our perception of the universe. At other times he will also express anxiety over philosophy's lapse into contemplation and stress its ability to enhance our power to act and to live. Philosophy for Bergson is not a rarefied, aristocratic activity, something reserved for the best or the most wise, but a popular activity that all can potentially participate in as a way of being creative. On the one hand, the paradoxical theoretical task of philosophy is, above all, to find some 'absolute' in the moving world of phenomena. On the other, it is more dynamic than this and, through this restoration of the absolute, we will gain in a feeling of greater joy and power. Like Whitehead, then, Bergson links philosophy and education with the task of becoming masters in the art of living. Bergson writes:

Greater joy because the reality invented before our eyes will give each one of us, unceasingly, certain of the satisfactions which art at rare intervals procures for the privileged; it will reveal to us, beyond the fixity and monotony which our senses, hypnotized by our constant needs, at first perceived in it, ever-recurring novelty, the moving originality of things. But above all we shall have greater strength, for we shall feel we are participating, creators of ourselves, in the great work of creation which is the origin of all things and which goes on before our eyes. (CM 105)

Typically we exist – both in terms of our species history and our individual development – as slaves of certain natural necessities. Philosophy is a practice and a discipline that can enable us to go beyond the level of necessities and enable us to become 'masters associated with a greater Master' (CM 105–6).

We exist as masters in two main forms: through science and the mastery of matter and through philosophy and the mastery of life. One is more free than the other for Bergson: the mastery of matter is part of the human condition and is a necessity for us, but the mastery of life takes us beyond the human condition and represents a free activity. Moreover, while the former activity serves to provide us with security and is bound up with securing a life of convenience(s), the latter is something different. Philosophy can become complementary to science with respect to both speculation and practice. More than this, it supplements science, since science offers us only the promise of well-being and the pleasure of it – philosophy can give us *joy*, and this joy is bound up with the move beyond the limited character of the human condition. This supplementary aspect of philosophy provides us with an insight into the role Bergson accords to intuition. Let me now focus on this in the next two sections.

Towards Intuition

Bergson calls intuition the attention that the mind gives to itself 'over and above, while it is fixed upon matter, its object' (CM 78). It is a 'supplementary attention' that can be methodically cultivated and developed. We need to begin by noting the distinction between life and matter that characterises Bergson's thinking. For the most part he writes of 'inert matter', though he also refers to 'organised matter' and also of matter as made up of vibrations and to which slight durations can be attributed (CE 201). However, marking a distinction between matter and life is a central feature of Bergson's thinking, whether he is attempting to explain the character of evolution or exploring the meaning of the comic.[8] Roughly speaking, it works as a distinction between inertia and vitality, between rigidity and suppleness, between automatism and creative effort, between necessity and freedom, and so on. However, matter and life/'consciousness' (delay, hesitation, a latitude of choice) are not to be explained apart from one another, and the two have a common source.[9] If the determinism of matter were absolute, to the point of admitting no relaxation and showing no elasticity (which Bergson thinks it does), then life would be an impossibility. Life is an insinuating energy, an impetus, that draws matter away from pure mechanism but only by first adopting this mechanism; life installs 'itself in matter which had already acquired some of the characters of life without the work of life' (ME 20). However, if matter were all that there is then it would have stopped at this point. This is akin, Bergson thinks, to the work of our scientific laboratories where we are seeking to manufacture matter that resembles living matter and is an enterprise that one day, he says, may well be successful. However, he adds, 'we shall reproduce, that is to say, some characters of living matter; we shall not obtain the push in virtue of which it reproduces itself and, in the meaning of transformism, evolves' (ME 20).

We also need to note that Bergson is puzzling on action and we can only resolve the difficulties generated by the puzzle by recognising that he is putting forward different types of action and activity. This is best seen in the way he seeks to demarcate the difference between metaphysics (and intuition) and science (and intelligence). Both are related to action but the action is different in the two cases. So, Bergson writes:

To metaphysics, then, we assign, a limited object, principally spirit, and a special method, mainly intuition. In doing this we make a clear distinction between metaphysics and science. But at the same time we attribute an equal value to both. I believe they can both touch the bottom of reality. I reject the arguments advanced by philosophers, and accepted by scholars, on the relativity of knowledge and the impossibility of attaining the absolute. (CM 37)

It is important to appreciate that Bergson is positing between science and metaphysics a difference of method and not a difference in value (CM 43–4). The task of metaphysics, as he conceives it, is to concern itself with the actual world in which we live and not with all possible worlds, so philosophy embraces realities (CM 44). Science for Bergson is attached to a specific task, one that he does not wish to negate the importance of, namely, the mastery of matter. Positive science relies on sensible observations as a way of securing materials and it does this by elaborating, through methods and faculties, abstraction and generalisation; in short it establishes the order of intelligence through judgement and reasoning. Its 'original domain' and its 'preferred domain' is the domain of inert matter, or of matter stripped of the vitality of life: 'it clings to the physico-chemical in vital phenomena rather than to what is really vital in the living' (CM 38). If our intelligence can be construed as the prolongation of our senses, then we can see the force of science and its aid to life, at least life in its aspect of calculability and manipulation. Prior to pure speculation – seeing for the sake of seeing – there is the imperative to live, and so life demands that matter be made use of, and this takes place through our organs (conceived as natural tools) and with tools, properly so-called, as artificial organs. Although science has pushed far the labour of intelligence, it has not changed its essential direction, which is to make us masters of matter. Bergson argues that even when it speculates, science continues to devote itself to acting, and here it is evident that he has a specific kind of action in mind, namely, action of a utilitarian and instrumental character. Bergson further holds that between intellect and matter there is 'symmetry, concord and agreement': 'On one hand, matter resolves itself more and more, in the eyes of the scholar, into mathematical relations, and on the other hand, the essential faculties of our intellect function with an absolute precision only when they are applied to geometry' (CM 39).

To break out of the social circle it will become necessary to appeal to experience. Experience is of two main kinds: if it is an affair of knowing material objects, then we are dealing with exterior perception; if it is question of encountering the mind, we refer to the name of 'intuition' and raising ourselves above our human state (CM 50). What of 'metaphysics'? Here Bergson holds that the task is 'to develop new functions of thought' (CM 41). The focus of metaphysics is with 'mind' and 'spirit', especially with ourselves and our internal lives. He acknowledges the difficulty: is it not, he asks, much more difficult to develop knowledge of oneself than it is knowledge of the external world?

Outside oneself, the effort to learn is natural; one makes it with increasing facility; one applies rules. Within, attention must remain tense and progress becomes more and more painful; it is as though one were going against the natural bent. Is there not something surprising in this? We are internal to ourselves, and our personality is what we should know best. (CM 41)

Bergson notes, then, a point that is crucial to his own attempt to contribute to how philosophy can aid the art of living, namely, that within the field of instrumental action, a certain *ignorance* of self is what is found to be most useful and answers to a necessity of life, since here we encounter a being, ourselves, that must exteriorise itself in order to act. Hence his claim that mind finds itself in a strange place when it encounters life, in contrast to its habitual feeling at home in the realm of matter (it knows what it must do when it comes to acting in the world). He is not denying, of course, that when it comes to such effective action we are distinguished from animals, for example, in having capacities that enable us to reflect on our actions. But, he notes, nature requires that we only take a quick glance at our inner selves: 'we then perceive the mind, but the mind preparing to shape matter, already adapting itself to it, assuming something of the spatial, the geometric, the intellectual' (CM 42). It is in this context of problems that he appeals to intuition as a mode of mental attentiveness: 'This direct vision of the mind by the mind is the chief function of intuition, as I understand it' (CM 42). But we still do not know what this intuition is and how it can amount to a new function of thinking. Part of the difficulty is our reliance on metaphor and ready-made concepts as a way of thinking reality and reflecting on our experience of the real. This is why Bergson stresses that in order to gain access to intuition – since there is nothing immediate about it as a method – an entire labour of clearing away is required as a way of opening up the way to 'inner experience': 'True, the faculty of intuition exists in each one of us, but covered over by functions more useful to life' (CM 47).

In order to gain access to the practice of intuition it is necessary to break with society, in particular with the subdivision and distribution of the real into concepts that society has deposited into language for the sake of the convenience of existence. Society or the social organism cuts out reality according to its needs, and Bergson asks why philosophy ought to accept a division that in all probability does not correspond to the articulations of the real – except, of course, in terms of our mastery of matter. The challenge here for thinking about the art of living is a serious one: it means not accepting the claim 'that all truth is already virtually known, that its model is patented in the administrative offices of the state, and that philosophy is a jig-saw puzzle where the problem is to construct with pieces society gives us the design it is unwilling to show us' (CM 50). Contra this position, Bergson maintains that in philosophy – and not only in philosophy – it is question of *finding* the problem and of positing it, rather than of solving it: 'stating the problem is not simply uncovering, it is inventing' (CM 51). The difference between the two is paramount since in the one case we are uncovering what already exists actually or virtually, and in the other what does not exist and might never have happened: 'Already in mathematics and still more in metaphysics, the effort of invention consists more in raising the problem, in creating the terms in which it will be stated' (CM 51).

Bergson gives an example to illustrate his point, and it serves as a good way of indicating how a Bergsonian philosophy of education can be developed from the insights I am staging. He imagines the question being set: 'Is pleasure happiness or not?' To answer the question, we could examine the conventional meaning of the words involved and take it as a question of vocabulary; alternatively, we could grasp 'realities' and not simply re-examine conventions, and so endeavour to *transform* the problem being posed. Bergson elaborates as follows:

Suppose that in examining the states grouped under the name of pleasure they are found to have nothing in common except that they are states which man is seeking; humanity will have classified these very different things in one genus because it found them of the same practical interest and reacted toward all of them in the same way. Suppose, on the other hand, that one arrives at an analogous result in analysing the idea of happiness. Immediately the problem disappears or rather is dissolved in entirely new problems of which we can know nothing, and in whose terms we do not even possess, before having studied in itself the human activity of which society had formed from the outside, in order to arrive at the general ideas of *pleasure* and *happiness*, views that were perhaps artificial. Even then one must be assured that the concept of 'human activity' itself is in accordance with a natural division. In this disarticulation of the real according to its own tendencies lies the principal difficulty, as soon as one leaves the domain of matter for that of mind. (CM 52)

Intuition and Sympathy

Let me now look in some more detail at Bergson on intuition and in particular seek to illuminate its connection with the mode of perception he calls 'sympathy'. Intuition is said to be a mode of sympathy 'by which one is transported into the interior of an object' (CM 135). The contrast is with the mode of 'analysis', which is an operation that reduces an object to elements already known and that are common to it and other objects. Intuition involves a special kind of attention or attentiveness to life (Bergson speaks of performing an 'auscultation' and in accordance with a 'true empiricism', CM 147). Bergson contends that even the most concrete of the sciences of nature, namely, the sciences of life, 'confine themselves to the visible form of living beings, their organs, their ana-tomical elements' (CM 136). The task at hand is to understand precisely what Bergson means when he says that intuition leads us to the 'very inwardness of life'. Intuition is important to Bergson since he holds that, taken as a mode of sympathy, it will enable us to resolve – indeed, to *dissolve* – many of the problems that are often taken to be the genuine puzzles of metaphysics, such as 'what is the first cause of existence?' and 'why is there something rather than nothing?' So, he writes: 'To the extent that we distend our will, tend to reabsorb our thought in it and get into greater sympathy with the effort that engenders things, these formidable problems will recede, diminish, disappear' (CM 62).

As Deleuze notes, intuition is the method peculiar to Bergson's phi-losophy. He stresses that it denotes neither a vague feeling or incom-municable experience nor a disordered sympathy. Rather, it is a fully developed method that aims at precision in philosophy. Where duration and memory denote lived realities and concrete experiences, intuition is the only means we have at our disposal for crafting knowledge of experience and reality. 'We may say, strangely enough,' Deleuze notes, 'that duration would remain purely intuitive, in the ordinary sense of the word, if intuition – in the properly Bergsonian sense – were not there as method.'[10] However, intuition is a complex method that cannot be contained in a single act. Instead, it has to be seen as involving a plurality of determinations. The first task is to stage and create problems; the second is to locate differences in kind; and the third is to comprehend 'real time', that is, duration as a heterogeneous and continuous multiplicity. Let me now note some salient aspects of Bergson on intuition and then draw on Deleuze to indicate how intuition aspires to operate as a method of precision in philosophy.

Bergson acknowledges that other philosophers before him, such as Schelling, had tried to escape relativism by appealing to intuition. He argues, however, that this was a non-temporal intuition that was being appealed to, and, as such, was largely a return to Spinozism, that is, a deduction of existence from one complete Being. Bergson locates a failure of empiricism in Spinoza. For a system like Spinoza's, Bergson notes, true or genuine being is endowed with a logical existence more than a psychological or even physical one: 'For the nature of a purely logical existence is such that it seems to be self-sufficient and to posit itself by the effect alone of the force immanent in truth' (CE 276). Spinozism is an attempt to make 'the mystery of existence', such as why minds and bodies exist, vanish, and instead of making actual observations of nature, the philosopher advances a logical system in which at the base of everything that exists is a self-positing being dwelling in eternity. Bergson's main engagement, however, is with Kant, and for obvious reasons. He argues that in order to reach the mode of intuition, it is not necessary, as Kant supposed, to transport ourselves outside the domain of the senses:

After having proved by decisive arguments that no dialectical effort will ever introduce us into the beyond and that an effective metaphysics would necessarily be an intuitive metaphysics, he added that we lack this intuition and that this metaphysics is impossible. It would in fact be so if there were no other time or change than those which Kant perceived . . . (CM 128)

By recovering intuition Bergson hopes to save science from the charge of producing a relativity of knowledge (it is rather to be regarded as approximate) and metaphysics from the charge of indulging in empty and idle speculation. Although Kant himself did not pursue thought in the direction he had opened for it – the direction of a 'revivified Cartesianism' as Bergson calls it – it is the prospect of an extra-intellectual matter of knowledge by a higher effort of intuition that Bergson seeks to cultivate. Kant has reawakened, if only half-heartedly, a view that was the essential element of Descartes' thinking but which the Cartesians abandoned: knowledge is not completely resolvable into the terms of intelligence. Bergson does not, let it be noted, establish an opposition between sensuous (infra-intellectual) intuition and intellectual (what he calls an 'ultra-intellectual') intuition but instead seeks to show that there is a continuity and reciprocity between the two. Moreover, sensuous intuition can be promoted to a different set of operations, no longer simply being the phantom of an unscrutable thing-in-itself:

The barriers between the matter of sensible knowledge and its form are lowered, as also between the 'pure forms' of sensibility and the categories of the understanding. The matter and form of intellectual knowledge (restricted to its own object) are seen to be engendering each other by a reciprocal adaptation, intellect modelling itself on corporeity, and corporeity on intellect. But this duality of intuition Kant neither would nor could admit. (CE 230)

For Kant to admit this duality of intuition would entail granting to duration an absolute reality and treating the geometry immanent in space as an ideal limit (the direction in which material things develop but which they never actually attain).

Deleuze thinks we can learn some valuable philosophical lessons from Bergson on intuition, so let me now to turn to his account. He argues that we go wrong when we hold that notions of true and false can only be brought to bear on problems in terms of ready-made solutions. This is a far too pre-emptive strategy that does not take us beyond experience but locks us in it. This negative freedom is the result of manufactured social prejudices where, through social institutions such as education and language, we become enslaved by order-words that identify for us ready-made problems that we are forced to solve. True freedom lies in the power to constitute problems themselves. This might involve the freedom to uncover certain truths for oneself, but often discovery is too much involved in uncovering what already exists, an act of discovery that was bound to happen sooner or later and that is contingent upon circumstances. Invention, however, gives being to what did not exist and might never have happened, since it was not destined to happen, there was no pre-existing programme by which it could be actualised. In mathematics and in metaphysics the effort of invention consists in raising the problem and in creating the terms through which it might be solved but never as something ready-made. As Merleau-Ponty notes in a reading of Bergson, when it is said that well-posed problems are close to being solved, 'this does not mean that we have already *found* what we are looking for, but that we have already invented it'.[11] For Bergson, the genuine philosopher, as opposed to the amateur, is one who does not accept the terms of a problem as a common problem that has been definitively posed and which then requires that she or he select from the available solutions to the problem (the example Bergson gives to illustrate his point is that of Samuel Butler rejecting Darwin's solution in favour of Lamarck's) (BKW 370).

A second rule of intuition is to do away with false problems, which are said to be of two kinds: first, those that are caught up in terms that contain a confusion of the more and the less; and, secondly, questions that are stated badly in the specific sense that their terms represent only badly analysed composites. In the first case the error consists in positing an origin of being and of order from which nonbeing and disorder are then made to appear as primordial. On this schema, order can only appear as the negation of disorder and being as the negation of nonbeing (CE 222). Such a way of thinking introduces lack into the heart of Being. The more or less errs in not seeing that there are *kinds* of order and forgetting the fact that Being is not homogeneous but fundamentally heterogeneous. Badly analysed composites result from an arbitrary grouping of things that are constituted as differences in kind. Bergson wants to know how it is that we deem certain life forms to be superior to others, even though they are not of the same order, and neither can they be posited in terms of a simple unilinear evolutionism, with one life form succeeding another in terms of a progress towards perfection in self-consciousness. Life proceeds neither via lack nor the power of the negative but through internal self-differentiation along lines of divergence. Indeed, Bergson goes so far as to claim that the root cause of the difficulties and errors we are confronted with in thinking creative evolution resides in the power we ascribe to negation, to the point where we represent it as symmetrical with affirmation (CE 287). When Deleuze says that resemblance or identity bears on difference *qua* difference, he is being faithful to Bergson's critical insight into the character of negation, chiefly, that it is implicated in a more global power of affirmation.

It is through a focus on badly analysed composites that we are led, in fact, to positing things in terms of the more and the less, so that the idea of disorder only arises from a general idea of order as a badly analysed composite. This amounts to claiming, as Deleuze recognises, that we are the victims of illusions that have their source in aspects of our intelligence. However, although these illusions refer to Kant's analysis in the *Critique of Pure Reason*, where reason is shown to generate for itself in exceeding the boundaries of the understanding inevitable illusions and not simple mistakes, they are not of the same order. There is a natural tendency of the intellect to see only differences in degree and to neglect differences in kind. This is because the fundamental motivation of the intellect is to implement and orientate action in the world.

To bring into play a different kind of intelligence is to introduce the element into philosophy that will enable us to go beyond the human state and to widen the canvas of its experience. It is intuition that allows this novel tendency to express itself through two procedures: the discovery of differences in kind and the formulation of criteria for differentiating between true and false problems. But at this point things get even more complex. If intuition is to be conceived as a method that proceeds via division – the division of a composite into differences of kind – is this not to deny that reality is, in fact, made up of composites and mixtures of all kinds? For Bergson, Deleuze argues, the crucial factor is to recognise that it is not things which differ in kind but rather tendencies: 'a thing in itself and in its true nature is the expression of a tendency before being the effect of a cause'.[12] In other words, what differs in nature are not things (their states or traits) but the tendency that things possess for change and development. A simple difference of degree would denote the correct status of things if they could be separated from their tendencies. For Bergson, the tendency is primary not simply in relation to its product but rather in relation to the causes of productions in time, 'causes always being retroactively obtained starting from the product itself'.[13] Any composite, therefore, needs to be divided according to qualitative tendencies. Again, this brings Bergson close to Kant's transcendental analysis, going beyond experience as given and constituting its conditions of possibility. However, these are not conditions of all possible experience but of real experience (for example the experience of different durations).

Bergson thinks that all the great masters of modern philosophy are thinkers who have assimilated the material of the science of their time. He adds that the partial eclipse of metaphysics in recent times can be explained by the fact that today it is a difficult task to make contact with a science that has become scattered. However, the method of intuition, which is to be attained 'by means of material knowledge', is something quite different to a summary or synthesis of scientific knowledge.

Although metaphysics has nothing in common with the 'generalisation of experience', it is possible to define it 'as the whole of experience' (*l'expérience intégrale*).

Intuition is not duration, but rather the movement by which thought emerges from its own duration and gains insight into the difference of other durations within and outside itself. It both presupposes duration, as the reality in which it dwells, but it also seeks to think it: 'to think intuitively is to think in duration' (CM 34). Without intuition as a method, duration would remain for us a merely psychological experience and we would remain prisoners of what is given to us. Informing Bergson's thinking, therefore, is a philosophical critique of the order of need, action and society that predetermines us to retain a relationship with things only to the extent that they satisfy our interest, and of the order of general ideas that prevent us from acquiring a superior human nature.

Bergson insists that his method of intuition contains no devaluation of intelligence but only a determination of its specific facility. If intuition transcends intelligence this is only on account of the fact that it is intelligence that gives it the push to rise beyond. Without it intuition would remain wedded to instinct and riveted to the particular objects of its practical interests. The specific task of philosophy is to introduce us 'into life's own domain, which is reciprocal interpenetration, endlessly continued creation' (CE 115). This is different to what science does when it takes up the utilitarian vantage point of external perception and prolongs individual facts into general laws. The reformed metaphysics that Bergson wishes to awaken that commits itself to an intellectual expansion of reflection and intuition is, in fact, intellectual sympathy.

For Bergson, then, the key move for thought to make lies in the direction of sympathy. By means of science intelligence does its work and delivers to us more and more the secret of life's material or physical operations. But this gives us only a perspectivism that never penetrates the inside, going 'all round life, taking from outside the greatest possible number of views of it . . .' (CE 176). By contrast, metaphysics can follow the path of intuition, which is to be conceived as 'instinct that has become disinterested, self-conscious, capable of reflecting upon its object and enlarging it indefinitely' (CE 176). Bergson has recourse to the example of the aesthetic to develop this insight. It is the aesthetic faculty that gives us something other than what is given for us by normal perception. The eye, he notes, perceives the features of the living in terms of an assembling and not as something involving mutual organisation and reciprocal interpenetration: 'The intention of life, the simple movement that runs through the lines, that binds them together and gives them significance, escapes it' (CE 177). It is just this 'intention' that the artist, he says, seeks to regain, 'placing himself back within the object by a kind of sympathy . . . by an effort of intuition' (CE 177). In his essay on Ravaisson, Bergson alludes to the importance of art for metaphysics: 'The whole philosophy of Ravaisson springs from the idea that art is a figured metaphysics, that metaphysics is a reflection on art, and that it is the same intuition, variously applied, which makes the profound philosopher and the great artist' (CM 231).

It needs to be pointed out, however, that Bergson himself does not subscribe to the identification of art with philosophy. He holds that philosophical intuition goes further than aesthetic intuition since it is capable of capturing the vital before its dispersal into images (BKW 450). Aesthetic intuition has a limited character, which resides in the fact that it gives us only the individual case. He thus invites us to pursue an inquiry that is turned in the same direction as art, but 'which would take life *in general* for its object, just as physical science, in following to the end the direction pointed out by external perception, prolongs the individual facts into general laws' (CE 177). He concedes the obvious point, namely that such a philosophy of life will never obtain a knowledge comparable to that which science acquires: 'Intelligence remains the luminous nucleus around which instinct, even enlarged and purified into intuition, forms only a vague nebulosity' (CE 177). In default of knowledge properly so-called, however, intuition provides us with a supplement that enables us to grasp that which intelligence fails to provide. More than this, it is intuition that can disclose to us in a palpable form what the discoveries of modern biology have established.

Just what this means is explained well by David Lapoujade in an incisive treatment of intuition and sympathy in Bergson.[14] I will now draw on his inquiry and cover only the essential points. Intuition is a reflection of the mind upon itself and there is no intuition of the material or vital as such. Given this constraint, how can we, with the aid of intuition, open ourselves up to different levels of reality and enlarge our perception of life? This is where sympathy intervenes and assumes an important role. Lapoujade argues that sympathy is not a fusion without distance and so cannot be crudely assimilated to some miraculous intuitive act. Rather, it relies upon reasoning by analogy. The reasoning Bergson has in mind here is not one that appeals to fixed terms but rather to movements. One way to think this is in terms of an analogy between tendencies, in which the 'structure' at work is not one of what is similar but of what is common. So, it does not work through an exterior relation of resemblances, but rather through 'an interior *communication* between tendencies or movements'.[15] Analogy comes into play for us between the movements of our own interior existence and those of the universe, and we uncover ourselves intuitively as material and as vital through a series of explorations into ourselves. Bergson expresses it in just these terms in his lecture of 1911 on 'Philosophical Intuition':

the matter and life which fill the world are equally within us; the forces which work in all things we feel within ourselves; whatever may be the inner essence of what is and what is done, we are of that essence. Let us then go down into our own inner selves: the deeper the point we touch, the stronger will be the thrust which sends us back to the surface. (BKW 299)

As Lapoujade pithily expresses it, for Bergson, 'we are analogous to the universe (intuition), and inversely, the universe is our analogue (sympathy)'.[16] In making the effort, then, to think 'beyond the human state' we come into contact, through intuition, with movements, memories and non-human consciousnesses deep within us. Deep within the human there is something other than the human. This means that, for Bergson, the 'sources' of human experience are more obscure and distant than both common sense and science suppose, and these are sources that, Bergson contends, Kant failed to penetrate in his attempt to philosophise about the conditions of the possibility of experience. In essence, this is what Bergson means when he writes of 'dissolving into the whole' and experiencing 'the ocean of life'. Although this dissolving experience may approach the insights of poetry or mysticism, Bergson is after philosophical precision and clarity. He never ceases to emphasise the extent to which intuition requires long and stubborn effort.

As Lapoujade further notes, Bergson is according primacy in reality to alterity: 'it is because the other is within us that we can project it outside us in the form of "consciousness" or "intention"'.[17] What we 'project' on to the world is our own alterity. However, it is clear that, for Bergson, when we experience sympathy it is not merely sympathy for others that we subject ourselves to, but equally sympathy for one's self and recognition of the alterity that lies concealed within ourselves: 'one thing is sure: we sympathize with ourselves' (CM 136). Such an insight perhaps allows us to reconfigure the 'in-itself': 'The in-itself no longer designates the way in which things will never be "for us" but the way in which, on the contrary, things will be very much within us'.[18]

To conclude this treatment of intuition: intuition is the primary method of philosophical thinking for Bergson, and from sympathy it gains an extension that enables it to be deployed as a general method. Intuition puts us into contact with other durations and ensures that we do not exist simply or only as internal duration. This constitutes a fundamental part of what it might mean for us to be able to go beyond the human state.

Education beyond Intelligence

Bergson's thinking provides us with a mode of philosophy that enables us to prize an education that is not based solely or simply on the possession and acquisition of intelligence. Although he holds intelligence in high esteem, which is 'the human way of thinking' (CM 78), he discloses that the 'intelligent human being' is to be regarded with a low opinion since this kind of cleverness only consists in talking about all things with a show of truth (CM 83). In short, such a human being has been merely socialised in truth. At work here we can detect a conservative mode of thinking, since it is a 'conservative logic which governs thought in common' (CM 82). Moreover, does not conversation greatly resemble conservation? As Bergson notes, 'conversation should bear only upon things of the social life. And the essential object of society is to insert a certain fixity into universal mobility. Societies are just so many islands consolidated here and there in the ocean of becoming' (CM 82). Although he does not explicitly posit legislation as the true goal of philosophising, Bergson does follow Nietzsche in exposing the hollowness of mere criticism as the endeavour of intellectual activity. Somewhat sarcastically, Bergson writes: 'Clever in speaking, prompt to criticize' (CM 83). In teaching someone to be critical the aim is not to get them to work on the thing in question, or on things themselves, but to appraise what others have said. Bergson thus expounds an education in being 'unreasonable', which is a philosophy of education based on the desire for *searching* that casts aside ready-made ideas. Only in this way can education disturb society and resist the socialisation of truth. In addition, the new education needs to aim well beyond the inculcation of encyclopaedic knowledge. Bergson clarifies his position as follows:

I value scientific knowledge and technical competence as much as intuitive vision. I believe that it is of man's essence to create materially and morally, to fabricate things and to fabricate himself. *Homo faber* is the definition I propose. *Homo sapiens*, born of the reflection *Homo faber* makes on the subject of his fabrication, seems to me to be just as worthy of esteem as long as he resolves by pure intelligence those problems which depend upon it alone. One philosopher may be mistaken in the choice of these problems, but another philosopher will correct him; both will have worked to the best of their ability; both can merit our gratitude and admiration. *Homo faber, homo sapiens*, I pay my respects to both, for they tend to merge. The only one to which I am antipathetic is *Homo loquax* whose thoughts, when he does think, is only a reflection upon his talk. (CM 84–5)

If education is to centre on the creative needs of the child, then the focus should be on the child as a seeker and an inventor, 'always on the watch for novelty, impatient of rule, in short, closer to nature than is the grown man' (CM 86). Bergson locates a tension between the educator, who is essentially a sociable human being, and the child to be educated, who is free of social conventions and expectations. The educator seeks to be encyclopaedic in the sense that they place primary importance on the need to impart to children the entire collection of acquired results that make up the social patrimony. Bergson does not doubt for a moment that these results fill us with pride and each one is precious. But it is not these acquisitions that education needs to be focused on if our interest is in the cultivation of the child and its original being: 'Rather, let us cultivate a child's knowledge in the child, and avoid smothering under an accumulation of dry leaves and branches, products of former vegetations, the new plant which asks for nothing better than to grow' (CM 86).

For Bergson, then, education appears to have two core aspects: socialisation and anti-socialisation! On the one hand, we are to be educated, but not loquaciously, in the domains of intelligence, which is 'science' broadly conceived and which centres on practical truths. On the other hand, we are to be 'educated' in the domain of intuition, which centres on art, literature (including the rhythms of reading) and philosophy, and here there is no pragmatism at work but rather a creative evolution and a style of life or way of life that Bergson calls 'sympathy'. The former mode of education provides us with tools of criticism and serves the needs of society; by contrast, the latter mode provides us with superior vision or extended perception and serves only the desires of life for creativity and originality. But in both cases we are dealing with reality, or with different aspects of it, and it is an education in realities that Bergson wants above all. In the case of the 'higher' form of education, it is clear that a Bergsonian philosophy of education seeks to make learning relevant to the tasks of the art of life: 'In this speculation on the relation between the possible and the real, let us guard against seeing a simple game. It can be preparation for the art of living' (CM 106).

Conclusion

Bergson's thinking is highly relevant to the concerns of the philosophy of education since it takes us beyond the idea of a ready-made world in which the child is simply exposed to ready-made ideas and concepts, be it through a scientific education or a philosophical one, with both modelled on intelligence. As he notes, education is needed simply because nature rarely produces in a spontaneous manner 'an emancipated soul that is master of itself', and here education's task is primarily to remove obstacles, rather than to communicate an élan, to lift a veil rather than to shed light (BKW 427). A Bergsonian-inspired education would take us beyond the realm of the natural and the necessary, in which the ready-made holds us in tutelage. Ready-made philosophy and science are to be accepted but only provisionally and as a means of climbing higher: 'Beyond the ideas which are chilled and congealed in language, we must seek the warmth and mobility of life' (BKW 428).

I agree with one commentator who has recently sought to show that Bergson's non-utilitarian thinking about 'the creative mind' and 'creative evolution' works profoundly against the logic of capital. Bergsonian thinking does not want human beings to be passive receivers − or consumers − of truth, but participants in the shaping and reshaping of truth, including the truth of their individual and collective lives (BKW 428–9). Bergsonian thinking thus works against the 'reductive and homogenising neoliberal landscape'.[19]

Notes

1. H. Bergson, *The Creative Mind*, trans. Mabelle L. Andison (Totowa, NJ: Littlefield, Adams and Co., 1965), p. 87. Subsequent references to this work are given in the text as CM.
2. *Bergson: Key Writings*, ed. K. A. Pearson and J. Mullarkey (London:

Continuum, 2002), p. 424. Subsequent references to this work are given in the text as BKW.

3. H. Bergson, *Creative Evolution*, trans. A. Mitchell (Lanham, MD: University Press of America, 1983), p. 123. Subsequent references to this work are given in the text as CE.

4. On this modesty, see H. Bergson, *Oeuvres* (Paris: Presses Universitaires de France, 1959), p. 658; *Creative Evolution*, p. 123.

5. Compare Nietzsche's definition of philosophy as 'spiritual/mental vision' (*geistigen Blicks*), in *Beyond Good and Evil*, trans. R. J. Hollingworth (London: Penguin, 1983), Section 252.

6. G. Deleuze's 1960 lecture course on Chapter 3 of Bergson's *Creative Evolution*, trans. B. Loban, *Substance*, 114 (36:3) (2007), lecture for 21 March.

7. Deleuze's 1960 lecture course on Chapter 3 of Bergson's *Creative Evolution*, lecture for 2 May.

8. For Bergson, the comic does not exist outside what is human and is to be explained in terms of the mechanical being encrusted on the living. He writes: 'The comic is the side of a person which reveals his likeness to a thing, that aspect of human events which, through its peculiar inelasticity, conveys the impression of pure mechanism, automatism, of movement without life'; H. Bergson, *Laughter: An Essay on the Meaning of the Comic*, trans. C. Brereton and F. Rothwell (Copenhagen; Los Angeles: Green Integer, 1999), p. 82.

9. H. Bergson, *Mind-Energy*, trans. H. Wildon Carr (Westport, CT: Greenwood Press, 1975), pp. 17, 20. Subsequent references to this work are given in the text as ME.

10. G. Deleuze, *Bergsonism*, trans. H. Tomlinson and B. Habberjam (New York: Zone Books, 1988), p. 14.

11. M. Merleau-Ponty, 'Bergson', in *In Praise of Philosophy and Other Essays*, trans. J Wilde, J. M. Edie and J. O'Neil (Evanston: Northwestern University Press, 1988), p. 14.

12. G. Deleuze, 'Bergson's Conception of Difference', in *Desert Islands and Other Texts 1953–1974*, ed. D. Lapoujade, trans. M. Taormina (New York: Semiotext(e), 2004), p. 34.

13. Deleuze, 'Bergson's Conception of Difference', p. 34.

14. D. Lapoujade, 'Intuition and Sympathy in Bergson', *Pli: The Warwick Journal of Philosophy*, 15 (2004), pp. 1–18.

15. Lapoujade, 'Intuition and Sympathy in Bergson', p. 8.

16. Lapoujade, 'Intuition and Sympathy in Bergson', p. 9.

17. Lapoujade, 'Intuition and Sympathy in Bergson', p. 11.
18. Lapoujade, 'Intuition and Sympathy in Bergson', p. 12.
19. S. O'Sullivan, 'A Diagram of the Finite-Infinite Relation: Towards a Bergsonian Production of Subjectivity', in J. Mullarkey and C. De Mille (eds), *Bergson and the Art of Immanence* (Edinburgh: Edinburgh University Press, 2013), p. 182.

5 The Master and the Professor are Dead, and I am not Feeling Well Myself

Mladen Dolar

On 26 December 1817 G. W. F. Hegel received an invitation to take a professorial position at the recently established university in Berlin. The university was founded in 1809 in the aftermath of the Napoleonic devastation of Prussia – and one must remember the iconic moment of Hegel finishing his *Phenomenology of Spirit* in the midst of the cannon fire of the battle of Jena, witnessing the great Prussian defeat and seeing Napoleon on a white horse entering the city in October 1806. The new university was immediately known as the Humboldt University, after Wilhelm von Humboldt, Hegel's distant friend, who was commissioned by the Prussian ministry to draw up plans for its conceptual foundation. For the ideals on which this new university was based, I can do no better than to quote Terry Pinkard's very apt description:

the instructional goals were to be focused on promoting the *Bildung* – the self-determining self-cultivation and inwardly motivated love of learning and education – of the students there and preparing them thereby to be fully modern citizens of a fully modern state. To accomplish this, the university had to embody within itself the union of 'teaching and research' – two great watchwords of the Humboldt university which were to endure for virtually all modern universities down to our own day. The university thus had to be organised around the notion that *Wissenschaft*, the totality of the learned disciplines, was an end in itself, that academic freedom was therefore of utmost importance, and that the purpose of the university was to have students *taught* by professors who were to impart the state of the art in current *research* in which they themselves were engaged . . . The process would lead to students emerging from the university with the formation necessary to continue to progress through such *Bildung* in the rest of their lives. Moreover, in Humboldt's vision . . . the university was most emphatically *not* to be a training ground for the professions, it was an incubator for self-determining men of taste and learning, who would emerge as the proper leaders and state officials of a modern, free form of life.[1]

This was the blueprint for what was reputedly the first form of the modern university, the Humboldt model, emulated in various ways in the wave of modern universities established in the nineteenth and well into the twentieth century. This model clearly departed from the venerable medieval tradition that characterised the first universities and that could be described – at least after the initial antagonistic conditions of their *establishment* – under the heading of 'the discourse of the master' (to use Lacan's term which we will come to later), relying on authority, religion and tradition – the authority of established knowledge vouchsafed by the authority of master figures (*Aristoteles dixit*, as the famous adage had it – the fact the Aristotle said so was proof enough) – the Church Fathers, Thomas Aquinas as the new Aristotle, alternating with Plato in the Renaissance, and ultimately the authority of the Bible. In such a framework, philosophy was relegated to the position of *ancilla theologiae*, the maidservant of theology, and this was the setting in which Hegel himself was formed in his student days in Tübingen, much to his discontent. In the Humboldt vision, however, philosophy was to assume the central role of unifying all realms of knowledge and bringing them to totality – and who would be better suited for such a mission than Hegel, the man who proposed the all-encompassing system of philosophical sciences?

The first key feature of this model was that knowledge was an end in itself, knowledge for the sake of knowledge,[2] relying only on its own authority; and therefore the transmission of knowledge was to be intimately linked with research, the production of new knowledge, for knowledge was seen as subject to constant transformation, development, expansion, progress, conquering ever new territories of the hitherto unknown. The professor was but the bearer, the agent of the self-development of knowledge. The grandeur of a professor was not based on his authority alone, but rather on the humility with which he subjected his own authority to the authority of knowledge itself, as its servant. Hence the teachers formed a community with the students as equally taking part in this self-development of knowledge, propelled by no other authority than that of knowledge itself in its own self-justification. As the German pun would have it, *Wissenschaft* is *das Wissen dass das Wissen schafft* – science is knowledge breeding knowledge. Following the authority of knowledge alone, research should unfold in complete freedom in any direction required by its course, taking nothing for granted.

The second key feature was the connection of this view of knowledge with *Bildung*, the famously hardly translatable German word – formation, education, culture, cultivating. The implication of this concept is that knowledge involves subject formation, it informs a subject position, or rather a process of permanent self-forming and deployment of subjectivity. Growth of knowledge would go hand in hand with personal growth, entailing the development of independent judgement and autonomy. Knowledge grants autonomy and self-determination.

The third feature is that if knowledge serves no other end but itself, it cannot possibly be subservient to training for the professions, in view of the needs of state, economic and social requirements and pressures, the needs of the market. Yet there is a tacit assumption of something like a pre-established harmony between both parts: knowledge as an end in itself, forming autonomous subjects, is actually the best way to produce subjects most suited for the life of a modern state, subjects that would best be able to fill the positions needed by the state and the community and guarantee economic development and prosperity. By disregarding pragmatic social and political ends as secondary, one actually eventually serves them better than by taking them as an immediate goal. Following its own ends regardless of the goals of state and economy, knowledge would thus be happily attuned to serve in the best way the goals of state and economy. It is ultimately in the interest of state authorities, and of society at large, to allow the free and independent development of knowledge on its own grounds, without any other consideration and interference. The invisible hand, not of the market but of spirit, would see to the happy match.

Such was the university, at least in its ideal conception, to which Hegel was called to fulfil its mission. He took the professorial position in October 1818, and this was the place where he would achieve the peak of his glory, and where he was to die, at the height of his powers and influence, in November 1831. There is something iconic in this moment, in this encounter, just as iconic as Hegel encountering Napoleon twelve years earlier, perhaps anecdotally less picturesque but conceptually more spectacular: the last metaphysician meets the first modern university.

Hegel, the Last Master, the First Professor

In 1969–70 Jacques Lacan, then at the height of his fame and influence, held the seminar entitled *The Other Side of Psychoanalysis*.[3] The seminar was held in fevered circumstances, in Paris in the aftermath of the 1968 student revolt. In the seminar Lacan tried to develop, among other things, a theory of the university that would meet the pressing needs of the moment. His take is highly relevant for our purpose, since this particular juncture – between the old type of knowledge placed under the banner of the master and the new type of university knowledge placed under the authority of knowledge alone – was very much at the heart of his concern. In his view, discourse is what forms a social bond, providing the assumptions on which fundamental social interactions are based, and the discourse of the university was for him what provided the social tie of modern societies and in many ways defined their demeanour. We do not need to enter into any detail regarding Lacan's grand and ambitious design, his proposal of the matrix of four discourses as paradigmatic social bonds, but we will concentrate only on the way that Hegel figures significantly in this theory as the symptomatic point.

One should first point out that the very idea of the discourse of the master – which would be the basic type of social bond – stems from Lacan's reading of Hegel's master–slave dialectic.[4] Since the discourse of the master is, in Lacan's view, the elementary type of discourse, all other discourses being deducible from it, it follows that the whole project of the theory of the four discourses is placed fundamentally under Hegel's banner; it hinges at its core on a certain account of the Hegelian dialectic. In short, the upshot of Hegel's master–slave dialectic was the passage from physical power, the life and death struggle between two individuals for supremacy, to the power of the symbolic, where the master, in his relation to the slave, is relegated to symbolic forms of domination, ultimately to the sign of the master, the master signifier as the core of symbolic efficacy. As Lacan strikingly put it, 'To make people work is even more tiresome than to work oneself, if one really had to do it. The Master never does it. He gives a sign, the Master-signifier, and everybody starts running' (OP 174). This master signifier is in itself senseless, yet it retains the key to the symbolic sway, the way that domination depends on a sign, not on superior strength. But the slave on the other side of this basic relation has to possess a knowledge, a know-how, in order to be able to carry out work, to crack the obstinacy of objectivity and by his work make it compliant to the needs and whims of the master. In such a constellation of mastery vs. knowledge, philosophy, since its origin, has presented a paradoxical and highly significant twist. Philosophy, to put Lacan's view in a nutshell, was initially based on a spoliation, a theft of the slave's knowledge; its major feat was to appropriate the slave's know-how and to turn it into an epistemic knowledge, extricated from its practical embeddedness and utility.

What does philosophy show in all its evolution? It's this – the theft, the robbery, the subtraction of knowledge from slavery by the operation of the master . . . The function of *episteme*, specified as transmittable knowledge . . . is always entirely borrowed from the techniques of handcraft [*techniques artisanales*], that is to say pertaining to the slave. What is at stake is to extract their essence so that this knowledge can become the knowledge of the master. (OP 21)[5]

There is an opposition: on the one hand we have the slave's knowledge, the starting point of knowledge, but it is a practical knowledge, a know-how, a *savoir-faire*, a knowledge pertaining to handcraft, to the crafts, a crafty knowledge which makes work possible, for there is no work without knowledge. On the other hand we have the *episteme*, the epistemological purified knowledge, the theoretical knowledge, knowledge to be transmitted as pure knowledge, which appears on the side of the master – and indeed philosophy was, from the outset, the pastime of masters. There was, at the very origin of philosophy, a transition from master to knowledge, yet firmly placed in the framework of the master's authority. At the end of the long line of development of philosophy Hegel still presents the figure of the master, its last avatar, the one who spells out this logic:

It is clear that his truth is hidden from him [from the master, in the discourse of the master], and a certain Hegel stated that it is delivered to him by the work of the slave. There you have it; however, it is a discourse of the master, this discourse of Hegel's, which relies on substituting the State for the master through the long pathway of culture, culminating in absolute knowledge. (OP 90)

So Hegel, the proponent of universal knowledge, is ultimately still endorsing the master. The master–slave story is but a nutshell, a bud from which a political theory is to be developed, its consequences drawn out. The structural inequality that the master–slave relation was based upon has to be overcome, superseded by recognition among equals (*Anerkennung*), by the ethical substance of community and by the rule of universal law, that is, of an ideal abstract common master in relation to which all are treated as equals. The master had to become disembodied, or rather, in a further step, he is incarnated in the state. And Hegel, notoriously, was the Prussian state philosopher, or so the story goes. So we have the slippage from the master to the state, the substitution of the state for the master, as Lacan compresses the story, as Hegel's way of endorsing mastery. The pathway of culture (*Bildung*) is the long process of education leading from enforced obedience to the master to the freely chosen obedience to the state as the incarnation of reason. If the master was from the outset relegated to a sign, the master signifier, then at the end of this story the master is dethroned, as it were, by being enthroned as the Hegelian monarch, merely relegated to his signature and to putting the dot on the 'i'; the figure of mere sign and of impotence in the midst of reason. So in this view Hegel still endorses philosophy as the discourse of the master and maintains mastery in its ultimate emptied out and universalised form.

Yet a hundred pages on in this same seminar we are surprised to find the following:

Hegel is the sublime representative of the discourse of knowledge, that is, of university knowledge. Among us in France you can only find philosophers walking the streets, as members of provincial societies, like Maine de Biran, or among people like Descartes who wander around Europe . . . Among us you don't find philosophers in universities. This can be seen as our advantage. But in Germany you find them in the University. (OP 200)

Hegel is now cast in another role, that of the key proponent of the university discourse – has Lacan changed his mind from February to June 1970?

First of all, what is at stake is not only the fact that Hegel happened to be a university professor by profession. The problem is that the university is already inscribed in the position from which he speaks. As a philosopher, he places himself in the paradigmatic place of the representative of the university. According to his habitus, his fundamental bearing, he couldn't possibly be anything else – a lens grinder, a cosmopolitan traveller, a persecuted sage or an eccentric genius. The formative place of expression of his knowledge is the university, which, historically, at this point, for the first time really appears in its modern sense. But this is not all; one could say that Hegel universalises university, he turns the whole of the world, all regions of being, logic, nature and culture alike, all philosophical attitudes and theories, all subject positions, he turns all this into a single progressive path of knowledge, the self-development of a universal system of knowledge, the most massive university imaginable. The world is part of the university, not the other way round; all of our activity is caught up in university discourse; in the Hegelian system we are all students (including and in the first place Hegel himself), we are always studying for exams, taking more and more advanced courses and acquiring more and more grades; we are trapped in a programme of permanent education, until the ultimate grade, the absolute knowledge, the PhD to finish all PhDs. World history is the world university.

Is Hegel, then, the paramount university professor? It seems that he fits this role as well as, or rather better than, that of the master. Or rather, the two roles are not really in contradiction – he can appear as an ideal agent of the master precisely insofar he is an agent of universal knowledge, presenting precisely the point of transition between the old forms of mastery and the modern ones. The ideal professor has, for the first time and the last, succeeded in resolving the universality of knowledge into an all-encompassing system, where he can construe the authority and the state as an embodiment of philosophy, an incarnation of reason. In the discourse of the university, knowledge is in the position of the agent and in a *quid pro quo* it can appear that authority, along with all institutions of power, stems from knowledge; it is knowledge that institutes power as a moment of its own internal self-development which can posit all its presuppositions and thus abolish them. It is mastery universalised to the degree that the master himself can be reduced to the mere impotent figure of the monarch.

By qualifying Hegel alternately as the vintage figure of the master at the moment of the demise of the metaphysical tradition (framed by the discourse of the master), and the vintage figure of the professor at the moment of the birth of university discourse, Lacan places Hegel at the most spectacular juncture. Historically, it is not only that Hegel is placed precisely at the point of inauguration of the modern university, but also at the point of the aftermath of the French Revolution, that event which inspired so much enthusiasm in Hegel, and its normalisation in modern societies – the slide from revolution to normalisation where knowledge appears as the ideal medium of both. After all, university is, among other things, to this day the best neutraliser of revolutions; it receives them happily into its bosom and turns them into an affair of knowledge – the best witness is May '68. The university particularly adores the label of 'subversive knowledge'; it alleviates its bad conscience, it swallows it with enhanced appetite. Hegel was the one who, through the shattering break of revolution, passed from master to professor, from one universe to another, from the pre-modern underpinnings to full-blown modernity.

Since Lacan opposes the French and the German ways of treating the university, the subsequent vagaries of the German and French fates of philosophy and university are highly telling. Most significantly, the philosophers who one cannot find in the German university, this otherwise ideal place for philosophers, are Marx, Nietzsche and Freud (preceded by Kierkegaard). There is no way around this fact: the major breaks in the post-Hegelian philosophy, the crucial points of our inspiration today, happened outside the university framework. In the twentieth century one can consider the strange case of Wittgenstein, who despite his foothold in Cambridge in the 1930s, arrived at his major breakthroughs outside of university and was by his life and demeanour anything but a professor. A most paradoxical place would have to be reserved for Heidegger: one could say that his project was a return to a fundamental thinking that would be recalcitrant to the university discourse, a way of thinking that would retain the symbolic efficacy of knowledge that the university discourse has neutralised and thwarted, the capacity of knowledge to stir truth, something that university discourse, for all its promotion of knowledge, has rendered virtually impossible. Yet from this radical critical stance, this project produced its most catastrophic moment precisely in its intersection with the university, in the *Rektoratsrede*, which one can read as a programme for a university not based on university discourse – the moment when the thought opposed to university discourse provided, in a highly political gesture, the starting point of a proposal to reform the university that was inextricably mixed with the most fateful new form of domination. Anyway, in the time after Hegel, philosophers were actually not so easy to find in German universities; the greatest moments of German philosophy were perhaps produced outside, and then eventually recuperated by the university.[6]

In France, it seems that in many respects the situation was the reverse of the German one: there is, to be sure, a whole tradition of grand philosophical figures outside the university, above all Sartre and Lacan, but also Bataille, Blanchot and several others; but the telling thing is that even the philosophers in the university, and often those holding the most prestigious positions, actually see themselves, are generally perceived as, and behave like outsiders. They present themselves as an underground movement inside the university, a bunch of guerrilla fighters who have to take on a temporary disguise, an alias – consider the cases of Althusser, Foucault, Derrida, Deleuze, Badiou, to name just the most famous. Is this to be read as a disavowal of their position, so that the ideal proponents of university discourse are ultimately those who present its inner opposition, the salient subversion complementing and secretly endorsing the mainstream; or are they really introducing something else and essentially different, offering a way out of the impasses of university discourse? I will leave this question in suspense. I can only add as an aside that on a more common level, leaving aside the big names, it belongs to the most conformist academic behaviour to rant against academia. 'I am not an academic' is most often to be read on the model of Freud's 'This is not my mother'.

Who is Afraid of the Absolute Knowledge?

But let us go back to Hegel. Is he to be seen as the master or the professor, and does one have to decide? Or is he the seamless transition and the secret alliance between the two? Or should one rather see him as the intersection of the two circles, to use Lacan's favourite didactic prop, where the intersection belongs to neither yet secretly holds both together, but as an entity which has to fall out in order for the two areas to be established, circumscribed and opposed – something that becomes invisible in the neat division into two discourses?

On closer inspection, the two roles attributed to Hegel, master and professor, actually do not fit him as well as it may seem, if one looks at the historical evidence of his legacy. It is obvious that neither the state nor the university ever followed Hegel's footsteps; their subsequent development took a completely non-Hegelian or even anti-Hegelian course. Hegelianism as a state philosophy and Hegelianism as a model of university knowledge have rather acquired the status of a fantasy, or even of a horror show, an object of dread, a figure against which it was deemed necessary to establish fundamentally different models of politics and knowledge. Hegel's ghost, in the disguise of the master and the professor, largely served as a warning and as a straw man, not as a model to follow. Obviously, the subsequently prevailing liberal political theory, in its assumptions about the nature of state and political power, is at the opposite end to Hegel, and it took an incredible feat of imagination, a masterpiece of conjuring, to see the triumph of liberal democracy as the Hegelian end of history (as in Fukuyama's notorious book, which marked another historical moment of transition). And if we cast a superficial glance at the entire development of post-Hegelian philosophy, if I may take the liberty of simplifying the general thrust to the outmost, we can easily see that it basically defined itself as a farewell to Hegel, a way out of the Hegelian trap, be it in its Marxist or Nietzschean variety, or in the whole analytical tradition and the theory of science, the phenomenological and the Heideggerian tradition, down to structuralism, poststructuralism and postmodernism. The slogan of 'the end of metaphysics', shared in one way or another by all these extremely varied traditions (even if understood in very different ways), always meant, in the most immediate sense, the departure from the last, that is, from the paramount and the most notorious of all metaphysicians. Hegel, the instigator of modernity and of the era of university discourse, had to be retroactively obliterated and expelled for modernity and university to function. He may well appear to be the paradigmatic case of the discourse of the master and the university discourse, yet the modern forms of domination and of knowledge rather took him as the model opponent (or a model straw man) against which they established themselves. Paradoxically, the university discourse could only function as the disavowal of Hegel, its initiator and vanishing mediator.

If an ultimate proof was needed of the untenable nature of Hegel's position, one could always produce the most obvious exhibit, absolute knowledge, the ostensible shorthand for the Hegelian fallacy. The mere mention of this term was enough and – unfortunately – Lacan followed the general thrust in this respect. One can put it in a simple thesis: Hegel may well have stood at the origin of university discourse, but it is clear that someone who raises a claim to absolute knowledge cannot possibly be placed within its framework, so that this extreme point had to be repressed and abandoned in order for the modern university to be established. For knowledge, the protagonist of university discourse, can only be assessed, gauged, weighed, judged, proven or refuted on the condition that it is not absolute; one has to scrutinise any knowledge with a cool and impartial eye in order for it to be admitted as justified. University is the great leveller and neutraliser of knowledge.

The paradox of absolute knowledge is that it appears as an antiquated remainder of the metaphysical tradition, its cumbersome refuse, but it occupies this position of the remainder precisely in its extreme claim to universality, as if the very excess of universality starts to function as the remainder, as a moment recalcitrant to universality. The extreme claim to reason is what appears unreasonable in Hegel; the excess of reason defies post-Hegelian reason. The figure of absolute knowledge is refractory to knowledge, the claim to an all-encompassing system cannot be quite encompassed. This is the point where the slogan of absolute knowledge starts functioning as its very opposite: the refuse of knowledge, something to be excluded and disposed of, an outrage, a scandal.[7] Lacan keeps coming back to it throughout his seminar, following the general course of indignation. His argument is that absolute knowledge 'would only be to mark the annulment, the failure, the disappearance at the conclusion of the only thing that motivates the function of knowledge – its dialectic with enjoyment'.

'Absolute knowledge is supposed to be the abolition of this term, purely and simply' (OP 35). It would be *un tout-savoir*, a knowledge forming a whole in its own self-transparency and self-sufficiency, the union of knowledge and mastery, knowledge as the ultimate gesture of the master. But couldn't one see in this gesture precisely that intersection between the discourse of the master and the university discourse that had to fall out, the symptomatic unplaceable point which exceeds both types of discourse while presenting their overlap? And couldn't one argue that this point, which was supposed to abolish the dialectic of knowledge and enjoyment, started to function precisely as the left-over, the surplus produced by philosophy, the remainder which points to its real? The refuse, the remainder emerging in the form of universality and absoluteness, the universality gone a bit too far, the universality run amok, the rest of the all-encompassing totality, not as something that this totality would be unable to cover, but in the very gesture of its totalisation. The absolute knowledge is thus a symptom of post-Hegelian philosophy, its monster, its impossible. If it seemed that absolute knowledge was the point that condensed the master and the professor, it appears that at the very same point it may offer an exit, a way out, a pass, a point with which to persevere, to work with it, to envisage its symptomatic value.

The Posthumous Revenge of the Master and the Professor

Let me return to the beginning. Belonging to a certain generation, I cannot read the description of the ideals of the Humboldt university without some sentiment of nostalgia mixed with bemusement. The generation of student revolts tried to put into question not merely the antiquated forms of the traditional university but also, beyond that, in some of its aspects, the very rule of university discourse as such. Lacan, in 1969, provided the name and the diagnosis, intervening into the tumults of the time. The main target of the revolts was precisely the model of the Humboldt university. The description I gave at the beginning may appear rosy and praiseworthy, but it contained many hidden clauses that Lacan spelled out: the self-justifying unfolding of knowledge for the sake of knowledge secretly relied on the disavowed master, all the more intractable since hidden under the bar.[8] The revolt was in part directed against the hidden and insidious mastery that had underpinned the university since its Humboldtian beginnings, particularly ostensible in the figure of the professor who, under the guise of a humble servant of the authority of knowledge, rather tended to arrogate the authority of its master, so that the modern universities, following the Humboldt model, were always intertwined with a feudal hierarchy, reproduced within the pursuit of pure science and under its guise. This is what Lyotard, in the aftermath of '68 and its dubious success, would call 'the end of the age of the Professor'.[9]

Secondly, the target was 'academic knowledge', precisely 'knowledge for the sake of knowledge', which seemed to yield an academic sphere cut off from the quickly changing modern world, a sphere closed in on itself, distant from the interests and the antagonisms of buzzing social reality. The catchword was 'the ivory tower'. Thirdly, another hidden clause of the Humboldt model was its elite nature, the presupposition of what was in Hegel's time called *die Gelehrtenrepublik*, the republic of the learned, the community of scholars, clearly designed for an enlightened minority, tacitly reserved for a small portion of the population, the select, supposedly the brightest, who would by university education and its *Bildung* be called upon to fill the ruling posts in society. The general counter-demand was a call for democratisation, for the free access of all to all levels of university education, with special concern for the underprivileged. And fourthly, there was a poignant demand for the inclusion of 'subversive knowledge', the knowledge hitherto excluded from the purified and rarefied realm of academic knowledge. At the time subversive knowledge was epitomised by Marxism and psychoanalysis, soon to be followed by women's studies, queer studies, post-colonial studies and a host of others.

The relative success of these demands turned out to be a very mixed blessing. The downfall of the professor did not defuse the hidden authority, but rather made it impalpable and even more pervasive. The undoing of the academic enclosure tended to be translated into a quest for mass-produced marketable knowledge, where the main concern was no longer truth, but efficacy, 'the optimization of the global relationship between input and output', to refer again to Lyotard[10] – knowledge that best fulfils social demands, that trains for the professions, attuned to the market, knowledge assessed by utility and functionality, not on its own grounds and merits; instead of *Bildung* in the light of autonomy, instruction in the light of production.

The supposed pre-established harmony between the autonomy of knowledge and its social benefit became an enforced imposition, the happy match transformed into a forced marriage. Democratisation yielded the mixed blessing of the massification of universities that we have witnessed in the last decades, making universities accessible more than ever before, yet with the concomitant lowering of academic standards, the proliferation of testing, the replacement of knowledge by information, the quickly transmissible and the quickly digestible, delivered in a host of underfunded and understaffed institutions with more students than could possibly be decently dealt with. Subversive knowledge in its different aspects most often turned out to be far more amenable to university discourse than anyone in '68 could have imagined. It could not only be rather easily integrated but positively flourished in the guise of new academic disciplines, often emulating the common patterns of old disciplines as their caricature, often alleviating the bad conscience of the conservative academic enterprise, now displaying its magnanimity in embracing the margins, and often, once it got its academic credentials, turning out to be equally boring. This is a somewhat makeshift and no doubt simplified list, but anyone working in academia can recognise the patterns, although they are seasoned with more ambivalent and complex processes.

What, if Anything, is to be Done?

To sum up, at the risk of simplification: what promised to be a revolt against the university discourse, this paradigmatic modern social bond, rather turned into its prolongation, all-pervasiveness, universalisation, general implementation, its strengthening. The demotion of the authority of knowledge, its functionalisation, actually reinforced and bolstered the university discourse. Lacan tried to show that in the university discourse, knowledge in the position of agent, 'knowledge for the sake of knowledge', was a mask, a deceptive surface under which one should see underpinnings in mastery, the enforced social distribution of power under the guise of pure knowledge. The cynical twist that has befallen the university discourse in the last decades could be seen as its coming out: 'We know full well that knowledge for the sake of knowledge is just a mask, so let's stop pretending and let's subsume it to its social function and efficacy. We are just doing what you were telling us all along.' Thus what started as a protest against Humboldt, with the ambition of dismantling the university discourse, ran out into a process whose main labels now abuse the names of the heartbreakingly beautiful Italian cities, Bologna and Pisa,[11] to the point that in retrospect Humboldt seems like a paradise lost. What devil pushed us to protest against it?

So what is to be done? Is there some way out of the university discourse, the structure that concerns not merely universities, but the very core of our modern social demeanour, the modern social bond, according to Lacan? I have no answer, but let me, in conclusion, suggest four strategies, as a provisional stand-in for a proper answer. Something we can perhaps engage in immediately.

First, one can enlist the forces of the Humboldt model, make a tactical alliance with it as it were, conservatively standing up for academic standards which seem to be dwindling under the pressure of quick evaluations, market feasibility, standardisation, testing, allotment of funding, infinitely expanding administration. There is something to be said for knowledge for the sake of knowledge, in defence of lost causes, despite all the dangers of the narcissism of the lost cause. There is something to be said for the futility of knowledge, in the face of its growing utility, for the nonchalant disregard for its social function. Secondly, one should adamantly oppose the rites of evaluation, the enforced measurement of the immeasurable, counting quotations, impact factors, citation indexes, gathering points for promotion and funding, ratings (why does one always have the impression that academic evaluation is modelled on the credit rating agencies? Our Standard and Poor's?) Anyone working in the humanities (and indeed in corporations generally!) knows to what extent the criteria imposed by evaluation are irrelevant, how the academic world is run by those criteria against everybody's will,[12] and how insidious they are (and just as all the great credit rating agencies failed to foresee crisis, they infallibly fail to register intellectual disasters). Thirdly, to reach for the impossible. I have insisted at some length on the Hegelian absolute knowledge as an impossible point to sustain in the university discourse, not as a point of some venerable wisdom that one should hold on to (absolute knowledge is precisely not a wisdom, anything but, it is but an empty point, the maximal opposition to wisdom), but as an extreme claim that blurs the lines. At the same time as defending strict academic standards, one should look for the points of academic impossibility, something that stands up against the tacit academic manners, against consensus and against the neutralisation of knowledge, something that can engage anew the symbolic efficacy of knowledge that university tries to deactivate.

The three grand figures of non-university knowledge, Marx, Nietzsche and Freud (not to forget Kierkegaard), despite their non-Hegelian or even anti-Hegelian demeanour, all produced points that continue to be not quite palatable for the university discourse, and the widespread attempts to integrate them into university frameworks have always produced trouble; they are oddly still sources of embarrassment, despite efforts to turn them into cultural icons. Instead of absolute knowledge, one could also use 'how to do philosophy with a hammer' (or with a hammer and sickle!). And fourthly, one should try to establish extra-mural communities. The Center for Wild Analysis, a group of five Danish theoreticians, seems to me to present an excellent model – a group whose members have to pursue academic careers for survival, but nevertheless engage in collective intellectual work which exceeds academia, is indifferent to academia, to its insignia, hierarchies and evaluations. The point is to make stark interventions into the ambient social texture with theoretical innovations, while maintaining intellectual freedom and autonomy, the spirit of collectivity, independent intellectual pursuit and the best standards of knowledge, independent of university frameworks. It sounds like a Utopian community, but it is a strategy that can be started and deployed in different ways at all times, by all of us, within and without academia.

The four strategies don't amount to some grand proposal, but maybe they are good places to start, and I am sure they can be multiplied, so as not to subscribe to the death-warrant of knowledge that is going around under the label of its promotion in what is currently heralded as 'the society of knowledge'.

Notes

1. T. Pinkard, *Hegel. A Biography* (Cambridge: Cambridge University Press, 2000), pp. 427–8.

2. The slogan of knowledge for the sake of knowledge can be put into parallel with the slogan *l'art pour l'art*, art for art's sake, which emerged at precisely the same time. The parallel is even more striking than one would imagine: the first to use the slogan *l'art pour l'art* was actually Victor Cousin, Hegel's French friend who introduced Hegel's philosophy in France. Both slogans can be read, in the spirit of Luhmann, as the autonomisation of particular social spheres in modernity after the French Revolution.

3. *The Seminar of Jacques Lacan, Book XVII: The Other Side of Psychoanalysis*, ed. J.-A. Miller, trans. R. Grigg (New York: Norton, 2007). Subsequent references to this work are given in the text as OP. In what follows I am somewhat retracing my steps in an essay that deals with this at more length, 'Hegel as the Other Side of Psychoanalysis', in J. Clemens and R. Grigg (eds), *Jacques Lacan and the Other Side of Psychoanalysis* (Durham, NC: Duke University Press, 2006), pp. 129–54.

4. I retain this common though inaccurate translation since Lacan uses it constantly. The Hegelian terms *Herr und Knecht* are more appropriately rendered as lord and bondsman; they refer to medieval conditions and not to slavery. In the interpretation of this dialectic Lacan largely followed the footsteps of Alexandre Kojève, the person who introduced Hegel in France in the 1930s and played the role of the master-figure for a whole new generation of French intellectuals, including Sartre, Beauvoir, Georges Bataille, Raymond Aron, Raymond Queneau and many others.

5. There is a lot more along these lines, for example: 'Philosophy has played its role in constituting a master's knowledge by subtracting it from the slave's knowledge. Science . . . consists precisely in this transmutation of the function, if one may say so . . . Anyway, there is certainly a difficulty in knowledge which resides in the opposition between know-how [*savoir-faire*] and *episteme* in the proper sense. *Episteme* was established by an interrogation, a purification of knowledge' (OP 173–4).

6. The case of the Frankfurt School is also highly indicative: people who started outside the university and continued in exile were eventually recuperated as the grand figures of the German university.

7. Derrida presents perhaps the most telling point in this respect. He was the only one of the (post)structuralist generation to engage with Hegel at length, as his most intimate enemy. In his major engagement in *Glas* (1974) (J. Derrida, *Glas*, trans. J. P. Leavy Jr and R. Rand [Lincoln: University of Nebraska Press, 1986]), he took SA (short for *savoir absolu*, absolute knowledge) as a formula, an abbreviation running through the whole book as a sort of matheme of the Hegelian enterprise. The subtitle of the paperback edition runs *Ce qui reste du savoir absolu*, 'What remains, or what is left over, of absolute knowledge'. But couldn't one argue that what is left over of absolute knowledge is absolute knowledge itself? Not some remainder that it couldn't cover but the very gesture of its production?

8. Lacan, in his schematic presentation of the university discourse which I cannot develop here, proposed the most economical way of presenting it: S2 in the position of the agent of university discourse has its counter-part in the S1, the master signifier under the bar, displaying its hidden truth.

9. 'The process of delegitimation and the predominance of the perfor-mance criterion are sounding the knell of the age of the Professor: a professor is no more competent than memory bank networks in transmitting established knowledge, nor more competent than interdis-ciplinary teams in imagining new moves or new games.' J.-F. Lyotard, *The Postmodern Condition: A Report on Knowledge* (Manchester: Manchester University Press, 1984), p. 53.

10. Lyotard, *The Postmodern Condition*, p. 11.

11. To add insult to injury, Bologna has reputedly the oldest university in the world, dating back to 1088. PISA stands for the Programme for International Student Assessment.

12. For a recent massive collective effort to counteract this, see B. Cassin (ed.), *Derrière les grilles: Sortons de tout-évaluation* (Paris: Fayard, 2014). Cf. also A. del Rey, *La tyrannie de l'évaluation* (Paris: La Découverte, 2013), and A. Abelhauser, R. Gori and M.-J. Sauret, *La folie évaluation* (Paris: Fayard, 2011).

6 Herod, the Ogre . . . and Miss Cooper's Rifle: Education as a Refuge for Childhood and the World

Jorge Larrosa

Translated from the Spanish by Elke Wakefield

There was a pedagogue:
he was called Herod.

Antonio Machado, 'Juan de Mairena'

If you have children,
think always of the ogre,
for he always thinks of them.

Michel Tournier

1

Hannah Arendt's celebrated words are now well known: 'the essence of education is natality, the fact that human beings are born into the world'.[1] For Arendt, natality is related to the human capacity for beginning: 'the new beginning inherent in birth is felt in the world only because the newcomers possess the capacity to start something new'[2] and, elsewhere, 'men, though they must die, were not born for that, but rather, to begin'.[3] We might say, therefore, that education is a sort of apparatus [*dispositivo*] inserted at the point of entry into the world. The function of this apparatus is to establish a particular relationship between the world and the newcomers (an *educational* relationship, one that must be distinguished from other relationships)[4] in which the capacity for beginning is preserved. In the final paragraph of *The Crisis in Education*, Arendt puts it like this:

Education is the point at which we decide whether we love the world enough to assume responsibility for it and by the same token save it from that ruin which, except for renewal, except for the coming of the new and young, would be inevitable. And education, too, is where we decide whether we love our children enough not to expel them from our world and leave them to their own devices, nor to strike from their hands their chance of undertaking something new, something unforeseen by us, but to prepare them in advance for the task of renewing a common world.[5]

Thus education involves a dual love and a dual responsibility, in which both the protection of infancy and the renewal of the world are at stake.

Education could be described as the way that those who are already in the world receive those who are born, or more concretely, the way that we position the world in relation to those who are born, and position those who are born in relation to the world. I will provisionally refer to this manner of receiving the new as 'openness'. At birth, the human being is characterised by his or her openness to the world. That openness requires, as its correlate, an open world. The newborn is open to a world that is itself open; in other words, he or she is new to a new world. On the other hand, for those already in the world – for the old – it is no longer open; it has become an old world. Moreover, it is education that must open the world, each time anew, for the newcomers. Thus, for those who are born, educational apparatuses can present two faces. The first, which we will call the hospitable face, is education insofar as it shelters infancy. It nurtures new beginnings and affirms the possibility of the world's rebirth. The other face, which we will call the hostile face, rejects outright this capacity for fostering renewal. It is here, in this hostility towards birth and renewal, that we encounter the 'corruption' of education.

In what follows I will depict that hostile face – that subordination of educational apparatuses to the continuance of the old world (and therefore, to its ruin); that 'corruption' of education – using the figures of Herod and the ogre, two characters who have traditionally embodied hostility towards newborns, enmity towards beginning, and the threat of kidnapping and murder that always accompanies childhood. Education is corrupted, we might say, when Herod and the ogre appropriate its apparatuses for themselves in order to ruin the world and to suppress the new beginnings that education enables. I will conclude with a brief account of the other face: education as refuge or apparatus of hospitality. In this aspect education is a construction of protected time and space – one separate from the ogresque logic – in which both infancy and the world are shielded from the destruction and ruin that threatens them, such that they are able to save themselves. Education is thus in constant tension with its own corruption, which is to say, it must permanently confront the many faces of Herod and the various guises of the ogre.

2

Childhood is not a natural fact, but rather a recent invention, inseparable from the existence of an educational apparatus that has – traditionally and most prominently – taken the form of the school.[6] For childhood can only take place to the extent that an educational apparatus is inserted at the point of entry into the world, one that takes charge of, or responsibility for, the newcomers. Education, therefore, is that apparatus which makes a place for children, or which gives them a space in which childhood can take place. It is an apparatus that operates by producing a partition of times and spaces. It constitutes the space and time for childhood (for the opening on to the world), by separating children from other spaces and times, in particular, from the spaces and times of the family, society (biopolitics) and the economy (labour). Education produces and separates out a specific chronotope for childhood such that children are not determined by their position (either present or future) in the family, society or economy. Nonetheless, although the educational apparatuses afford childhood a place of its own, this absolutely does not amount to infantilisation – quite the contrary. Education infantilises when it turns children into 'students', namely, when it determines them as subjects/objects who occupy positions defined by some body of knowledge and set of teaching practices, which make children visible and tangible in terms of their needs, talents, achievements, qualities and interests. However, as Jan Masschelein notes, childhood is constituted in the void that 'separates the student from herself'; that 'breaks and exceeds the identification of the student with herself'.[7] Moreover, education also infantilises when it adopts the modes in which society and the economy conceive of children, which is to say, the methods by which they fix the present or future position of the child in relation to a world already given, already determined, one which they always take for granted. If infantilisation occurs by the determination of children in relation to the world, then childhood takes place by virtue of their indetermination, their openness. Hence childhood has little to do with age; rather it pertains to the manner in which we relate to the world.[8] It is a specific relationship with the world that is, in Arendtian terms, oriented towards the capacity for starting something new and the possibility of renewing the world.

Moreover, if we agree with Hannah Arendt that the purpose of education is to establish a particular relationship between childhood and the world, then this chronotope – this separate space and time, this hetero-chronic and heterotopical apparatus – not only ensures that childhood has a place (and a time), but also that the world (a particular form of the world, of opening-of-the-world) has a place and a time. Therefore education is an apparatus that opens and separates a chronotope for the world, in that it offers childhood a space and time from which to take on the world in a manner that is childlike, but not infantilised.

3

Education is an apparatus that not only takes responsibility for child-hood but that also, most importantly, takes responsibility for the world. And it does this by considering the world from the point of view of its transmission and its renewal. In Arendtian terms: 'the function of school is to teach children what the world is like and not to instruct them in the art of living'.[9] From this point of view, an educational apparatus would involve enabling an 'opening-up' of the world, in which the world itself, upon coming into contact with childhood, is also carried to its infancy, to its novelty, to its own capacity to start over, or to self-start. This is because, like childhood, the world is not a fact, a given, a reality in-itself, a thing; rather it only emerges as a function of the way that we relate to it. There is no world as such, only particular ways of making-world. Therefore, to enter the world is to enter into certain relations with the world. And it is these relations that constitute the world, that make pos-sible the different ways in which the world first becomes world. It is for this reason that taking (or opening) the world from the point of view of its 'transmission-renewal' [*transmisión-renovación*] – or, in other words, estab-lishing an educational relationship between childhood and the world – enables the world to become world without being taken for granted. Hence education does not remove children from the world, but it does isolate them from certain ways of relating to the world, fundamentally those in which the world is taken as already given. In our times these relations are those in which the world appears as an object for domi-nation or appropriation, as an object of production or consumption, as an object of use, value or exchange, as something to be exploited, monetised or utilised – a veritable commodity. An exclusively economic and utilitarian relationship with the world literally destroys the world in that it predetermines it, and worse, predetermines it only from the perspective of its value or utility, thereby suppressing the opening of other possible worlds.[10]

The opening of the world is not the production of the world. Opening the world for childhood cannot mean manufacturing or designing it, nor selling it as a product or submitting it as a plan. Only by establishing a non-economic and non-utilitarian relationship between childhood and the world can education open the world, or rather, open up 'world possibilities'. For education, the world is neither there to be dominated, nor to be exploited (made to produce), nor to be managed (ordered and administered), nor to be consumed (devoured), nor to be transformed, but instead, to be transmitted. Transmitted, that is, from the point of view of its possible renovation, which is to say, transmitted not in its determination but in its indetermination, its openness.[11] Therefore, insofar as the function of education is to take responsibility for the indetermination of childhood and the world, the social and economic 'corruption' of education presents a danger to both childhood *and* the world. One's entry into the world reduces to an insertion into a world that is already economically and socially determined and planned out – a world that is not merely disposed in some manner, but rather presupposed or imposed.

4

There is a short film by Spanish filmmaker Víctor Erice that illustrates some of the conditions that attend our entry into the world.[12] Throughout the film the threat of death hangs over a newborn child: a drop of blood seeps through the white nightgown of a baby sleeping in its crib. Nearby, meanwhile, life goes on and the world around the baby unfolds before our eyes. The film pulses with a series of rhythms that punctuate the life of the place: the tick-tock of a grandfather clock, the rocking of a girl on a swing, the dripping of water into a bathroom sink, the beating of a hammer as it sharpens a scythe, the movement of the pedal of a sewing machine, the scrubbing of a brush as it shines a shoe, the swinging of a scythe as it cuts grass, the folding and unfolding of hands as they knead dough on a wooden table. The owners of the house are enjoying a siesta, the employees are working and the children are playing. As well as this life-time, composed of immemorial rhythms, the film also pulses with what we could call a biographical time, into which the birth of Luisín is inserted. On the walls of the room in which his father and grandfather are napping, there are photographs of a family business. The car, in which some children play at being adults, has plates from Havana. It would seem that the newborn belongs to a Spanish family that has returned to Spain after growing rich in Cuba. Finally, certain images allude to the historical moment in which Luisín is born, the tyrannical, ultra-Catholic dictatorship of post-war Spain: there is a scarecrow in uniform, complete with military helmet, there is a young, wounded man plaiting a cord tied to the big toe of his remaining leg, and the table on which the family kneads the dough is covered by a newspaper featuring military uniforms and a date in 1942.

But there is something more: at the start of the film, a child, alone in a barn, opens a window to let the light in and then, moistening a crayon with saliva, draws a watch on his wrist and raises it to his ear. It is as though, in addition to the life-time, the biographical time and the historical time, the possibility of another time is opening for Luisín, a species of time outside time. As if, in addition to the clearly defined social spaces in which the various characters move, the possibility of a new space is emerging, a space that is not only separate but separating. After the servant restitches Luisín's umbilical stump and returns him to his parents in a kind of second birth – this time under the attentive gaze of all who inhabit the place – a servant sings a lullaby behind a freshly hung white sheet, the bloodied nightgown is washed, someone finishes embroidering Luisín's name on a bib, and the solitary boy in the barn (the only one absent from the circle of witnesses) wipes off his crayon watch and closes the window; the group dissolves, the various times resume. And perhaps, as an apparatus inserted at the point of entry into the world, education requires as its condition of possibility this separation of times and spaces to which the solitary boy in the barn alludes: the possibility of a distinct time that interrupts the continuity of the aforementioned 'times', as well as a distinct space that suspends the social order of attachments and belongings. In short, the possibility of a heterochrony and a heterotopy in which something other can take place.

The table at which the servant stitches the bleeding umbilical cord is the same table at which we have already seen her making bread, the one covered in the newspaper bearing the date. It is as though Luisín's second birth were presided over by a symbol of life and of the immemorial (bread), as well as a symbol of history and the world (the newspaper). After dressing Luisín's wound, the servant delivers him to his parents and thus to a bundle of familiar, biographical and social affiliations whose continuity he is destined to guarantee. Moreover, immediately after this delivery, his name appears embroidered on his bib, now complete and finished. Another umbilical cord has thus been constituted, this time a social one, which not only guarantees his survival (the bread) but at the same time ensures that the child is connected with the spaces and times (biographical, geographical, social, cultural, historical) in which he was born. Spaces and times that will determine his identity, his name, what he is and what he must become, his destiny, everything that will form and mould him. It would seem that for Luisín there is no escape. But there does exist a place where he can find refuge, a safe place, a hospitable place, in which a separated time and space will give him the opportunity to explore other possibilities – precisely because this time of the painted-on watch, this space of solitude, does not determine him but rather, in some sense, makes him indeterminate.

5

Erice's film reminds us of the both hostile and hospitable character of the world into which we are born, or, to put it more dramatically, of the promise of life and the menace of death that hang over any newborn, and that not only threatens her life but also (and especially) her infancy, her capacity for beginning. The film brings to mind the shadow of Herod that is cast over every new birth. In our tradition, the figure of Herod embodies the murder of children brought about by the fear of new beginnings. If, for Hannah Arendt, the words that herald the birth of Jesus of Nazareth express the faith and hope that stems from the human capacity for new beginnings,[13] Herod's infanticide could be said to express the way in which:

terror, as an obedient slave to natural or historical movement, must eliminate from the process not only liberty in any specific sense, but also the very source of liberty that stems from the fact of man's birth and resides in his capacity to make a new beginning.[14]

The figure of Herod emerges vividly in a beautiful quotation from Peter Handke, a note written after a visit to the museum with his young daughter, a museum that includes a painting of the mythical massacre of the children:

with each new consciousness the same possibilities as ever were beginning, and the eyes of the children in the midst of the throng – look at them! – conveyed the eternal spirit. You are the poorer if you cannot perceive their gaze! Finding himself, one day, in the museum in front of the legendary painting that depicts the Massacre of the Innocents: a child, in the snow, extends its arms towards its mother, who has one foot turned backwards, a shawl on her head and an apron. A thug, with pointed index finger, gets ready to grab the child; and, as if all of it were happening at that very moment, the observer thinks quite literally: 'This cannot be!', with the firm intention on their part of creating a different tradition.

The first few lines, clearly Arendtian in inspiration, are a call to perceive the eternal spirit, that spirit of beginning that flickers, fragile and pleading, in the eyes of children. The vivid description of the massacre of the innocents illustrates the danger that looms over this spirit, thereby underscoring the extreme vulnerability of children. However, the painting does not represent something that happened, but rather, in the words of Handke, something that is happening at every moment, something connected to the danger that threatens, time and again, and each time anew, the spirit of beginning. It is for this reason that the paragraph closes with a horrifying thought: 'This cannot be!', and with the intention to 'create a different tradition'.[15] And perhaps education, as an apparatus of hospitality inserted at the point of entry into the world, is really about this capacity to perceive the spirit that flickers in the eyes of children and this sensitivity to the multiple faces of Herod. Perhaps it is about creating refuges, themselves fragile and vulnerable, forever under attack, to shelter those who come.

6

In the popular imagination, the figure that looms most menacingly over children is the ogre, that abductor of children and devourer of infantile flesh. Michel Tournier develops this figure in his novel *The Ogre*.[16] In his *The Wind Spirit: An Autobiography*, Tournier tells the story of his childhood in Germany, during the expansion of Nazism, 'in an era – that of Tom Thumb – that was of chief interest to ogres'. It is a feature of Nazism, says Tournier, to convert infancy and youth into value. Nazism is a paedophilia and hebephilia that whips itself into a frenzy over the biological substance of the state:

To be good, fresh meat must be blond, blue-eyed, and dolichocephalic, and it follows that there is also a bad meat, dark, brown-eyed and brachycephalic. The continuation demonstrates that the system leads inevitably to the destruction of both the bad and the good, the bad through murder, servitude and other forms of extermination, and the good because it is the cannon fodder for the Thousand-Year Reich.

And then, almost at once, a terrible detail that confirms the fascist regime's ogresque calling:

that date, the nineteenth of April, when every girl and every boy who had celebrated their tenth birthday that year – one million children in total, a lovely, round number! – was solemnly assimilated into the Jungvolk and the Jungmaedelbund. Why the nineteenth of April? Because Hitler's birthday was on the twentieth. The Fuehrer embodies the figure of the Great Ogre, the Minotaur to whom, on whose birthday, they offered an entire generation of children.[17]

The vampirism in Tournier's novel echoes that of Himmler's 1944 *Heuaktion* ('Operation Fenaison') ('Hay Operation'), in which 50,000 Ruthenian children were transported to Germany in order to enrich its 'biological capital', and impoverish that of the Soviet Union. The novel also explores the operation of the *Napolas* (*Nationalpolitische Erziehungsanstalten*), elite schools for children hand-picked by the SS, and the *Adolf-Hitler Schulen*, schools for the children of party members. Indeed, the protagonist of the novel, Abel Tiffauges, works as a carer in the *Napola* of Kaltenborn. Tiffauges, like all ogres, loves children. He is not a pederast, but he is a paedophile, and it is in relation to this paedophilia that the novel explores the meaning of the ogre myth, in this ambivalence of love, in this malignant and destructive love, in this loving wickedness, which, like Herod, is the enemy of beginning. And so, in the *Napola* they celebrate Christmas not as the rebirth of the sun but as its death. And the midsummer celebration, with the children jumping over the flames of the bonfire, reminds Tiffauges of 'the diabolical invocation of the Massacre of the Innocents'[18] – a massacre that is indeed finally realised with the death of the *Jungmannen,* when the garrison commander refuses to surrender to the Russians and thereby consents to the sacrifice of the children.

We know that, for Hannah Arendt, Nazism consists in a *revolutionary* totalitarianism, which is to say, it aims at the construction of a new world, even if this construction must occur over scorched earth. Tournier's novel, however, stresses that this revolutionary character draws upon a perverse tradition: 'Hitlerism is refractory to any idea of progress, creation, discovery and invention of a virgin future. Its force is not in rupture but in restoration: it is a cult of race, ancestors, blood, the dead and homeland.'[19] Hence the idols before which the children kneel 'are called Patriotism, Sacrifice, Heroism, Honour'.[20] Like Handke's Herod, the ogre of Tournier also represents a tradition of death. And although Tournier portrays the ogre as specifically Nazi, he is aware, as Handke is with respect to Herod, that the ogre is capable of multiple metamorphoses and that its malignant love for children continues to act over and over in the world: 'the ogre is a character that exists in our neighbourhood and perhaps even in every one of us'.[21]

7

La revue des écoles was painted by Jan Verhas in 1880, two years after the creation of the Ministry of Public Education and the first secular schools in Belgium. An enormous painting at two-and-a-half by four-and-a-half metres, it depicts an event that occurred in Brussels in 1879: the procession of the professors and students of these first public schools in front of King Leopold II, the royal family, the government ministry, other notables of the city and a vast crowd, which, according to eyewitnesses, cried 'long live the King!' and 'long live the public school!' The size of the painting and the solemnity of the scene convey that this is an event of great importance, and it is clear why. The painting depicts the delivery of the children to the state, the nation-state of imperial calling, that political form which, at that time, had become a Great Ogre. The word 'nation' is related to the word 'natality', so that the nation is made up of those who are born within the territory of the state. And the state is a war machine as such. In being delivered to the school, the children are also delivered to the state. Therefore, birth is captured immediately by the state from the moment in which, in the era of nation-states, the principal job of the school becomes that of moulding those who are considered to be the 'future' of the state, those from whom the state derives its own permanence and power. Based on this, we might ask whether the delivery of the children to the state – to the state's cause, to the way the state imagines the world and its ways of relating to the world, and to the ways it determines the future – does not constitute in itself the sacrifice of childhood. Or, put another way, we might question whether this sacrifice – this logic of sacrifice, this sacrificial logic – isn't the same logic as that of the nationalisation of our entry into the world. It is not just primitive gods who demand human sacrifices. The logics of theocratic states, totalitarian states, nationalistic states and imperialistic states presuppose the existence of a cause to which is owing a sacrifice and, especially, the sacrifice of a child inasmuch as these logics ascribe to children, from the moment of birth, a destiny. But the educational relationship between childhood and the world is an indeterminate relationship, a relationship that is not designated or predisposed towards anything in particular, a relationship in which neither the destiny of the world nor the destiny of the child can be taken as a given. From the educational point of view, coming into the world cannot be the same as delivering or devoting the child to a cause, that is, sacrificing the indeterminate character of childhood by determining it in relation to a cause. And that is because the world itself, from the perspective of its transmission and renewal, from the perspective of its opening, is a world still becoming world; without destiny and without cause.

8

We spoke before about umbilical cords in the context of Erice's short film. In a series of lectures given in Frankfurt in the mid-1980s, Peter Sloterdijk formulated a poetics of beginning, a poetics of birth, a poetics, more concretely, of parturition. But as the German word for parturition is *Entbindung*, a word that also means 'release' or 'unbind', Sloterdijk has no choice but to speak of binding and unbinding, of knotting and unknotting, of connecting and disconnecting, of joining and unjoining, and of umbilical cords. For the German philosopher, birth is simultaneously *Entbindung* and *Anbindung*, binding and unbinding. It is an event in which the newborn is detached from the mother and, at the same time, attached to the world; that is, in the same moment that the child is untied from the mother, their connection to the world is initiated. In the first instance, birth gives over into openness, and only later, out of this original openness, does that set of content that we could properly call 'world' (to the extent that it occurs in language and for language) start to appear. Sloterdijk argues that for us, for human beings, language is the authority which properly gives us the world. Therefore, coming into the world is coming into language. Language is not just a means of transmission, but the very condition of transmission itself, that which Sloterdijk calls the a priori of transmission. This is why birth involves disconnection from the mother and the immediate initiation of a lengthy, complex process of binding, connecting or linking to language, which is, at the same time, a lengthy, complex process of binding, connecting or linking to the world.

When Sloterdijk talks about newborns connecting to language, he establishes a historical distinction. He argues that in the logic of the *Bildung* – the logic that dominated educational theories and practices from the end of the eighteenth century to the middle of the twentieth – the newborn was fundamentally connected to their national language. And through this language the newborn was connected to a nation, a culture, a tradition, to certain customs, a history, a homeland, a religion . . . and all of those elements that constituted a sense of belonging or, as Sloterdijk says, a totalitarian folklore. To be born was to be 'born-within' a nation. The nation was the extra-uterine framework to which newborns were connected. The coming into the world was only conceivable as a connection or bonding to that linguistic community that was both a national and a historical community. The destiny of the newborn was bound to the destiny of the nation. In Sloterdijk's own words:

the primary preoccupation of any nation is to connect those 'born-within' to the so-called mother tongues. The detachment from the mother at birth as an attachment of children to the gravitational centre of national reality has, as a necessary consequence, a fundamental arabisation, brazilisation, britanisation, japonisation, russification, sudanisation, etc. of the newborn. Children are converted time and time again into the prisoners of the state of their nations and linguistic communities, whenever they are rightly treated as the future of their people.[22]

The question is whether this tradition is not already anachronistic, whether, in this globalised world, the language to which newborns are bound is anything other than a vehicle for transmitting competencies, knowledge, abilities and identities which are totally stateless and defined by the new necessities of transnational capitalism. In our age, Sloterdijk says:

the learning of German, which is the heritage of the majority of our citizens, has led to completely different regions of national linguistic life. In these regions, the *a priori* of transmission has operated in such a way that one cannot but speak of the urgent German of business people [. . .], the ambitious German of the future-builders, the German of those who look forward, of the newspaper columns, of the moralists, of the dead souls worried about national unity. This flux of national transmissions, concerns, miseries and powers also generates the German of the news and the German of newspapers, as well as the German of the spirit of the times, the German of committees, the German of the media, the German of the commissions, of pedantic objectivity and cynical pap.[23]

Hence today we might wonder what it is that we are 'born-within', what it is that the taught language binds us to, what world it connects us to, in which terms it defines the world and in which terms it captures and understands our entry into the world. It is possible that today there is no longer such a thing as a historical destiny for people and nations. In this sense, it is possible that we live in post-historical and post-national times. It is possible that the newborn is no longer destined to perform historical or national tasks. It is possible that our time is defined by the denationalisation, dehistoricisation and depoliticisation of human societies. And it is possible that the ogre does not abduct children and Herod does not sacrifice children in the name of the nation or history, but rather in the name of the full deployment of the economy and biopolitics, that is to say, in the pragmatic, utilitarian management of individuals and populations that have finally been transformed into goods. The cultural, national traditions (literature, philosophy, art and culture in general) are already mass spectacles or private experiences without historical efficacy. And it is the languages of the global economy, of social management and of the permanent constitution and reconstitution of flexible, empty and interchangeable personal identities, which now seem to determine the world to which newborns are fundamentally tied.

9

The novel *The Night of the Hunter*,[24] brought to the screen by Charles Laughton, depicts the hard years of the Depression. Ben Harper, a family man tired of unrelenting misery, robs a bank and is subsequently executed. His children, John and Pearl, are with him when he is detained and know where the stolen loot has been hidden, though they have promised to tell no one. Before he is hanged, Ben Harper shares a cell with a man called Harry Powell, known as the Preacher because he hides behind religion to commit his crimes and has the words 'love' and 'hate' tattooed on his knuckles. Upon being released from prison, the Preacher ingratiates himself into Ben's family (seducing and then murdering his widow), before starting on a drawn-out pursuit of the children in order to steal the hidden money. In the most beautiful and dream-like part of this pursuit, the children flee down the river (a metaphor for the river of life) in a boat that belonged to their father. The Preacher, played by Robert Mitchum in the film, is a kind of ambiguous ogre, a killer of children yet also friendly and seductive, driven by the evil principle that runs through the whole film: money. The sinister figure of the ogre of children's stories is already creepily present in the first paragraphs of the novel. A girl he has tried to con says that he is 'as handsome and old and cruel as Herod'.[25] And almost at the end, in the magical interior monologue of Miss Cooper (the old lady who finally offers protection to the two children), the threat of the ogre is turned into the essential feature of the condition of childhood:

with every child ever born of woman's womb there is a time of running through a shadowed place, an alley with no doors, and a hunter whose footsteps ring brightly along the bricks behind him. With every child – rich or poor – however favored, however warm and safe the nursery, there is this time of echoing and vast aloneness, when there is no one to come nor to hear, and dry leaves scurrying past along a street become the rustle of Dread and the ticking of the old house is the cocking of the hunter's gun [. . .] And in the shadow of a branch beneath the moon a child sees a tiger and the old ones say: There is no tiger! Go to sleep! And when they sleep it is a tiger's sleep and a tiger's night and a tiger's breathing at the midnight pane [. . .] For each of them has his Preacher to hound him down the dark river of fear and tonguelessness and never-a-door. Each one is mute and alone because there is no word for a child's fear and no ear to heed it if there were a word and no one to understand it if it were heard.[26]

At the end of the book (and the film), John and Pearl, tired and hungry and drifting down the river in their father's boat, wash up in a reedbed. They are taken in by Rachel Cooper, a thin, old, solitary woman, irritable and isolated from the world, who devotes herself to sheltering the many children who wander the fields and roads, having been driven out of their homes by poverty. Miss Cooper's refuge appears in the final chapter of the novel, which is called 'A Strong Tree With Many Birds', and also in a brief epilogue: an anxiously hopeful ode to the fortitude of children, entitled 'They Abide'. Rachel Cooper protects children from the prowling ogre (with a repeating rifle even bigger than she is) and assuages their fears by telling them Bible stories. The first story she tells, which she tells twice, is an episode that is especially affecting to John: the story of Moses, abandoned like him and his sister and carried by the river like them, until his adoption by the old Pharaoh's daughter.[27] Secondly, she tells the story of Herod, whose tale, in the novel, concludes like this:

'And when little King Jesus's ma and pa heard about that plan what do you reckon they went and done?' 'They hid in a broom closet!' gasped Clary. 'They run under the washhouse', said Little Mary. 'No', said John. 'They went a-runnin'.' 'Well, now, John, that's just what they done!' cried Rachel, angry all over again at what King Herod had done to all these little, helpless things. 'Little King Jesus's ma and pa took and saddled a mule and rode clean down into Egyptland.' 'Yes', said John. 'And that's where the queen found them in the billy rushes.' 'Pshaw, now!' scolded Rachel. 'That warn't the same story at all . . .'[28]

John conflates the two stories but he isn't wrong – the word 'Egypt' evokes the place to which they flee (the refuge, the goal of the fugitives, the place where they will finally find safety) as well as the place of adoption. At some point, every child hears the echo of the hunter's footsteps. Every child feels fear and the necessity of hiding herself. But only some, like John, know that it is necessary to flee, and that one can only feel safe when somebody with a rifle keeps the ogre away.

We should make three further observations regarding the film. First, it explores not only the opposition between good and bad, but also the ambiguities between the two and their possible inversion. Hence, when the Preacher, flourishing his tattooed fists, portrays the war between good and evil to his blessed audience, the 'good' that triumphs is tainted by the will to power and therefore is actually bad. Bad disguises itself as good, hatred as love. Hatred and evil seduce, taking the form of good and of love. And it is interesting that only two people, little John and old Miss Cooper, refuse to be seduced – and not because they know things that others don't, but rather because in some enigmatic way they are able to sense evil. Both are taciturn and wary of words, and it is as though they are able to recognise instantly, in an almost bodily way, that the 'love/hate' battle the Preacher recounts so as to win over the naive is actually a trap. For Miss Cooper,

The years alone in the nights of river silence and river wind had taught her the wisdom of stable beasts; the cunning of the small creatures of the woods. And now while she looked at the boy and listened while Preacher prattled and joked with the little girl Rachel, she felt the skin of her back bunch and twist like the hide of a frightened mare when something prowls the midnight yard and her new foal bleats with mortal dread.[29]

Handke pities those unable to perceive the spirit of beginning shining in the eyes of children: 'You are the poorer if you cannot perceive that gaze!' Likewise, Davis Grubb seems to pity those unable to sense the ogre-spirit gleaming in the eyes of the preachers in this world.

The second point relates to the fact that Miss Cooper knows her refuge is not only threatened by the hunter (a threat that forms part of the very condition of childhood, given that, at some moment, all children feel the echo of his footsteps) but also by the family and the state. She fears that the children's parents, mumbling their rights and excuses, or some social worker regurgitating set phrases behind the mask of authority, will come and reclaim them. Family and the state have legitimate rights to the children, but for Miss Cooper there is another right, based in love, which is the only one capable of building a refuge. The third point relates to the current of evil running through the film that contaminates everything it touches: money. The stolen money is hidden in Pearl's doll. During the entire pursuit of the children, the money is inside the toy. The toy is also contaminated by money, that money to which the entire world directs its ambition, and to whose protection John must be constantly attentive. Having to guard the money and the secret regarding the money, as well as the promise made to his father to protect the money, enslaves the child. So John is also imprisoned by the curse of the money. At the end of the story, John hits the Preacher with the doll, the doll breaks and the money spills out – though John doesn't care any more. It is then, when he renounces money, when he is liberated from money (and the promise he made to his father to protect it) that the child finds peace. It is then that the toy once again becomes a toy.

10

The 'different tradition' that Peter Handke proposes after his encounter with the painting of Herod finds one of its most beautiful images in the day that he first takes his daughter to school. The date is framed by two ideas of tradition. The first, which represents the school to which he takes the little girl, is the tradition of a scattered people without prophets, kings, victims, idols or even a name. The second, which the girl belongs to by birth and by language, is the infamous tradition of a metaphysically dead people, condemned to endlessly wander the world, without happiness and without aim. The father, who declares himself incapable of any tradition, nevertheless takes his daughter to a building that 'looked like so many of those urban schools, with a small, dusty patio, smaller classrooms, bad lighting and the rattle of the Metro right there beneath the earth. But the fact of accompanying the girl towards this place always gave the man the sense that he was on the right path.'[30] Perhaps John would say that the 'right path' is the path towards Egypt, towards the place of refuge and adoption. In any case, towards a place where the children must be taken to find refuge from Herod and his death-tradition, a place where a new and different tradition can be invented. Confronted with the girl, the father 'perceived in himself a totally new desire to educate, but the only thing he could have taught her stemmed from that language of "I am stronger than everyone else"'. It may be for this reason – the fact that education has nothing to do with a difference in strength or power, but rather a difference in knowledge, love and attention to the world – that the father reflects,

but to be heard by the child, one would have to be much more succinct. And so the child remains the teacher, for she teaches him to have more time for the colors of the world outside, to see forms more accurately; and therefore (not only as a matter of atmospherics but in a deeper sense) to read the changes of the seasons in an uncurled fern, in the leatheriness of a leaf, or the new rings on a snail shell.[31]

11

There is a short film by Samira Makhmalbaf that elucidates something of the logic of this refuge.[32] The film is characterised by a kind of inverted symmetry: it begins in a well and ends in a tower. As the film begins, some children are stomping on clay to make bricks. We learn that the well is drying out from overconsumption. We also learn that the bricks are to be used in the construction of a bomb shelter. Around the well the children are speaking of the village. The teacher passes through, assembling them for school, informing them that the bomb shelter will not save them from bombs, that their destiny is part of a common destiny bound to the fate of Afghans in Iran, and that they have to go to school because there are books there. In this sequence we see that education begins with a displacement. Children must be uprooted from the demands of survival and from local history in order to take them to a new place that is connected to the world and the common, a place characterised by books. The shelter that the children are constructing will not save them, though neither will the school because school has nothing to do with salvation. School is, first and foremost, a summons, an accessible and available place to which one is called, a place one must go to. And perhaps the question is: in which name is one summoned? In this film, the first answer is that one is not summoned in the name of necessity or salvation, but rather in the name of books. The school provides a space in which books are made available. We watch some children set up a precarious school space beneath some archways. And so begins the educational scene, but it is not, as one would have thought, a scene of the children reading. The teacher asks the class to name something important that has happened in the world, and the children respond with stories about the village. One of the girls says that she will speak but only if she is allowed to whisper in the teacher's ear. The teacher refuses and eventually the girl narrates a personal drama. Education is not related to each person's dramas, or their personal history, and it therefore rejects intimate confidences. That which is said must be made public because that is what education is about; the public, which is to say 'everybody', and with the act of 'making public'. Therefore, school summons in the name of the public. And in the name of the books, which are one form of publication, one form of creating experiences that transcend their personal or private meaning, and which are capable of acquiring, through consideration by the public, a public meaning such that they become a common issue or concern. Immediately, another child repeats the story, smiling, and the magic happens: a private event is repeated, and in being repeated, loses the quality of personal trauma to become the experience of everybody. But the teacher does not pursue this line of thought; instead she talks about the attack on the Twin Towers, and makes the children look at the chimney of the kiln where the bricks are baked, before proposing a minute of silence in memory of the victims. She draws a clock on a small blackboard that she holds between her hands and, using her finger as the hand of a clock, creates the minute. But the children do not respect this silence and, in front of their indifferent teacher, enter into a prodigious conversation about whether it is God or men who fly planes. One of the children says that God destroys humans to create new humans, because the world needs new humans – an almost Arendtian statement. The teacher does not draw on or engage with the children's conversation. She is not interested in colonising this conversation, in turning it into pedagogical material. But without the liberating time of the drawn clock or the open, public space of the archways, this conversation would never have occurred. Therefore school has made this time and space, that is, has made time and disposed a space for the children to discuss the meaning of what has happened. Eventually, because the children have not performed their minute of silence, the teacher conducts them to the foot of the tower and demands again a minute of silence.

The film illustrates a displacement: the route of the children from the well to the tower, led by their teacher. A well that is drying out because the water is being used to make bricks that are fired in the tower. Like the children, the water goes from the well to the tower, and in this trajectory is transformed from being an element of life to an element of construction. The teacher calls the children to school and later takes them from the school. And between these two opposite and symmetrical poles, an educational scene occurs. It occurs inside a space and time made separate so as to enable a particular relationship between the children and the world. The tower around which the children congregate at the end of the film is no longer just the kiln where bricks are fired, and the smoke that rises from the kiln is now intermingled with other kinds of smoke. Now the children are located at the tower, a site of human construction and human violence. No one can save them from that. But, in these intermediary moments, education has functioned as a refuge, though a refuge totally different from the shelter that the adults are building; for the educational refuge suspends the war (even as the children talk about it and draw it out) while the adult refuge forms part of the war.

12

There is a short film by Johan van der Keuken that resonates strangely with Makhmalbaf's. The film, 'Reading Lessons', is set in a school in Amsterdam in 1973, during the military coup in Chile.[33] As is well known, the bombing of La Moneda Palace, in which Salvador Allende died, also took place on an eleventh of September. Both films are about dates and bombings, about the way in which an educational apparatus converts a date and a bombing into a component of the world, and thus converted, offers it to the children and puts it at their disposal. The children in Amsterdam learn to read by connecting words with images. On the walls of the school corridors there are newspaper clippings about the events in Chile, and it appears as if the children are drawing pictures about torture for an Amnesty International magazine. One supposes that the teacher of this class has made the same gesture as the Iranian teacher: he has marked a particular event as something that is important for everyone, as something that forms part of a common world. He has set tasks for the children to do in relation to this event. Both films are about death. But in both it is a fake death. It is a death made academic; the death of a toy, a fiction, like the Bible stories Miss Cooper tells the children to counter the threat of the hunter. We could say that it is there so that the children can play with it, that is to say, so they can elaborate, in relation to it, their own thoughts, their own emotions and their own words. Fire recurs throughout van der Keuken's film. It is one of the words the children learn, written beneath a picture of a fire drum from which flames rise. Smoke billows from the windows of the Chilean presidential palace in a manner similar to that which pours from the windows of a house fire nearby, which the children go on to the street to watch being extinguished. The children of Amsterdam also enter and leave the school. In addition, one child reads a North American comic in which a heroic fighter pilot opens fire on an enemy plane. At the end of the film, the command of 'Fire!' and a burst of machine-gun fire overlap with images of the school. The children go through all these fires. They play with each of them without burning themselves. It is these fires which make up the world, but it is only here, in the school, that the children can play with them.

13

The theme that structures Tournier's novel is *-phoria* or, rather, *pedophoria*. The term *-phoria* comes from the Greek *phoresis*, to bring or carry (the word 'metaphor', which in Latin is literally trans-port or trans-late, comes from this root), and so a pedophor would be a bearer of children, he who carries children, which, in principle, can be as easy as 'the simple gesture of carrying a child on your shoulders'.[34] Taking this basic gesture as a point of departure, Tournier develops the variations, inversions, metamorphoses and extremes of pedophoria, and above all, the fatal, excessive inversions represented by the figure of the ogre. The title of the book refers to a poem by Goethe in which a child, carried by his father through the night, hears the seductive and fatal call of the King of the Alders, he of the gloomy trees that live in stagnant waters, so different to the green willows that grow in flowing waters. Abel Tiffauges, the protagonist of the novel, embodies this figure of the malignant pedophor, the ogre, until his final inversion into a white, benign and protective phoria, effected through an almost literal transfiguration of Saint Christopher, the Christ-carrier, that giant bearer of Christ who appears in the texts of Jacobus de Voragine. The deadly pedophor of the Kaltenborn *napola* transforms into a benign phoria when, faced with the deadly attack of the Soviet soldiers on the *napola* and the suicidal defence by the young SS, he chooses to protect and carry on his shoulders, blind and allowing himself to be led, Efrain, a young Jewish boy he found at the side of the road who he has healed and cared for. The pedophor who carries the children to the place of their murder transforms into the pedophor who carries them to a safe place. Hence,

the good giant who becomes a beast of burden to save the child is very close to the man of prey who devours children. Whoever carries a child, makes off with a child. Whoever humbly serves the child, murderously crushes them. The shadow of Saint Christopher, carrier and saviour of children, is the King of the Alders, abductor and killer of children.[35]

It is as though the very same figure, the pedophor, without changing anything structurally, can invert its value at any moment, as though it has two inseparable sides: serve and dominate, love and kill. If we consider that the pedagogue, that slave who led children to school, was also a pedophor, a carrier of children, we are moved to think that all pedagogy is a pedophoria, and, as such, is necessarily ambivalent and susceptible to corruption. Taking a child to school could be 'finding oneself on the right path' or, on the contrary, putting oneself on the wrong path. You can lead children to Herod or to Egypt. And if we consider that this slave does not lead children to school in their own name but rather in the name of others, we can conclude that only a free slave can serve education, a pedagogue who does not obey anybody, a pedophor who does not carry children in the name of anybody but is simply guided by that dual love or responsibility for childhood and the world of which Hannah Arendt speaks.

14

After making this historical distinction that differentiates between being connected to a nation (though a national language) and connected to commodities (through the language of businessmen, which embodies the spirit of the times), Sloterdijk also traces what we could call an ontological distinction. And he does this by asking if there is a language that does not make one a member but rather absolves one of all belonging, or, put another way, a language that allows us to be reborn, to catch the breath of the original opening. In short, a language that does not tie but unties, that does not bind but releases, that does not connect but disconnects, that does not identity but de-identifies, that does not determine but makes indeterminate. A language that cuts the umbilical cord that binds us to the constituted linguistic communities, to the poisoned traditions, to the affiliations and identities, to the spirit of the times, to the construction of the future, to harmful modes of being. Moreover, a language that does not mould the world but rather opens possibilities of worlds or, in Slotderdijkian terms, 'world promises'. This language is poetry. Not, of course, poetry understood as a literary genre, but rather as that which language still has of the poetic, which is to say that by which human language is (still) something more and something other than a means of communication. Language, says Sloterdijk,

does not only consist in the transmission of national ties and the prejudices that give meaning to the world. Language, which articulates and distributes the summons among those entering the world, also consists in the breath of absolution. This separates us from the nationality in which we have naturally taken root, and from falling into inherited violence; it evokes the first moments of being-in-the-world in which the experience of air anticipates all outside contact.[36]

At this point we might wonder whether we don't also need the breath of that time outside of time, of that world outside world; whether disconnection, as well as connection, is not just as constitutive of that which is human. Whether we shouldn't attend urgently to that dimension of language that does not bind but rather releases, that allows us to breathe, that enlivens us, that opens the possibility or the promise of a different time and a different world. To quote Sloterdijk once more, this depends on whether 'our texts are directed towards spaces of liberty or whether they are made into wallpaper with which the unseparated cover their cave walls'.[37] This depends on the possibility of a new tradition, or of finding ourselves on the right path. The possibility, in short, that our coming into language could also be a coming into the opening of language, and that our coming into the world could also be a coming into the opening of the world.

15

The ogre loves children, and so we bring them to him. There was a time when we gave children over to the Church to be educated. Later, we gave them to the state. Sometimes, as in the novel of Tournier, we have even given them to a totalitarian state in which Adolf Hitler plays Supreme Ogre. And sometimes we have given them to an imperial state, as in the painting by Verhas, in which the Supreme Ogre is Leopold II, surrounded by those lesser ogres, his ministers and functionaries. The question now could be: to which ogres do we deliver our children when we take our children to school today? I will recount two anecdotes that may provide an answer. The first took place at a Brazilian airport, when a group of school students, accompanied by their teachers, boarded my plane on their way to Disneyland. On their shirts was emblazoned a motto that reminded me of the chapter in Pinocchio in which he is lured from his path to school by the tempting signs of the Land of Cockaigne: 'Welcome to the world of fun.' And I couldn't help but imagine Mickey Mouse as the ultimate incarnation of the great paedophile and pedo-phor of our times. Because Mickey Mouse also loves children, he also makes off with them (or rather, we also take them to him), and he also nourishes himself on the lifeblood of children. The second anecdote relates to the fight against budgetary cuts to education that we are expe-riencing in Spain, and to be sure, in all those countries where public education is being progressively and implacably dismantled. Teachers from the school of a friend's daughter made each child write the same phrase on the wall: 'My name is X, I am not an expense, I am an invest-ment.' And I thought that it could have been the very same Herod, dressed up as an economist, who put these words in the mouths of the children. We could make a contemporary version of Verhas's painting in which Mickey Mouse (as representative of the world of consump-tion) and the president of the board of directors of a huge investment corporation (as representative of the world of production) inspect the procession of children. No longer is it the teleological-religious logic that appropriates the educational apparatuses, nor the logic of the state or the teleological-political logic, but rather the logic of commerce, which is also a murderous and sacrificial logic.

I would like to suggest that what all these ogresque logics have in common is precisely the future. For the state, children are the future of the nation, and they must be sacrificed to this future. For consumption and investment, children are the future of the economy, and they must be taken hostage to this future. Because both the state and the economy (if they can even be distinguished) take the world for granted. They know what has to be done with children, because they know what the world that the children come into is, and they know what their position in the world should be. For the apparatuses seized by the state and by capital, both children and the world are already known. School determines the *infans* as a student and, from this point of view, assigns her tasks to complete and instructions to follow, and the educational apparatuses are turned into a prelude to something else, such that the principles that regulate education are outside of education itself, beyond education. Education becomes a means of constructing the future, the future of the children and the future of the world. Therefore, the educational apparatuses, insofar as they are distinct from the logic of Herod and the ogre, can only be apparatuses without a future. Hence, education does not have a future nor should it have one; indeed it does not have anything to do with the future. Educational apparatuses are only worthy of that name when they are inhabited by people without a future who, precisely for that reason (because their time is not oriented towards the future), have free time. Because free time is a time liberated from necessity, from work and, of course, from leisure and consumption, but also, most importantly, it is a time liberated from the future. It is a simple passing of time, a lost time, a time to lose, which is not oriented towards the future of the world or to the future of the children. And for this we need Miss Cooper's rifle, so that she can ensure that that the evil ogre does not tear down the children's refuge, that Herod does not reign there, and that there, in Egypt, the children do not have to worry about the future of the world or, above all, their own future.

Today, the ogre is not outside the refuge but inside. Perhaps he has always been there. Thus far I have tried to convey that the educational apparatuses have been specially arranged for the relationship between childhood and the world, but that somehow the various Herods and ogres have captured and appropriated them for their own ends, as if they do know what children are (and should be) and what the world is (and should be). It appears, I have suggested, as if apparatuses organised for the indetermination of childhood and the opening of the world – in this manner, indifferent to the future – had been domesticated and put to the service of those who own the future. I have argued that Miss Cooper's rifle should protect this refuge (for childhood and the world) by keeping the ogre out, by guarding the door. But it is possible that Herod and the ogre have themselves designed the educational apparatuses so as to ensure the orientation of and control over entry to world (even though their own form, their own heterotopic and heterochronic configuration, makes them dysfunctional). In such a case, the function of Miss Cooper's rifle is more complicated than simply guarding the door of the refuge. Instead, it must open refuges (moments of refuge, refuge-events, times and spaces for refuge) inside a house already occupied by the ogre. Miss Cooper perceives the spirit of commencement that shines in the eyes of children and she also perceives the evil that gleams in the seductive face of the ogre. But the children have already been delivered up, are already inside the ogre's house – and there is clearly no outside to this house. Therefore her responsibility is not so much to avoid this giving over of the children, or even to flee from the house of the ogre, but rather to transgress its rules and invent ways of making it work differently.[38] Education is not what there is (in schools, in the varied ambit of the work of social educators, in art or cultural institutions) but what one does, that is to say, what happens when in any of these places a space and time is opened for an undetermined, undestined relationship between childhood and the world.

We might say that education, as a relationship between childhood and the world, is not a structural component of every society; and that, in our society, which calls itself a 'society of learning', it has acquired a primordial importance. Education, as we understand it here, is something exceptional. What is structural is the social and economic management through a 'corrupt' education, one seized and governed by the big and little ogres of our age. Education, nevertheless, configures times, spaces and logics that interrupt this massive management and exploitation of the world. That is why it can be understood as suspension, as novelty, as dissent, as a cut or deviation from the social and the economic modes of operation. Education, as it is understood here, is an activity without a destiny, without a vocation, without effects, without any result that can be calculated by the logics that govern normality. Education is precisely an interruption – always ephemeral and provisional, always exceptional – of these logics. Because what the ogre does is subordinate educational apparatuses to ends that lie outside them, submit them to teleological imperatives, mould them to the notions of result and future, put them into the service of purposes that are not educational, but rather social and economic. And, as Handke cried before the painting of Herod: that cannot be!

16

The world opened up by education, that is transformed into a kind of toy or plaything and made available to childhood so that it can be renewed and transmitted, is, as Hannah Arendt puts it, a common world. For Arendt, education intends 'to prepare them in advance for the task of renewing a common world'.[39] It is there, it seems to me, that the greatest danger of education's 'corruption' lies, in these times when the ogre's principal job seems to be to occupy the educational apparatuses as part of a global logic of privatisation of the common and the demolition of the public. Because opening up the world and making it available means, precisely, making it public, positioning or disposing it in public, placing it inside a public sphere. For Arendt, 'the term "public" signifies the world itself, insofar as it is common to all of us and distinguished from the place we privately possess in it'; this is because 'a world always exists between those who have it in common, in the same way that the table is already located between those who sit around it; the world, like everything that is in between, both joins and separates men at the same time'.[40]

Education, therefore, must make the world interesting, not only because it puts or disposes it 'amidst', because it situates it in an 'in-between', *inter-esse*, but also and above all because it directs the attention of each and every person towards this world that it makes common. From this point of view, education is not a relationship between individuals, that which we nowadays call 'intersubjectivity', but rather a relationship with the world. And a relationship with the world that is neither individual nor collective (if we understand the collective as an aggregate of individuals). Education is not a relationship between consciousnesses, perspectives, interests or individual opinions (if we understand the subject to be the owner-bearer of a consciousness, of a perspective, position, interests), but rather a relationship with the world that can only

occur in common. Therefore education cannot be about the individuali-
sation of the relationship with the world, but rather its communalisation.
So, the common or the 'in common' of education is not the result of a
summation of individuals or an abstraction of relationships, but rather
of a suspension of individuality – that which is attributable to this or that
particular individual, this or that consciousness, this or that interest – in
order to open an anonymous singularity.

Furthermore, we might say that every child is *somebody* in the family
(i.e. is determined by her private condition or history in a network of
personal relationships) and that every child is one thing or the other in
society (i.e. is determined by her condition or position in a network of
social positions). But insofar as the educational apparatuses constitute
a public space, every child is liberated from any condition; that is, they
are suspended from any conditioning, from any private history or social
position, so that they may become *anybody*. Or, said in another way,
childhood only appears (only takes place) insofar as the educational
apparatuses suspend the conditions, the determinations, the histories
and the positions that make each child a particular individual. Or, as
Rancière would say, education emancipates from the point of view of
'equality', that is, it emancipates every child from her social and economic determinations and positional fixations – both the ones they
have and the ones they are supposed to have.[41] That is what education
is about: displacing the private and individual for the shared and the
public, the particular for the common, and inequality for equality. And
it is this while showing equal respect to both childhood and the world.

Therefore education must also be about disappropriating the world,
communalising it, making it public and shared, and suspending the ways
in which it has already been appropriated and privatised. This is especially important, and ever more difficult, in the present period of privatisation of existence (by the configuration of the 'I' as a subject who owns
her possessions, identity, rights and interests – who is owner of herself,
ultimately – and who owns an immunised and anaesthetised life, isolated
from others and the world), privatisation of the collective (through the
constitution of 'us' as a collective 'owner' of goods, interests, identities
and rights), of the privatisation of culture (understood from the point of
view of its profitability and utility, its production and consumption, its
economic value and private appropriation), the privatisation of knowledge (through its constitution as a commodity or capacity that should
be individually appropriated), the privatisation of the world (through its

constitution as a whole that can be economically exploited and socially managed) and the privatisation of education (through the implementation of individualised learning environments and technological mediations which are, consequently, individualised from the relationship with the world, and through the insertion into the educational apparatuses of that entrepreneurial mindset that makes every person owner and administrator of herself). Therefore, education is not concerned with appropriating for itself either children or the world (that is what the ogre does with an insatiable appetite), and still less with making children appropriate the world for themselves or making the world appropriate children for itself. In education, neither the world nor children are anybody's property, because both childhood (as a mere opening of 'someone') and the world (as a public fact) have been arranged in respective and mutual disappropriation.

17

A Spanish philosopher once said that 'education arises from the fundamental idea, as persistent as it is stupid: that we know what a child is'. He adds, 'the worst thing for any child is that it should be mine'.[42] Perhaps this is what it is about – abandoning the pretension that we know what children are or should be, abandoning the notion that children are 'ours'. Perhaps education consists in the creation of an apparatus that disappropriates children, in the creation of a refuge in which children do not belong to anybody and where they are not known in advance, so that childhood, the novelty of childhood, is made possible. And we might also say that the worst thing for any *world*, for any form of world, is that it should belong to someone. Perhaps then education also consists in this, in the creation of an apparatus that disappropriates the world, in the creation of a refuge in which the world's becoming-world can take place without belonging to anyone, such that the renewal and communalisation of the world become possible.

Notes

1. H. Arendt, 'The Crisis in Education', in *Between Past and Future* (New York: Penguin, 1977), p. 174.
2. H. Arendt, *The Human Condition*, with an introduction by M. Canovan (Chicago: University of Chicago Press, 1998), p. 9.

3. Arendt, *The Human Condition*, p. 246.

4. Apparatus (*dispositivo*) is a loaded term, above all due to the systematic use that authors such as Foucault, Deleuze and Agamben have lent to it in order to speak of power relations. Here I use the word (from the Latin *dispositio*) to signal that education is neither synonymous with socialisation (as training in the ways of life) nor with learning (as a psychological process), nor is it something that is produced in just any interhuman transmission of knowledge, competencies, values etc. In this text, education is something that is produced inside certain material forms of disposing (*disponere*) spaces, time, bodies, relations, objects, technologies, disciplines, languages and ways of doing things that make the world available to infancy, and infancy available to the world. With the word apparatus ('*dispositif*'), I am here interested in emphasising the question of disposition, but above all the question of availability. In this sense, an educational apparatus is a device or artefact (such that we could talk about 'the art of education' in the same way as we talk about 'the art of fishing') in which the world and infancy are made mutually available to each other: the world is put at the disposition of, or made available to, infancy, and infancy is put at the disposition of, or is made available to, the world. An educational apparatus is therefore a certain way of composing (*componere*) the forms of relationship between infancy and the world, in which neither infancy nor the world are taken for granted/given in advance. Or, put another way, education is not about starting from certain determined assumptions about infancy or the world but, on the contrary, is about suspending these assumptions to make possible a relationship between infancy and the world in which nothing (neither infancy nor the world) is taken as given and in which, precisely for that reason, novelty is possible. To that end, education has nothing to do with propositions, proposals or projects about what infancy or the world should be. To understand education as an apparatus is to denaturalise it and, at the same time, to denaturalise or defamiliarise infancy and the world insofar as they can only be considered in the way the apparatus arranges or disposes, or composes them.

5. Arendt, 'The Crisis in Education', p. 196.

6. Maarten Simons and Jan Masschelein, 'School: A Matter of Form', in P. Gielen and P. De Bruyne (eds), *Teaching Art in the Neoliberal Realm: Realism versus Cynicism* (Amsterdam: Valiz, 2012), pp. 69–83. Cf. from the same authors, *In Defence of School: A Public Issue*, E-ducation, Culture

and Society Publishers (2012), https://ppw.kuleuven.be/home/ english/research/ecs/les/in-defence-of-the-school/jan-masschelein-maarten-simons-in-defence-of-the.html (accessed 9 January 2017). In this chapter I will discuss education, educational apparatuses, educational artifices, and not the school. But it should be made clear that one can only speak of education insofar as the educational apparatuses show 'scholastic' features. One could say that the school (the school form) is the material, spatial-temporal refuge of education. I think, nevertheless, that the form of the school is disappearing, in that classrooms are being converted into 'learning environments' and telematic workstations, and that the extensive and ever-proliferating domain of so-called 'social and cultural education' is nothing other than the proliferation of mechanisms for the rational and instrumental management of individuals and populations. In other words, if the scholastic form is disappearing, we will have to speak more and more of a certain exceptionalism of education.

7. J. Masschelein, 'El alumno y la infancia: a propósito de de lo pedagógico', *Cuadernos de Pedagogía*, 11 (2003), pp. 123–4. See also J. Larrosa, 'El enigma de la infancia, o lo que va de lo imposible al lo verdadero', in *Pedagogía Profana* (Buenos Aires: Novedades Educativos, 2000). Perhaps the text that still best captures the logic of infantilisation/'studentification' is Witold Gombrowics' classic, *Ferdyduke*. For more on this logic, see J. Larrosa, 'Educación y empequeñecimiento', in *Entre la lenguas. Lenguaje y educación después de Babel* (Barcelona: Laertes, 2003).

8. Infantilisation occurs when children are determined according to closed codes of meaning. Some Spanish speakers use the Argentine term 'pibe' (kid) as an alternative to both 'student' and 'child'. In relation to the question of equality in education as it has been raised by Jacques Rancière in *The Ignorant Schoolmaster: Five Lessons in Intellectual Emancipation*, trans. K. Ross (Stanford: Stanford University Press, 1991), Gerte Biesta discusses what would be the appropriate term for those who are brought into the educational apparatus in 'Learner, Student, Speaker: Why it Matters How We Call Those We Teach', in M. Simons and J. Masschelein (eds), *Rancière, Public Education and the Taming of Democracy* (Oxford: Wiley-Blackwell, 2011). Natality (the capacity for beginning) cannot be reduced to an empirical and punctual fact of birth, not even if we consider infancy as a stage of life. The activity of coming into the world never stops and, in this sense, it is a quality of existence itself, one of the elements of the human condition. Humans

never stop being born, given that they can have constantly the experience of beginning. And this experience is produced whenever there is an opening onto the indeterminate.

9. Arendt, 'The Crisis in Education', p. 195.

10. J.-L. Nancy, for example, begins one of his books by affirming that 'the world has lost its ability for world-forming', that what is occurring nowadays is that 'the world is permeated by a death drive that wants nothing else but to destroy the world', that 'the destruction of the world is not a hypothesis: it is, in some sense, the realisation of that which all thoughts of the world feed on', and that the destruction of the world is essentially related to the circulation of everything in the form of commodities, with the absorption of all signification into commodities. See *The Creation of the World or Globalisation*, trans. F. Raffoul and D. Pettigrew (Albany: SUNY Press, 2007), pp. 34–5.

11. Transmission is a particular way of positioning the world in time, which necessarily supposes its conservation and renewal. With transmission, the world is conserved inasmuch as it is renewed, and it is renewed inasmuch as it is conserved. In this respect, see J. Larrosa, 'Dar la palabra. Notas para una dialógica de la transmisión', in J. Larrosa and C. Skliar (eds), *Habitantes de Babel. Políticas y poéticas de la diferencia* (Barcelona: Laertes, 2000).

12. The film is called 'Life Line' and is included in the collection *Ten Minutes Older: The Trumpet* (Road Movies Filmproduktion, 2002).

13. Arendt, *The Human Condition*, pp. 246–7.

14. H. Arendt, *The Origins of Totalitarianism* (Cleveland: Meridian, 1958), p. 466.

15. P. Handke, 'Child Story', in *Slow Homecoming* (New York: NYRB Classics, 2009), p. 219.

16. M. Tournier, *The Erl King*, trans. B. Bray (Baltimore: Johns Hopkins University Press, 1997). Also in English as *The Ogre*.

17. M. Tournier, *Le vent Paraclet* (Paris: Gallimard 1975), p. 106. In English: *The Wind Spirit: An Autobiography*, trans. Arthur Goldhammer (Boston: Beacon Press, 1988).

18. Tournier, *The Erl King*, pp. 244–5.

19. Tournier, *The Erl King*, p. 229.

20. Tournier, *The Erl King*, p. 219.

21. 'L'Ogre Tournier', interview with M. Brandeau in *L'Express*, 1403 (May 1978), pp. 149–50. Quoted by A. Bouloumie in *Michel Tournier. Le roman mythologique* (Paris: Jose Corti, 1988).

22. P. Sloterdijk, *Venir al mundo, venir al lenguaje: lecciones de Frankfurt* (Valencia: Pre-textos, 2006), p. 145.
23. Sloterdijk, *Venir al mundo, venir al lenguaje*, pp. 146–7.
24. D. Grubb, *The Night of the Hunter* (New York: Dell, 1953). The film of the same title is from 1955 (screenplay by J. Agee) and was produced by United Artists.
25. Grubb, *The Night of the Hunter*, p. 88.
26. Grubb, *The Night of the Hunter*, p. 105.
27. Grubb, *The Night of the Hunter*, p. 85.
28. Grubb, *The Night of the Hunter*, p. 96.
29. Grubb, *The Night of the Hunter*, p. 93.
30. Handke, 'Child Story', p. 222.
31. Handke, 'Child Story', p. 222.
32. The short is called '11'09"01 September 11', and forms part of a collection of the same title from 2002.
33. 'Reading Lessons' (Lucid Eye, 1973).
34. Tournier, *The Erl King*, pp. 257–8.
35. Tournier, *The Erl King*, p. 125.
36. Sloterdijk, *Venir al mundo, venir al lenguaje*, p. 152.
37. Sloterdijk, *Venir al mundo, venir al lenguaje*, p. 159.
38. Regarding this point, and many others, I am grateful for the comments of Joan-Carles Melich, whose reading of a previous draft of this text was a great help to my preparation of the final version.
39. Arendt, 'The Crisis in Education', p. 196.
40. Arendt, *The Human Condition*, p. 52.
41. Rancière, *The Ignorant Schoolmaster, passim*.
42. A. G. Calvo, '¿Qué es un niño?', prologue to I. Escudero, *Cántame y cuéntame. Cancionero didáctico* (Madrid: Ediciones de la Torre, 1997).

7 Parlomurs: A Dialogue on Corruption in Education

Alessandro Russo

Translated from the Italian by Laura Lotti

PRUDENTIA: (*walking alone on a wooded hill that overlooks a plain with blurred ruins shrouded by thick vegetation*) What godforsaken ruins down there. From above they look less sinister, but still they are. Only someone like Demoval could call a meeting at 7 a.m. I haven't seen him in so long that I almost forgot about his timing – today he's late though. Sure, women are always early . . . and must have to wait.

DEMOVAL: (*previously unseen*) You are wrong, Prudentia, I have been here for a while, and have already started to survey the scene.

PRUDENTIA: I was surprised you weren't here already.

DEMOVAL: By all means! Never keep a lady waiting. I don't think women are always early though. According to Freud, you ladies slow down the progress of civilisation.

PRUDENTIA: Demoval, since when have you been studying psycho-analysis? And who told you that Freud was all for virile acceleration? Or is it you who projects upon him your irrepressible desire for progress?

DEMOVAL: Never mind, just saying.

PRUDENTIA: Long time no see, Demoval. Perhaps you've become slightly maximalist in the meantime?

DEMOVAL: I got here at 6.30. On time as always – today as represent-ative of the Division for Evaluative Competencies for the Department of Communication – as I was yesterday as a school principal in my office.

PRUDENTIA: I remember well, in the office at 6.30 a.m. Your chronic governmental insomnia is incurable. Not even Freud could treat you.

DEMOVAL: Insomnia is my business, but I do stay awake for the well-being of institutions.

(*Parlomurs and Diorthos enter the scene.*)

PARLOMURS: Good morning, Prudentia, good morning Your Excellency.

DEMOVAL: I am no Excellency, (*good-natured*) but I do watch over excellence.

PRUDENTIA: Demoval excels in paronomasia.

DEMOVAL: (*now serious*) You, Prudentia, excel in witty remarks, and you, Parlomurs, you may well be a free thinker but you've never been a man of institutions. I am afraid I will waste my time with you. Mind you, my time is subject to quota.

PARLOMURS: Mine isn't, Demoval, I take the time I need; the governmental libido for quotas never appealed to me. It is that fate makes us meet again; do not believe I have done something for this to happen.

DEMOVAL: Nor I, God forbid.

PARLOMURS: Well, now that we are all here, let me introduce you to Commissioner Diorthos. He comes from very far away – we should update him on the situation.

DEMOVAL: Excellent, here comes the foreign commissioner. He guarantees the levels of internationalisation required by the regulations, which as you know impact on the ranking for the evaluation of our commission.

PRUDENTIA: Welcome, Commissioner Diorthos, I am Prudentia, teacher; I am an old colleague of Parlomurs. Demoval was our principal a long time ago, and today fate makes him the president of this commission. A nice reunion, as they say.

DIORTHOS: Good to meet you, Prudentia. Good meeting you too, Mr President . . .

DEMOVAL: Demoval, please. The pleasure is mine. I am the first-level executive of the General Division for the Democratic Valuation of the Department of Communication.

PRUDENTIA: (*to Diorthos*) You see? It happens sometimes that one identifies with his own name. Once we had a police commissioner named Truncheon.

DIORTHOS: Really? That's incredible.

PRUDENTIA: I am serious. Anyway, Parlomurs and I are the two teachers called to be part of this commission to conduct a preliminary survey upon the ruins of this school building. The great earthquake destroyed it some ten years ago. (*pointing towards the plain*) There, you see, there is only debris covered in thorns and shrubs. Who would tell that there was a school there? And to think that it was a great scandal when it happened, with journalists and media involved. They failed the anti-seismic measures. But then nothing happened, neither here nor elsewhere, so the majority of the buildings have been left to ruin.

DIORTHOS: And why this commission now?

PRUDENTIA: There has been a change in the government. The heads of the Coalition for Governmental Harmony tore each other to pieces during the last financial scandal and after the protests in the square – in this region there have been loads, as you may know – the New Tribunate of the Plebs came to power.

DEMOVAL: (*shaking his head*) Well, the Tribunes are doing what they can, you know. A government is made of mediations, negotiations, you-give-me-something-I-give-you-something, (*looking at Prudentia*) no maximalisms. The better is an enemy of the good.

PRUDENTIA: Your wisdom is proverbial, Demoval, but the people at the Tribunate are uncompromising on certain matters. I read it, you know? Among the 'reform' priorities there is 'integrated scholastic communication'. I didn't get in which sense it is 'integrated', though it was written very clearly: 'educational communication is at the basis of communicative democracy'.

DEMOVAL: I read it too, what do you think? It is certainly so, education rhymes with communication.

PRUDENTIA: Are you also a poet, Demoval?

DEMOVAL: Things are very easy. The Department of Democratic Communication, which today also manages the old services of Educational Communication, nominated a series of commissions, such as this one I chair, with the goal of surveying the old areas hit by the earthquake in order to verify the possibility of opening local busi-nesses [*Azienda*] for *EduTainment*. On this topic, however, I have already advanced the proposal for a more precise name, *EduInfoTainment*. They are discussing this issue 'upstairs'. (*turning his finger towards the sky*) Do you understand?

PRUDENTIA: Pardon me, what does that profanity mean?

DEMOVAL: (*spelling it out loud*) *E-du-in-fo-tai-n-ment*, shortened as E-I-T. Therefore, LoBEIT. It means an education that is informative but that would also capture its audience with apt communicative forms – multi-media, performative . . .

PRUDENTIA: They will need special training courses for teachers, won't they? You can't improvise yourself as multimedia and performa-tive from one day to the next.

DEMOVAL: You are so backward, Prudentia. There is no need for train-ing programmes. Just look around – the media, television, everything is online. Do you know that today the Tribunate has included American

TV series about politicians in their Educational Communication programmes for future ministers?

PRUDENTIA: Yes, I heard; something like 'Sex in the Government' if I remember correctly.

DEMOVAL: There is a great one for the school system, with excellent pedagogical value. It is called 'The Enjoyment of Empowerment'.

PRUDENTIA: You really cannot resist a rhyme.

DEMOVAL: You teachers should get some inspiration too – why not? – from talk shows and TV contests. You seem 'choosy', Prudentia, as that minister used to say to spoilt students. You should understand that time has changed: teachers' performance evaluation needs to include integrated scores now. This is integration, you know? – objectively recording teachers' competence in educating, informing, and *entertaining*. 'Entertainment' is a key concept, whose meaning is very hard to grasp.

PRUDENTIA: Well, it sounds very straightforward to me. It means 'leisure'.

DEMOVAL: Well, you make it so easy but there are all these pedagogical implications – there is empathy, and sympathy, also.

PRUDENTIA: You really have a natural talent for rhyming couplets.

DEMOVAL: Teachers have to educate, that is for sure, no need to talk more on that, but above all they must maintain a suitable flow of information, and have to – why not? – create a feeling of well-being, of fulfillment: this is *entertainment*. This is the E-I-T mission that we have to instill into each local business. One could even open franchises . . .

PARLOMURS: Wait a moment, Demoval. Franchises? An E-I-T mission to be instilled into each local business? You are going too fast, we haven't even started the survey and you are already imposing the conclusions. What for, after all? A feeling of well-being. Is that all?

DEMOVAL: You, Parlomurs, you are very backward too. Or are you pretending not to understand? Don't you know that we are about to launch a chair in the Pedagogy of Well-being?

PARLOMURS: No, really, never heard of it.

PRUDENTIA: Me neither, I hadn't heard of such daring projects.

DIORTHOS: I am sorry, I don't think I understood either what the duties of this commission are, or how it was formed.

PRUDENTIA: Let me give you a rundown. The commission is chaired by the first-level department manager Demoval, as he said himself, who is in charge of ascertaining the objectivity of the assessment criteria in the prospect of a possible rebuilding. (*addressing Demoval*) The fact that they have to be E-I-T local businesses hasn't been decided by anyone, yet.

DEMOVAL: Prudentia, you are stuck in the past. (*addressing Diorthos*) Let me recap the situation more clearly. One of the members of the commission has to be a schoolmaster, or a mistress – (*to Prudentia*) please, do not misunderstand, I am a strong supporter of the pink quota, you know! – entrusted by the decree with the task of 'representing the needs of school plebs'. Given the retrograde mentality of today's teachers, one single teacher would have been enough, but since the regulations from the department prescribe that there also be one component 'hailing from the lists of the consultants provided with a national communicative qualification', Parlomurs was selected – I don't know why him, another teacher imbued with ideological archaisms, who gained the qualification of 'substitute complementary consultant'. Oh! Couldn't have been worse. Thankfully, we have Diorthos who, being a foreign expert, grants the score for internationalisation.

DIORTHOS: (*talking to himself, looking at the plain*) I was observing how the debris is displayed among the shrubs. In Olympia, the columns of Zeus' temple that Theodosius destroyed were pulled outwards with ropes and the marble discs that composed them are now laid almost tidily outside of the perimeter of the temple. It is as if the temple was flattened on the ground but so as to let its original shape transpire. Here instead, it looks like the building imploded inwards, it is all so confused, and the ruins seem to overlap on to various layers.

PRUDENTIA: Well, you know, the earthquake.

DIORTHOS: Tell me, what kind of school was this? It looks like there was a floor in that clearing. What could that be? A gym, a theatre hall, a lab?

PRUDENTIA: Who cares what it was? It has been destroyed, that's it. No one knows the name of that school any more.

DIORTHOS: I see. So, if I may, I would like to say something to give my contribution to the work of the commission.

DEMOVAL: You have the floor (*big grin*). Please, let's all listen to the international commissioner.

DIORTHOS: In front of this spectacle of ruin I would like to remind you of Plato's expression: 'if at any time education becomes corrupt, but can be put right again, this is a lifelong task which everyone should undertake to the limit of his strength'.

PARLOMURS: Sounds like a great starting point.

DEMOVAL: Oh no, this is a really, really bad start. The foreign commissioner can – and must – give his contribution, otherwise we won't reach the necessary score. However, believe me guys, this language doesn't fit our historical times. (*to Diorthos*) International Commissioner, let me say (*grins*) with the utmost respect towards the duties of internationalisation, you are influenced by outdated conceptions. Besides the fact that Plato doesn't seem to me that champion of democracy that we need today, what does it mean to say that education is 'corrupt' when it is evident that is deeply backward? If Plato meant backward then we agree. If so, I sign sight unseen. Done deal! (*big grin*) But, you see, education is corrupt because it hasn't caught up with the exigencies of a global communicative system. (*now serious*) We need tough but essential reforms, perhaps unpopular in the eyes of certain teachers – right, Prudentia and Parlomurs? – but historically necessary in order to keep up with the historical times.

PRUDENTIA: And you, Demoval, do you think you are historically necessary?

PARLOMUR. I think Demoval is telling us that our times are subject to quota.

DEMOVAL: Hey guys, you think you can get away with the usual jokes but you can't get into your head that we need to update education to the era of global information, and above all we must subject it to an objective evaluation. If you like the word 'right', then I use it too. We must right scholastic communication, so that the skills conveyed by the educational message could reach the receiver more directly, and the didactic transmitter could receive the feedback from the receiver just as directly, thereby being able to fully assess the cognitive performance.

PRUDENTIA: What a performance, Demoval!

PARLOMURS: Demoval, you are going too fast, we can't keep up with your historical times. Let's examine what Diorthos said about corruption in education, please, and you, Demoval, try to listen, at least for the sake of internationalisation.

DEMOVAL: Fine, let's hear about 'corruption', as long as you don't drag it out for too long. I have other things on my plate. Unfortunately we don't have a well-defined regulation about this commission's tasks that would specify the timing, the methods, and above all the criteria of evaluation. Ha, I wish we had a rule that would prevent wasting time in useless ideological chitchat.

PARLOMURS: On the contrary, I believe we must talk about it. Demoval, please, be kind enough to listen to us, that would get you scores for the evaluation.

PRUDENTIA: In the meantime we will look for clues about the truth of education, starting from the problem of corruption.

DEMOVAL: Stop it with this archaeological language!

PRUDENTIA: Pardon me? What do you mean?

DEMOVAL: I mean to say that it smells of mould, of antiquity, left behind by history. 'Truth' – come on, are you really still stuck with that? Don't you know there is a book by some philosopher titled *Bye-bye Truth?* Bold title, isn't it?

PRUDENTIA: Really? And what did truth answer?

DEMOVAL: What kind of a question is this? What do you think it may have answered?

PRUDENTIA: What do you think Diorthos?

DIORTHOS: Well, it could have answered: my dear, it doesn't seem like a very good deal to say goodbye. Perhaps truths can do away with philosophy but philosophy cannot do without truths.

PRUDENTIA: Please Diorthos, tell us. When Plato was talking about 'righting', did he mean righting communication?

DIORTHOS: Of course not. I don't even understand what righting communication means. According to Plato, education needs to be righted by virtue.

PRUDENTIA: Well, now we know that Demoval is not very platonic.

DEMOVAL: Well, this is certainly not my problem.

PRUDENTIA: We should also specify which kind of virtues we are talking about. There is the philosophical *aretè* and the revolutionary *vertu.*

DEMOVAL: Wake up all of you! You are still attached to antiquated ideological conceptions that caused so much evil – maximalism, terror-ism, totalitarianism. The better is always the enemy of the good.

PARLOMURS: I suggest that we interrupt these skirmishes and that we deal directly with the problem of corruption in education. Agree?

DEMOVAL: That's fine by me, as long as you don't waste my time. (*starts texting on his phone*)

DIORTHOS: At any rate, Plato considered education 'corrupt', 'deviated' but not 'backward'.

PARLOMURS: How do you say that in Greek?

DIORTHOS: *Exerchomai*, literally: 'deviated', in the sense of 'deviated from the right path', 'gone astray'.

PARLOMURS: Fine, so let's translate it as 'corrupt'. 'Deviated' would mean that there already exists a path on which to take education. I think that this 'path' needs to be constantly reinvented.

DIORTHOS: To Plato, things aren't quite that easy. Righting a corrupt education is a humungous enterprise, which requires life-long effort.

PARLOMURS: How do you say 'to right' in Greek?

DIORTHOS: *Epanorthousthai*, which means to straighten something that is bent, as a bent mast. It has nothing to do with communication.

PARLOMURS: Therefore, 'to right' is fine in the sense of 'to resolve something that is not going well'.

PRUDENTIA: In other words, as Mao used to say, 'the contemporary situation and our tasks' are still Plato's: education is corrupt and we must engage all our efforts to right it.

DIORTHOS: Sure, we can say so.

PARLOMURS: Should we then also consider the efforts of other people engaged in fighting corrupt education?

DIORTHOS: We certainly should.

PARLOMURS: If we reject the idea that there is a path already drawn for virtuous education, we can look better at the singularity of such efforts. Corruption in education has manifested itself in different circumstances and I believe that the attempts to right it have not only been different but also unique. Every invention in this area had to overcome the obstacles introduced by certain corrupt circumstances in new ways. Plato and we are talking about different things.

PRUDENTIA: He was fighting the Sophists.

DIORTHOS: There are enough Sophists today for that matter.

PRUDENTIA: There is never a shortage of them.

PARLOMURS: I think this has to do with a kind of corruptibility intrinsic to education.

DIORTHOS: How?

PARLOMURS: If there is corruption in education, it is because education is corruptible. There is no incorruptible education.

DEMOVAL: (*interrupting an intense text message exchange*). One needs to be incredibly patient with you all. Things are very straightforward. The human brain is a centre for the reception and transmission of information. Society is an information network, today more than ever. Setting aside your philosophising on the topic – (*looking at Diorthos*) no offence to Plato – educating means straightening the connections between the brain and society.

PARLOMURS: If this is the case, how come it sometimes goes astray? If we are all so communicative, the trajectory of education should always be spontaneously direct. Why would anyone have to right it?

DEMOVAL: Today information has accomplished enormous progress but education has been left behind.

PRUDENTIA: If this were the case, the point would be not to right it but to accelerate it in order to catch up with the progress of information.

DEMOVAL: Accelerate, of course.

PRUDENTIA: You just said that we have to accelerate the progress of civilisation – are you sure, Demoval?

DEMOVAL: (*hesitating*) Do you think that 'accelerate' sounds too maximalist?

PRUDENTIA: No, why, coming from you . . .

DEMOVAL: I mean, this is a historical necessity.

PARLOMURS: Demoval, looks like you are not that convinced about 'righting', though you are hesitant about 'accelerating' too. Perhaps something like 'limiting' would suit better? Limiting the corruption in education.

DEMOVAL: Stop going on about corruption! Anyway, that other thing you said, 'limiting', that would do, why not? It sounds less maximalist; as I say, the better is always enemy of the good. We must limit the lack of information in education. (*goes back to writing text messages*)

DIORTHOS: Well, I am sorry but I don't agree. Corruption is not about lack of information. Don't you see those ruins down there?

PARLOMURS: I think that we need to limit both actual corruption and intrinsic corruptibility.

PRUDENTIA: It still isn't clear what you mean by this distinction.

PARLOMURS: I just mean that, since education can become corrupt there must be some intrinsic tendency towards corruption, but this corruption manifests itself in different circumstances.

PRUDENTIA: But who corrupts education?

PARLOMURS: It doesn't depend on the corrupter's action. That is the norm. Indeed, a lot of people go along with it, and some even govern it.

PRUDENTIA: Therefore, it would be more accurate to assert that normally it is education that corrupts.

DIORTHOS: Well, the teacher's pedantry and her ludicrous authoritarianism are a comic *topos*.

PRUDENTIA: As a matter of fact it is not always like that, luckily. Sometimes students manage to make a mockery of it, and some teachers do not base their teaching on their own pedantry.

DIORTHOS: Excuse me, let me sum this up to see where we are at. Looks like the first hypotheses so far are: first, that it is useless to think of a main path to which education should go back; furthermore, that corruption in education manifests itself in different circumstances but this comes from an inner corruptibility; and lastly, that education is both corrupted and corrupter. These are all negative hypotheses, though. We should find an affirmative path.

PARLOMURS: There are exceptions. There are some moments in which the normality of corruption gets altered. Those forms of non-corrupt education are ultimately exceptions, rare moments, in which each time the invention of a didactic singular subjectivity shines through. There may be inventions that can effectively limit corruption. Weren't Socrates' teachings an exception?

DIORTHOS: They certainly were, although he was then sentenced to death for 'corrupting the youth'.

PARLOMURS: And wasn't he sentenced precisely by a corrupt education?

DIORTHOS: Of course.

PARLOMURS: Such an education never acknowledges its own corruption, but it fights spontaneously everything that limits it. The Sophists fought Socrates ferociously.

PRUDENTIA: Therefore we could also say that Lacan's seminar was limiting the corruption of education.

PARLOMURS: Sure. It limited the corruption in the training of analysts but it also had a huge value beyond that.

PRUDENTIA: As a matter of fact, the seminar was open to everybody.

PARLOMURS: Lacan was able to carry it forward while resisting violent attacks.

DIORTHOS: Those were rather 'defensive mechanisms', they were attacks to defend the *autonomous ego*. Luckily the International Psychoanalytic Association didn't use hemlock. They only excommunicated him.

DEMOVAL: (*interrupting his text messages again*) Hey, stop beating around the bush. Can't you see that information technology has taken giant leaps forward? 'Socrates' was a videogame invented about thirty years ago, if I remember correctly, and there was a nice comic about Lakant. But they are outdated, I don't know how one could recycle them in the new EIT programmes.

DIORTHOS: These authors aren't widely read in your department, are they?

DEMOVAL: I am sorry, but we have other issues to deal with. The programmes and methods of educational communication are completely obsolete. Today, in the internet era, academic teaching hasn't moved beyond the Middle Ages. This is ludicrous; some people can't even use PowerPoint. We are very, very behind the times.

PARLOMURS: Truth be told, Demoval, it is PowerPoint that is obsolete. It is out of fashion even in company briefings. After all, the medieval university was not that bad, they didn't even have real exams.

DEMOVAL: There you go again with your anarchic fantasies.

PARLOMURS: Look, this is not a fantasy. It is proved by historical documents. The Jesuits invented exams.

DEMOVAL: So? The Jesuits were the great precursors of the school of the future: centrality in communication and evaluation. Evaluation is the key to scholastic communication, get it stuck in your heads.

PRUDENTIA: Oh, Demoval, the great Evaluator.

DEMOVAL: I am not great, (*bantering*) I am democratic. (*solemn*) Evaluation is the midwife to democracy.

PRUDENTIA: That is maieutic, then. Is that like the Socratic one?

DEMOVAL: Sure, if you want to put it that way, why not? It doesn't sound that bad.

PRUDENTIA: So, only communication and evaluation matter to you. But is it enough?

DEMOVAL: Of course not! The democratic evaluation of cognitive competences is the objective foundation of educational communication but, beyond the normative factors, there are the psycho-relational ones, and let's not forget, as I always say, that pedagogy goes hand in hand with empathy, which is in fact another form of communication.

PARLOMURS: Demoval, so do you think the Jesuits invented democracy?

DEMOVAL: To be precise, I said that they were the precursors of democracy. Don't make me pass for a maximalist at all costs. Let's acknowledge that their exams were a serious system for democratic evaluation. Today we are much more advanced, that's for sure. We finally have scientific methods that guarantee objectivity. There are practically perfect tests for the evaluation of competences in any area. And I hope that the development of cognitive neuroscience will provide us with definitive results very soon. All we need is a well-calibrated pro-gramme of *neuroimaging* – you know? Those close-ups of the mind that turn to technicolour in a flash – see, we'll just need something like that to establish whether the sides of the brain that light up in one colour or the other correspond to the right or wrong answer. You are still stuck in the medieval university, but history runs.

PRUDENTIA: Unbelievable, the examiner will be replaced by the truth machine.

DEMOVAL: Forget about the truth. You really don't want to under-stand that the objectivity of the evaluation of the reception of cognitive competences is the keystone of every democratic educational system. Listen, all this 'philosophising' – to use a euphemism – is boring me.

(*Demoval answers a call on his mobile phone.*)

Hello, Demoval speaking. (*listening with great satisfaction*) Ha, excellent. Sure, I'll be there immediately. Absolutely, let me wrap this up and I'll be at the department. You know, I have been here since 6.30 a.m. to chair the survey with quite a – how shall I put it? – challenging commission. (*whispering*) This commission is an enormous pain in the arse . . . (*talking out loud and haughtily*). Of course, I am honoured by this task and, I venture to say, the work of the new board chaired by me will bring prestige to the department – I am hoping both you and the under-secretary will take this into account . . . Great, I will reach the new office as soon as possible. Talk soon. (*shuts the phone and addresses the three teachers*) There you go, we are done, the commission has fulfilled its duties.

PRUDENTIA: What do you mean that we are done? We haven't even started.

DEMOVAL: I have just been nominated General Director of LoBEIT

DIORTHOS: Excuse me? I am sorry but my knowledge of your language is limited.

DEMOVAL: Allow me to integrate your language skills. LoBEIT is the system of the local businesses for (*spelling*) E-d-u-I-n-f-o-T-a-i-n-m-e-n-t, whose constitution I proposed, as I said before. The minister has already approved it and he nominated me – (*smiling*) he did it *motu proprio* – he nominated me as the General Director of the EBLoBEIT, the evaluation board that presides over the project. Therefore, I am due back to the department to take up my new role.

PARLOMURS: And who is going to replace you in this commission?

DEMOVAL: No one. The commission is dissolved.

PARLOMURS: Dissolved? Just like that?

DEMOVAL: Since the minister just approved the regulations I proposed for the realisation of the LoBEIT, the surveys of the commissions previously nominated are not needed any more. We also have binding limits to our spending and, like it or not, our time is subject to quota.

PRUDENTIA: Have you just decided all this yourself, Demoval, or are you applying a regulation that the department has just tailored for you? How can you dissolve a commission on the spot?

DEMOVAL: What is there to quibble about this decision? You should consider it as the result of the personal approach of the EBLoBEIT director.

PRUDENTIA: What a true democratic evaluator.

DEMOVAL: I am democratic! This is very straightforward. As I told you, there is no specific regulation, so little so that you have been wittering on about your fantasies for the whole time. Since I am democratic, I have listened to your opinions but now I have been called to a superior function, so don't make me waste any more time. I have to be at the department as quickly as possible. Goodbye, Diorthos, I'll keep you in mind for some other commissions in which the score for internationalisation is required. (*pointing a finger at Prudentia and Parlomurs*) And I won't forget about you two either, we'll tighten up the procedure for the democratic evaluation, so you will stop being so irresponsible. (*walks away hurriedly*)

PRUDENTIA: Deo gratias! He's gone. Hopefully, we'll be the ones to forget about Demoval.

PARLOMURS: I'm afraid we won't be able to forget about him that easily. One way or another, Demoval will come back, he can't disappear completely.

PRUDENTIA: I hope he won't come back any time soon, at least. If you wish, we could continue this discussion among the three of us.

PARLOMURS: I agree, let's keep talking.

DIORTHOS: Sure, let's continue.

PRUDENTIA: Demoval's ministerial ascension freed us from a permanent obstacle to reflection, at least for the moment. Let's enjoy this breath of fresh air.

DIORTHOS: Why can't he disappear?

PARLOMURS: Because he represents the normality of education, or better, that which governs such a normality.

PRUDENTIA: But we are interested in exceptions. Let's talk about the exceptions then.

DIORTHOS: Exceptions to what?

PRUDENTIA: To everything we've said so far, the exception to ordinary corruption in education. Right?

PARLOMURS: My proposition is that this is the norm, unless education is limited by an exceptional invention.

DIORTHOS: There is a lot to clarify on this. At any rate, let's start with the exceptions: what are those exceptional moments of limitation to corruption in education? We have already mentioned Socrates and Lacan.

PARLOMURS: The medieval university was a great invention too, but we could give other examples. Someone could consider these examples even more 'archeological', and rightly so. For instance, Charlemagne's Schola Palatina, the *Ecoles centrales* of the French Revolution, or the educational revolution during the Cultural Revolution. In truth, the occasions in which corruption in education has been limited are countless. We only know of a small part, many are still to be rescued from oblivion, or have to be rethought in entirely new ways.

DIORTHOS: Here we may need a preliminary clarification. How does corruption in education become manifest? In other words, how can we recognise it?

PARLOMURS: It is not easy. Education – I mean education in its normality – depends on the governmental circumstances of a time and therefore it is usually wrapped in an everlasting fog that prevents one from seeing its corruption. Only the inventions that can limit corruption will allow us to clear this fog.

DIORTHOS: Although, if it is a matter of normality, that is, if corruption in education is a structural element of the governmental circumstances, there must be some constants, or at least some recurring manifestations of such a corruption.

PARLOMURS: I think so. For what we know about limiting inventions, I believe there are at least two constants in the normality of education. A first constant is the general tendency to transmit knowledge – or skills, as they say these days – and to consider thinking not only as a waste but also as a threat.

PRUDENTIA: Indeed, we are told that thinking for ourselves is a terrible habit that we should get rid of as soon as possible. A while ago there was an advertising campaign for a big IT company, whose slogans were precisely 'No Time to Think' and 'The End of Thinking, The Beginning of Knowing'.

PARLOMURS: This is the government programme for the 'knowledge society'.

PRUDENTIA: Mencius was more for a compromise. He said: 'knowing without thinking is useless, thinking without knowing is dangerous'. He kept himself in the 'golden mean', he made some concessions, he admitted that you can't do without knowledge completely, bless him, but all in all he saw thought itself as the source of a danger to avoid at all costs.

DIORTHOS: For any programme of government of others, if you know without thinking you are harmless after all, but if you think without knowing you are a suspect.

PARLOMURS: Today the obsession for 'multiple-choice tests' only aims to prevent this threat. 'No Time to Think' during exams either.

DIORTHOS: Well, a typical recommendation for American students to pass exams is 'Think less, learn more.'

PRUDENTIA: A newspaper recently praised the profound wisdom of the formula 'Think a little less, live a little more'. It's a whole programme of life.

DIORTHOS: By the way, do you have 'bibliometrics' too?

PRUDENTIA: Of course we have bibliometrics. We have shops that sell 'books by the metre'. Together with couches and bookshelves, you can buy metres of books intended as furniture. They even do bibliometric promotions, and you can pay in instalments.

PARLOMURS: 'Evaluation is midwife to democracy'.

DIORTHOS: I see. Therefore, a first manifestation of corruption in education is to promote a knowledge that claims that there is no need to think. What is the second constant?

PARLOMURS: I'd say that the second constant is that the experience of education, without limiting inventions, spontaneously tends to create a hierarchy based on knowledge – who knows stays on top, who doesn't stays at the bottom. If the teacher doesn't question honestly his or her desire – what does the teacher desire? – they inevitably hold to the discourse of the master. Today's 'evaluation' is what makes of educational experience one of the hierarchical rituals of social connivance, it establishes who is the master.

PRUDENTIA: The master of words, as Humpty Dumpty used to say. The refrain that comes from the institutions, however, is that we cannot do without assessment.

PARLOMURS: It depends on what one wants. One thing is to guarantee the teacher's superiority according to his or her function of setting a 'rank', based on the alleged 'objectivity' of the 'number'. Another is to take stock of one's teaching experience in order to be able to make some adjustments and to understand what works and what doesn't. In the medieval university there was nothing like the Jesuits' 'exams';

however, there were informal interviews in which the *magister* attempted to understand how his *lectio* was from the *discipuli*.

DIORTHOS: Therefore we could say that the two constants in which corruption in education is manifested are the tendency to marginalise thinking and the tendency of the teacher's discourse to model itself upon the master's.

PARLOMURS: Yes, we could say so.

DIORTHOS: However, if we can recognise these tendencies only through the inventions that limit corruption in education, then, vice versa, in the latter we should find great openings for the novelty of thought and for egalitarian possibilities.

PARLOMURS: Sure. Without these openings there would be no inventions. I believe there are always two forces at play in didactic inventions: an intellectual novelty in excess to the ensemble of the knowledge transmitted by ordinary education and, at the same time, egalitarian political inventions that dissolve the normal hierarchies of a certain historico-social world.

DIORTHOS: Exceptional moments, then. Intellectually and politically. Any examples?

PARLOMURS: I mentioned Charlemagne's Schola Palatina. That was a new wave of researches on language, of which Alcuin was the key figure. There was a fervour for the study of language from a grammatical point of view, somehow 'structuralist', also linked to the great philosophical themes popular in those days.

DIORTHOS: Yes, of course, there were never-ending disputes about the grammatical and philosophical value of *Ens*. These are themes that reverberate up to contemporary philosophy.

PARLOMURS: And they come from far away. It is the *present participle* that 'participates' both in the beings and in being.

PRUDENTIA: An ontic-ontological *joint venture*, right?

PARLOMURS: Charlemagne values above all the intellectual novelty of grammatical study for a precise reason: 'language', he writes in one of his *Epistles* . . .

PRUDENTIA: Well, an emperor couldn't express himself but through *Epistles* . . .

PARLOMURS: Language, Charlemagne says, could be an obstacle to 'truth'.

PRUDENTIA: An obstacle?

PARLOMURS: He said that, because language 'runs too fast', it might 'lie'.

DIORTHOS: It is remarkable that the problems are language and truth.

PARLOMURS: It is also remarkable that he chose grammar. In the Schola Palatina they used to study how language works from a strictly grammatical perspective. It sounds like extreme formalism but instead this is a great didactic invention, as Durkheim explains. The Schola Palatina teaches grammar in order to curb, we could say, the speed of 'communication'.

PRUDENTIA: The problem is how not to be spoken by language. Holding off the 'verbal parasite' is every poet's concern.

PARLOMURS: Knowing the structural functions of language to prevent thought from being overwhelmed by it. Charlemagne aimed to provide an unprecedented freedom in the ordinary education of the times. The invention of the Schola Palatina stems from a major intellectual novelty.

PRUDENTIA: At this point, Demoval would say that he is getting bored.

DIORTHOS: Are you already missing Demoval?

PRUDENTIA: (*surprised*) Why? I don't think so. We may not be able to forget him altogether, but at least when he is not here let's allow ourselves a moment of reflection. In truth, he is the one who wastes our time.

PARLOMURS: It should also be said that Charlemagne wanted the Schola Palatina to be open to students who didn't belong to aristocratic families. He was very wary of the intellectual capabilities of the young lords.

PRUDENTIA: Now that I think of it, there is another emperor that intervenes on language, but in a completely different way. I am talking about the invention of the *hangŭl* alphabet in Korea.

DIORTHOS: When?

PRUDENTIA: Mid-fifteenth century, by the Korean emperor Sejong the Great . . .

DIORTHOS: 'Magnus' too, then.

PRUDENTIA: Well, he deserves the title. Sejong personally intervened in the creation of the *hangŭl* alphabet to substitute Chinese characters that were not only difficult to learn, but were hard for Koreans to pronounce. This alphabet was created basically from scratch but with an immense precision, to the point that it is still used in Korea today.

DIORTHOS: It's not easy to invent an alphabet.

PRUDENTIA: It was an extraordinary undertaking, which anticipated some fundamentals of twentieth-century linguistics. Today linguists look at *hangŭl* with admiration, for its capacity to identify the singularities of Korean phonetics and for the elegance of the stroke. In short, for its great simplicity.

DIORTHOS: Also in this case we have an intellectual novelty in the field of linguistics.

PRUDENTIA: In order to create such an original alphabet *ex novo* they studied language properly at the level of the signifier. It is surprising how they managed to classify phonemes with the precision of modern linguists, in spite of the lack of acoustic instruments apart from their own hearing apparatuses, and how they transcribed them according to clever but simple rules.

DIORTHOS: What a great enterprise. And what was the scholastic novelty that corresponded to this linguistic invention?

PRUDENTIA: Sejong himself was a remarkable scholar; we could say that he was the 'research coordinator' of the project. He established a linguistic academy that worked on the details of *hangŭl* for many years in order to replace Chinese characters. The stated objective of the promulgation of the new alphabet was to spread the use of written language, which was a privilege of the Confucian aristocracy up until then, to laypeople. Obviously, he met with enormous resistance. It wasn't easy to compete with the cultural and aesthetic hegemony of the Chinese alphabet, and not only for aesthetic reasons. Sejong died too soon and the academy lasted only a few years before being wiped out by a *coup d'état*.

PARLOMURS: This is a major political issue.

PRUDENTIA: There were confrontations on several aspects: the independence of the Korean language, which is entirely different from Chinese; relations with China, which was Asia's cultural centre; the egalitarian value of the democratisation of writing, etc. The divergences were very strong on all these fronts. For the Confucians, who ruled over education in Korea and were very influential at court, the Chinese alphabet was the most suitable tool to think in Korean, or better, the only one. They opposed *hangŭl* also because it severely threatened the privileges of the Confucian élite, the holders of the knowledge of a very complex writing, even more so because it established a phonetic structure entirely foreign to Chinese.

PARLOMURS: It was like paying tributes to the empire for the usage of written language.

DIORTHOS: So, the coup was organised by the Confucians?

PRUDENTIA: They did it in the name of China's cultural centrality, which was key to their power.

DIORTHOS: And did they regain this centrality after the coup?

PRUDENTIA: The Chinese alphabet was immediately brought back, together with the primacy of Confucian education, but *hangŭl* survived below the surface. The Confucians considered it scornfully as 'the language of women and children', and as a matter of fact, it was the language of the people for centuries, at the margins of official culture. Only in the twentieth century, after many political vicissitudes, did it officially become the alphabet of the Korean language.

DIORTHOS: Therefore the academy that developed *hangŭl* is the scholastic invention and Confucian education is the corruption, isn't it?

PRUDENTIA: Don't let some Chinese hear you. Still, the academy provided a linguistic education of a high level, it was a scholarly formation linked to top-notch research.

PARLOMURS: This would have been highly regarded by Humboldt, for various reasons . . .

PRUDENTIA: I think that the *hangŭl* enterprise could be considered a scholastic invention with a national scope, with long-lasting consequences that concern the relation of any Korean speakers with written language to this day.

PARLOMURS: We could push ourselves even further to look for examples of scholastic invention. Let's take the Chauvet caves. They are an ingenious artistic invention from which a didactic invention may have certainly flowed. Not only are the paintings from different hands, but they are also thousands of years apart from each other. Therefore, there must have been a singular educational invention among these artists. There must have been a 'Chauvet School' – a school not only for new painters, but also for anyone who entered the caves.

PRUDENTIA: Sure, the Chauvet artists were geniuses, perhaps the best cave artists that we know of, but how was this limiting corruption in education?

PARLOMURS: We can only speculate, of course. For instance, we may guess that hordes of people gathered in those caves to be subjected to forms of ritual hierarchisation. Perhaps that is what ordinary education was like in those circumstances.

DIORTHOS: Inert gathering in the Platonic cave . . .

PARLOMURS: Something like that. After all, there must be something in the platonic myth that predates it. The 'Chauvet School', instead, brought an extraordinary artistic invention inside the cave; it provided the eyes with the capacity to look at the movement of those lions as figures of thought. It was a scholastic invention not only for the new painters but also for anyone who entered the cave, whether he was called for a ritual gathering or not.

PRUDENTIA: As a matter of fact, 35,000 years after, it still possesses a grandiose capacity to open our gaze. Should a contemporary artist paint that way, he would be considered a genius. A few years ago, I did a test. When the first catalogue of Chauvet's paintings was published, I showed the photos to a painter friend, who was very impressed. Then, without saying what it was, I asked, 'how old is the artist, for you?' Answer: 'thirty, thirty-five'.

PARLOMURS: It was enough to multiply by a thousand ...

DIORTHOS: (*looking toward the plain*) I apologise for momentarily interrupting this review of scholastic inventions, although I was the one to propose this. This discussion allows for a broader perspective from which to look down at those ruins. However, I feel that we haven't got to the core of the issue yet.

PARLOMURS: We did find something though, or at least some working hypotheses: the normality of corruption in education and the exceptionality of limitations to it. Furthermore, we found some constant manifestations of corruption that are opposed by educative inventions.

DIORTHOS: OK. So, in this optic, the problem is: what was the twentieth-century state school about? Was it an invention or another instance of the normal corruption in education? First of all, it is a state apparatus. Is this an element of corruption in itself? Or, vice versa, can we identify limiting factors?

PARLOMURS: I think we need first to separate these questions in order to discuss them. We know for a fact that the very existence of the state school was conditioned by a series of egalitarian inventions. We should distinguish these inventions from the state-owned nature of the twentieth-century school. It's not easy though. For decades, the school has been a primary ground for intervention by all kinds of governments, and even a ground for competition among opposite systems. This is also one of the reasons for its growth. Not only did socialist and capitalist states threaten each other on the military plane, but they also competed with each other through education systems.

DIORTHOS: Is there a relation between the end of that competition and the decline of the state school?

PARLOMURS: I think so, but we have to admit that on these questions, we are fumbling in the dark. All the previous conceptual maps – historiographical, sociological, pedagogical – are useless.

PRUDENTIA: Our big problem is that we have to create a new political perspective to orient ourselves on this ground. The classist perspective – the idea that school belongs to the dominant class – doesn't shed any light on those ruins. And ultimately doesn't say anything about the twentieth-century school.

DIORTHOS: Althusser maintained the thesis of the school as Ideological State Apparatus. His was no longer a classist perspective.

PRUDENTIA: That doesn't sound like an enlightening thesis. The school as dominant ISA, which inherits this function from the Church, describes an imaginary and Eurocentric picture, as they say.

PARLOMURS: That was a text written around 1968, with no mention of what was happening in France in those days. Ultimately, it is a first 'negation' of 1968, and for Althusser marks his comeback in the French Communist Party.

PRUDENTIA: In China, for instance, what was the ISA of the imperial age? Confucianism? State exams? Or even written language itself? After all, in China, the establishment of schools from the end of the nineteenth century happened under the thrust of major intellectual and political movements.

PARLOMURS: Not only in China. In Europe too, the state school was established through great political and intellectual movements. It was far from a transition to a new dominant ISA.

DIORTHOS: If the idea of the school as 'class instrument' doesn't help us make sense of these ruins, and the theory of ISA doesn't allow us to overcome this impasse – although I am not too sure about this – this means that we have to create new tools to think about the twentieth-century state school. Otherwise we either accept its destruction, or we keep waiting for a miraculous restoration.

PARLOMURS: Or we take the path of communication at full speed.

PRUDENTIA: Communicating through education, educating through communication – Demoval would say.

PARLOMURS: Do you think that he would be versed in the use of chiasm? Either way, our perspective is that the scholastic inventions capable of limiting ordinary corruption are the most varied and singular; however, they are all characterised by the capacity to open up knowledge to thought by way of an egalitarian force.

PRUDENTIA: Both the cases discussed previously had a novelty of thought intertwined with a political novelty at their source.

DIORTHOS: If the state school has been a limiting factor, it must have had a singular intellectual and political driving force.

PARLOMURS: Of course. The state school would not have existed without a series of great egalitarian moments and intellectual inventions.

However, it evolved in a very convoluted way – through anticipations, interruptions, periods of great expansion and a halting point.

DIORTHOS: The halting point being the sixties?

PRUDENTIA: That was an unusual impasse, though, since the sixties were also very inventive. I believe that the question of how to assess the sixties is decisive to the problem of the state school.

DIORTHOS: I have a question in this regard: we previously referred to the educational experiences of the Cultural Revolution as inventions – but weren't they instead within this impasse?

PARLOMURS: In truth they were a very experimental creative moment. They pointed to an entirely new conception of the school system and were driven by a radical questioning of the egalitarian character of the state school. Today the Cultural Revolution is regarded as the anathema of 'thorough negation'; it is dismissed as a destructive moment. Yet it also entailed experimentations in many fields, especially in education.

PRUDENTIA: In 1966 Mao Zedong wrote the famous 'May 7 Letter' for the 'revolution in teaching'.

DIORTHOS: He was writing *Epistles* too.

PRUDENTIA: He didn't have an imperial tone, though. If anything, in his early writings on education, he had the force of the radical reformer, the same that he had when he theorised and realised in Changsha, in Hunan province, the self-study university. That was in 1921, on the onset of the 'May 4 1919' movement. Then he wrote a 'Manifesto' for the creation of that experimental university, and chaired it for a couple of years. The key point was the questioning of the self-evidence of the teacher's role. The 'university' was based on 'self-tuition' because students had to learn by themselves, choosing the books they wanted to read from the libraries. The university had to be a place for the self-organisation of study.

DIORTHOS: Would you say that everybody could choose their teachers?

PARLOMURS: The choice of one's teachers is an ideal of free education. Ultimately, Mao had the same attitude towards the education system during the Cultural Revolution. How many people followed his approach is another matter.

PRUDENTIA: The core idea of the 1966 letter – which in China was called 'May 7 Directive', which is a more demanding term than *Epistle* – is to 'make a great school of society'.

DIORTHOS: What did he mean? Schooling society? Or socialising the school?

PARLOMURS: Not really. 'Society' was for him a political concept. It was the ensemble of all the possible egalitarian inventions. 'To make a great school of society' meant to put educational experiences to the test of those political experiments. Education had a value only if it promoted the reduction of the 'three great differences', as they used to be called – that is, the great barriers that protect the anti-egalitarian regime: the one between city and countryside, the one among different types of labour, and obviously the one between executive and subordinate positions.

DIORTHOS: A communist hypothesis for the school.

PARLOMURS: For a few months each year, everyone had to engage in activities that they had never done before: factory workers had to become farmers and farmers had to work in factories; soldiers had to work both in factories and in the country; students, teachers and all state functionaries had to have experiences in different activities. And those who were doing manual labour had to have the time to study.

PRUDENTIA: Some would say that everyone was required from time to time to change discourse.

DIORTHOS: You are talking about experiments that have fallen into the most complete oblivion.

PARLOMURS: A forced oblivion.

PRUDENTIA: I remember that Mao used to be very careful with details. When he talked about peasants who had to have the time to study, he clarified: 'even the ones engaged in fish farming and silviculture'.

DIORTHOS: We could say that, even in this case, there was an existential injunction addressed to everybody to devote every effort to resolve corruption in education.

PARLOMURS: The hypothesis of those experiments was that, in order to create new schools, there had to be participation in egalitarian inventions. The value of knowledge transmission was subjected to this condition. Those were experiments that aimed to limit the ordinary corruption of education.

DIORTHOS: I have two questions. The problem of equality was certainly crucial to that 'great school', but those experiments were drastically dismantled after Mao Zedong's death. Was that because of an internal impasse? Also: were those experiments aimed to radically overcome the state school, or did they retain something of it?

PARLOMURS: I think we should start from the second question. Egalitarian invention was crucial to the birth and evolution of the state school but it was a tortuous development and in order to investigate it, starting from its state character is not enough.

DIORTHOS: We cannot ignore it though.

PARLOMURS: I agree, but what we are discussing is whether there were elements of intellectual invention in the state school that limited corruption in education. I mean that we cannot look for those elements in an alleged bureaucratic rationality of the state apparatus – if anything, we would find the opposite in that regard – and we should not limit ourselves to considering the state school as the result of new governmental technologies.

DIORTHOS: Therefore, there would be non-governmental factors in the origin of the state school?

PARLOMURS: Distinguishing these factors is not easy, they are deeply intertwined.

DIORTHOS: A *case study?*

PARLOMURS: Let's look at the *Ecoles centrales* of the French Revolution. They were approved right after Thermidor but they are a fruit of the Convention, for which education was an extremely important theme. Also, they were a great rediscovery by Durkheim in *L'évolution pédagogique en France,* right at the beginning of the twentieth century.

DIORTHOS: That is the moment at which scholars were working on a modern historiography of the French Revolution.

PARLOMURS: That was also a moment of great advance for the generalisation of the state school. To Durkheim, the existence of the latter was due to the creation of the *Ecoles centrales,* even though its effects were dormant in the nineteenth century. He says that the nineteenth century wasn't particularly pregnant with novelties in this regard.

DIORTHOS: *L'évolution* is not read enough, unfortunately.

PARLOMURS: Perhaps also because it is not very 'Durkheimian'. Durkheim is really enthusiastic about this point. He highlights that the great novelty of the French Revolution was that for the first time the modern 'sciences' were taught – both the physical-natural and the historical-social. They were left out of the dominant educational form of the previous two centuries, the Jesuit College.

PRUDENTIA: Demoval's favourite.

DIORTHOS: Not only Demoval's. The college was highly regarded in academia in previous years. However, during the French Revolution, the Jesuits had already lost their authority and the prestige of the college had been challenged. The entry 'collège' in the *Encyclopédie* was final.

PARLOMURS: As a matter of fact, the revolutionaries aimed to invent something entirely new. First of all, they turned to the modern sciences for the first time. The question is: how did they hold it together? How did they organise the transmission of so many disparate kinds of knowledge in a single place?

DIORTHOS: This is the moment Foucault periodises as the passage from the classical episteme to the modern. The passage from one episteme to the next remains under-theorised in Foucault's dispositif, although it has been described in detail.

PRUDENTIA: I agree. There is something here left unexplained or willingly undetermined that resembles the passage from one ISA to the other, although from two completely different perspectives.

PARLOMURS: The less convincing aspect is that Foucault's problematic essentially concerns the relations between different kinds of knowledge. The fact that these relations are intertwined with inventions of thought remains secondary. It emerges at times but Foucault does everything to hide it. Like when he refers to the French Revolution, without ever openly mentioning it, as the key event for modern episteme. Grasping its importance, he says, requires an enormous effort, but then he leaves it completely outside of his 'archaeology'.

PRUDENTIA: That is a great virtuosity, like that novel by Perec written without the letter 'e'. Furthermore, his surname contains two 'e'.

PARLOMURS: Anyway, Foucault's foundational idea is that there exists a strong tendency towards a general unity of knowledge but also an equally strong opposed tendency, which periodically takes over. It happens then that a certain epistemic grid, which lasted for centuries, disarticulates itself – something that happens in fast processes, over a few decades – and new types of knowledge emerge that look beyond that general unitary space and constitute mutual relations in entirely different ways.

PRUDENTIA: Doesn't this remind you of the dialectic between 'relations of production' and 'forces of production'?

PARLOMURS: Perhaps. This may also relate to Durkheim's idea of the different 'epochs of knowledge', a formulation that seems to anticipate 'episteme'. But in Foucault there are two opposed 'epistemic drives', towards unity and disunity.

PRUDENTIA: In this case too there seems to be a strong model in the background.

PARLOMURS: Yet, I believe that, whatever the sources of inspiration, on this point Foucault helps us focus on our problem. When the *Ecoles centrales* are opened, we are in the middle of that epistemic passage – the previous general unity of knowledge is dissolving and the new one hasn't been fully constituted.

DIORTHOS: And it wouldn't be constituted so easily.

PARLOMURS: Sure. The remarkable thing is that, right at that moment, that problematic propels a very clever new didactic invention. What can keep those diverse teachings together? Since the teachers don't know yet, let the students decide. The very idea of the 'school class' as a principle of organisation is abolished – that was a tenet of the Jesuit educational discipline – and is substituted by a system based on courses. In essence, there is no preliminary unified didactic programme, but it is up to the student to choose the courses he wants to attend.

PRUDENTIA: Basically, that is a complete liberalisation of the curriculum. A much larger liberalisation happened here too from 1968 onwards.

DIORTHOS: Your friend Demoval would say that you are indulging in anarchic fantasies.

PRUDENTIA: Looks like you appreciated Demoval's subtlety too.

PARLOMURS: Foucault's argument is that the new sciences – those that emerge in the passage to the modern episteme: economy, biology, linguistics – aren't conceived as spontaneously converging on a single general plane of knowledge. Foucault says that each of them is 'enfolded into itself'.

PRUDENTIA: Do they become specialised?

PARLOMURS: Each of them is much more involved with the singularity of its object – work, life, language – and much less concerned with its inscription into a general order of knowledge. In those conditions, according to students the freedom to decide their subjects was a wise decision, and eventually realistic. In the first place, nothing was keeping together those disciplines to compose a unitary system, other than the student's desire, a certain *studium*. That would have been unthinkable in the Jesuit College or in what survived of the old university.

PRUDENTIA: Victor Hugo wrote that the Convention was looking for a point of the real in what is usually considered impossible.

PARLOMURS: The two great novelties are the opening up to the new sciences in every field, leaving the question of their didactic unity open, and the egalitarian character of education. Here too everyone could choose their teachers.

PRUDENTIA: In the medieval university students could also choose their teachers.

DIORTHOS: Therefore, in the *Ecoles centrales* also, the role of the one who knows little but wants to learn was valorised.

PARLOMURS: The novelties of the *Ecoles centrales* do not depend on new governmental technologies. Moreover, they are long forgotten. Even more so, in the nineteenth century they were considered as the apex of the scholastic disorder of the Revolution. It is Durkheim who revalues them as 'unprecedented inventions' that paved the way for the modern school.

DIORTHOS: Yet it took a century before the state school was generalised.

PARLOMURS: He considers the nineteenth century as devoid of scholastic novelty; in fact, as a regression. In truth, there are great intellectual novelties but they converge towards the generalisation of the state school only at the end of the nineteenth century.

DIORTHOS: Political and scientific novelties.

PARLOMURS: Precisely, and they are deeply intertwined. Political inventions principally stem from the organisation of the communists, especially from 1848. Beyond supporting political egalitarianism, the communists are also great supporters of modern science. Not only do Marx and Marxists consider Darwin a genius, even a precursor, but they also pay great attention and care to the study of scientific inventions as materialist openings that favour revolutionary politics.

PRUDENTIA: They also advocate mass education.

PARLOMURS: The communists have always organised the most varied forms of popular political education. The same *Manifesto* is the result of an educative experience; ultimately it is the synthesis of the 'theoretical seminar' that Marx and Engels held at the League of the Just in 1847. For the proletarians, theoretical study is the fundamental condition for becoming politically organised – 'to raise themselves theoretically', as the *Manifesto* says. The same historical materialism is both a principle for political organisation and a scientific vision; its pillar is the 'dictatorship of the proletariat' and its inspiration is the experimental nature of modern science.

DIORTHOS: The state school has been strongly supported by the Communist Party and all the workers' parties.

PARLOMURS: Indeed, but it has been a controversial issue since the beginning. Marx criticised the idea of a 'state-educator of the people'. He used to say: 'Don't tell us this is a future state'. In the *Critique of the Gotha Programme* he states that, on the contrary, it is 'the state that needs a rough education from the people'. He threw sarcasm at the 'blind faith in the state typical of the Lassallean sect', which precisely wanted a 'state-educator'. Marx proposed a series of governmental measures that warranted the appropriate resources to open local schools, and a few forms of supervision at most, but not a centralised state school system.

DIORTHOS: However, without the workers' parties, there would be no twentieth-century state school.

PARLOMURS: The threat of communism plays a crucial role. Late nineteenth-century European governments realise that they are facing a serious danger. The great political thrust of Marxism mobilises the proletariat to 'raise itself theoretically' in order to create forms of independent political organisation and welcomes modern knowledge as one of the conditions for the establishment of a 'dictatorship of the proletariat'. In response to this danger, the state school starts to become generalised.

DIORTHOS: Is this a concession that governments make to the egalitarian forces in order to contain them?

PARLOMURS: It is less risky to 'educate the masses' than to let them 'raise themselves theoretically'. It is not so much a benign concession as it is the necessity of facing a danger.

PRUDENTIA: Furthermore, the state school gains an unprecedented diffusion when the socialist countries – those that claimed to be the embodiment of the 'dictatorship of the proletariat' – made the generalisation of the state school one of the key points of their governments' programmes.

PARLOMURS: The Cold War gives its contribution too: the competition between the two main systems, capitalism and socialism, didn't happen only on the military front. It entailed a 'civil' competition, for instance, precisely on the issue of the state school system. Without the Cold War the enormous development of the American univerisity wouldn't have happened. The American university has achieved global supremacy only since the fifties, pushed by competition with USSR.

DIORTHOS: Excuse me, I would like to go back to an issue we previously discussed. Let's go back to the question of unity in the general space of knowledge. The *Ecoles centrales* invented the system based on courses freely chosen by students, and by doing so acknowledged the inadequacy of a unitary space for the modern episteme in the first place. But then, doesn't the state school have to face this problem?

PRUDENTIA: Perhaps it is no accident that the system of the 'school class' has been back in full force since then.

PARLOMURS: Let's try to orient ourselves through some Foucauldian mapping. At the beginning of the twentieth century Durkheim describes a unified picture of knowledge, and on this basis he outlines programmes for the secondary school with great foresight. In his writings one can find the best of what it could have been, and even more. For instance, Durkheim wanted to include anthropology in the secondary school programme, he emphasised that the modern disciplines cannot ignore the problem of the unconscious, the 'obscure conscience' as he called it. However, there is a fundamental element that allows him to affirm the establishment of a general unity of modern knowledge. Durkheim talks from the perspective of the recent academic acknowledgement of the 'human sciences', whose existence he theorises as an independent form of knowledge, not only as integrated into a new scientific order but also as integrating factors.

DIORTHOS: Of course, he promotes sociology as a science.

PARLOMURS: He also promotes the scientific independence of psychology; he researches in anthropology, history, even into the history of educational inventions, such as in *L'évolution pédagogique en France*. That is a posthumous title by the way, which poorly defines the spirit of the work, in which there is not after all much evolution.

PRUDENTIA: He could have named it *Les inventions pédagogiques en France*.

PARLOMURS: That would have been the right title. I think that the perspective of *Les mots et les choses* helps us better examine the moment at which Durkheim taught that course then titled *L'évolution pédagogique*, around 1905. According to Foucault, it is the human sciences that ultimately give unitary consistency to the modern episteme at the beginning of the twentieth century. Their development happens not only in proximity with the empirical sciences – psychology with biology, sociology with economy, the modern study of literatures with linguistics – but altogether they end up occupying the epistemic 'void' constituted by their relations, or better, non-relations. It is in this empty space that the figure of 'man' is constituted. The human sciences borrow concepts from the empirical sciences and 'translate' them on the plane of representations. 'Man' is the creature endowed with so-called 'mental representations'. He doesn't merely live, speak, work, but he is also capable of 'representing' his life, his labour, his language.

This 'man', therefore, plays a mediating role that makes up for the impasse constitutive of the modern episteme of not being able to be conceived as unitary.

DIORTHOS: Certainly, but here is a big problem. Foucault says that the figure of man is the precarious result of a certain epistemic conjuncture and therefore the human sciences are dangerous mediators in the general space of knowledge.

PARLOMURS: This is a diagnosis that was possible in the mid-sixties, which is fully manifested in the final image of *Les mots et les choses* – the image of 'man' as a footprint on the sand by the sea. Yet at the beginning of the twentieth century Durkheim could outline a systematic vision of secondary education by considering the general space of knowledge as fully unitary. The danger of those 'mediators' hadn't emerged yet; that is, in Foucault's sense, the instability of the unifying functions of the 'human sciences'.

PRUDENTIA: At the beginning of the twentieth century, then, Durkheim was at the crossroads between the first academic acknowledgements of the humanities and the generalisation of the state school.

DIORTHOS: This would explain the *décalage* of a century between the *Ecoles centrales* and the diffusion of the state school.

PARLOMURS: I think that the establishment of the human sciences at the end of the nineteenth century is a condition that allows for the expansion of centralised governments' school systems. An analogous 'delay' happens in the university as well: it is anticipated by Humboldt's ideas on the combination of teaching and research at the beginning of the nineteenth century but only in the eighties does it fully become a state institution, which encompasses the teaching of the whole system of modern knowledge.

DIORTHOS: However, if the nineteenth century wasn't very 'rich in novelties' on the education front, it was rich in political inventions that certainly influenced the establishment of the state school. But how would they be situated in this epistemic picture?

PARLOMURS: On this problem, the Foucauldian cartographies cannot give us much help. According to Foucault, Marx is merely the name for the primacy of a certain tendency of knowledge in a certain moment of the modern episteme. Instead, it is precisely Marxism as a space of political invention that gives a decisive boost to the consistency of a general picture of knowledge.

DIORTHOS: This happens because Marxism constitutes itself as a space of general knowledge, doesn't it? Not so much as an alternative to the modern episteme but rather as broader and better organised?

PARLOMURS: We must make a distinction. The ideological and organisational structure of socialist states had a sort of 'Marxist episteme' as a main stabilising factor. However, Marxism as a space for political invention plays a unifying role, not in relation to the state, but above all because it regards the ensemble of modern disciplines as an indispensable revolutionary resource, in order for the proletariat to 'raise itself theoretically'. For this reason it constitutes a threat, which in turn produces a certain responsive unification in academia. Governments' reaction to the danger of a 'dictatorship of the proletariat', which was even a supporter of modern science, becomes one of the main vectors for the establishment of historical and social sciences in the universities.

DIORTHOS: The first sociologists are very anti-Marxist.

PARLOMURS: Yes. Weber and Durkheim start precisely by refuting Marxist theories on the origins of capitalism and the division of labour.

PRUDENTIA: In turn, sociology is repaid by its exclusion from academic curricula in socialist states, at least up to a certain point. However, setting aside sociology, the socialist university has basically the same courses, and the programmes are compatible with those of other universities. In short, socialism completely inherits the university that was constituted at the end of the nineteenth century.

PARLOMURS: Not only that, but it also strengthens the university. It aims to make of the university one of its elements of maximum prestige.

PRUDENTIA: Lacan observed that the discourse of the university triumphed in socialism.

PARLOMURS: Not only the university, but also the whole state school was the area in which socialism had to show both its scientific and its egalitarian superiority.

DIORHTOS: At this point, however, if the nineteenth-century state school was the same everywhere, why not consider it a state apparatus – perhaps not the dominant but certainly a very prestigious one? What survives of the original political force in the state school? Isn't precisely the state character of the twentieth-century school a great source of corruption in education?

PARLOMURS: Yet that egalitarian political force has been a condition of the prestige of the state school, of its own existence. Whether the state school developed in order to face a threat, or whether it was the result of competition between political systems, it didn't originate from within the evolution of state forms and their apparatuses but it stems from a series of egalitarian inventions. A counterproof? Today the state school has no other choice but to become 'communicative' and 'entertaining' precisely because egalitarian political inventions are weak and dispersed. The birth, development and decline of the modern school are politically marked.

DIORTHOS: I agree but, going back to the criteria previously discussed, if it wasn't only due to the corruption of education, what were the educative experiences capable of opening knowledge to thought and of limiting the governmental tendency of the teacher's role in the twentieth-century state school?

PARLOMURS: There have been plenty of innovative, liberating experiences, both within and outside of the state school in the twentieth century, although we only know a few of them. In spite of all the bureaucracy, the state school could not completely close down the spaces of didactic invention, because of the egalitarian force that determined its existence. These were openings that many teachers managed to exploit in a clever way.

PRUDENTIA: Indeed. All of us remember some particular teachers, even only one, who could open up our perspectives. Not only for the knowledge they could transmit but above all for the acute way of looking at their discipline and at their own role.

PARLOMURS: There have been great collective moments of invention too. At the origins of the school system in China, since the end of the nineteenth century, there has been a succession of very original intellectual and political movements. Already at the end of the nineteenth century there is a great intellectual movement – the 1898 Reformers – that supports the creation of new schools open to modern science. During the 1911 Revolution there is the school reform promoted by Cai Yuanpei, a genius with an anarchic youth, who becomes Minister of Education for a few months. With great political and philosophical arguments, he designs a new school system based on the principle that education needs to be an experience of liberation of the spirit. That was a very short-lived but fundamental experience.

PRUDENTIA: Education in China also had to free itself from a long history of oppression. As the radical students of those days used to say, 'two thousand years of knowledge without thought'. Obviously, even in that context there were so-called limiting exceptions – you can't remain for two thousand years without thinking – but the imperial examination system was a nightmare. Learning by heart the Confucian classics could drive people mad. There is a famous tale by Lu Xun in which one student goes mad by studying the Confucian classics and eventually convinces himself that they are composed of only two characters, endlessly repeated everywhere, *chi ren*, 'eating men'.

DIORTHOS: He saw a deadly drive in Confucian education. It doesn't look as though the Chinese authorities appreciate this view these days.

PRUDENTIA: Lu Xun's ideas are unpalatable to the Marxo-Confucians.

PARLOMURS: Even the whole 'protracted people's war' was an altogether great educational experience. Becoming a soldier in the People's Liberation Army allowed peasants a formidable intellectual opening. There were real schools, too, with original experiments, in the liberated villages. One of their main polemical targets was that of 'circular education': the model in which the teacher teaches what he learnt from his teachers to his students, who in turn will teach that to their future students.

PRUDENTIA: Mao gave regular lessons in military strategy, politics and philosophy in Yan'an.

DIORTHOS: I don't think there have been similar experiences in Europe, especially among the communists, apart from Kruptskaja's attempts after the October Revolution.

PARLOMURS: I think there have been analogous situations at times. Let's not limit our thinking to the traditional idea of the school. For instance, the anti-Nazi Partisans' war in Europe was a period of great experiences of 'self-education'. There is an extraordinary novel by Luigi Meneghello, *The Outlaws*, originally titled *Piccoli maestri* [Little teachers], which passionately tells the story of those twenty-something boys – that is how old the Partisans were, or even younger – who had to completely rethink what they had learnt in the fascist schools about Italianness, Romanness, etc. For this reason, they were the 'little teachers' of themselves.

DIORTHOS: It makes me think of Bloch, who wrote *Apologie de l'histoire* (*The Historian's Craft*) while he was fighting with the Partisans. He wrote it in the name of a new way of teaching history – fighting against the prejudices transmitted by the historiographical didactics of his time. He said that historians had to free themselves from the 'virus of the present'. The war was for him a period of great intellectual tension, both as a Partisan and as a historian and teacher.

PARLOMURS: Here is another good example. Durkheim's course on the history of education in France also sounds like a didactic innovation. Besides, Bloch remembered those lessons with admiration. That was a course addressed to the training of future high-school teachers. Durkheim taught to discern the great educational inventions in the history of France's secondary school, he showed that they were the most diverse – for their duration, contents, methods, and above all because they were 'unprecedented'. That was a good omen for future teachers.

PRUDENTIA: So, there have been great openings in the state school, there were egalitarian factors that limited corruption, as we said. After all, that was one of the main governmental conditions of the twentieth century, which developed thanks to political inventions, but on the other hand also to fight egalitarian threats.

PARLOMURS: Until there were inventions on the horizon, the state school managed to lower inequality. Ultimately, it is precisely thanks to that political egalitarian factor that it kept a certain opening of knowledge to thought.

PRUDENTIA: After all, up to a certain point the Humboldtian ideal reigned – the ideal of a university able to teach a knowledge opened to the unknown, of a professor who teaches people willing to learn but who also paves the way for new kinds of knowledge – paths he can't see himself because he already knows too much.

PARLOMURS: He needs students, precisely because they know less than him. If they hadn't come to him, he would have to go and look for them. Here the hierarchy between the one who knows and the one who doesn't is blurred as well.

DIORTHOS: Ultimately, that is the same ideal of Lyotard in *La condition postmoderne* – professors who train future researchers by teaching them to assess their own ongoing research. One teaches what one knows but also what one 'doesn't know' – something one is not so sure about, something one is still searching after and would like to discuss among one's 'peers'. To form 'peers', he says.

PARLOMURS: The egalitarian dimension opens education to thought. It diminishes the master's discourse, always lurking behind a teacher.

PRUDENTIA: However, the governmental aspect of the state school is somehow the reverse of its egalitarian dimension. Once one could have said that, between these two planes, there was class struggle.

PARLOMURS: Which doesn't say anything about the universal affirmation of the state school, which happened in the twentieth century under every kind of government, whichever 'class' it claimed to 'represent'.

PRUDENTIA: At best one could say that it was jerked around by different tendencies.

DIORTHOS: Althusser theorises the state school as an Ideological State Apparatus traversed by 'class struggle'. Perhaps we could say it was 'jerked around' between different classes?

PARLOMURS: I think this is the least consistent point in the whole text, the symptom of a political and philosophical impasse. At the end he concludes quickly that what counts politically is the class struggle within the ISA. But this is sheer *flatus vocis*, juxtaposed to the rest of the argument.

PRUDENTIA: However, Althusser's text is still a remarkable philosophical effort. From its impasse, others found new ways.

DIORTHOS: The question then is: if it wasn't class struggle, what were the contrasting vectors that 'jerked around' the state school?

PARLOMURS: The state school is determined by an egalitarian condition, as it entails the opening of knowledge to thought, but it is also one of those modern governmental circumstances, and as such it operates not only to contain egalitarian inventions but also to replace them through training in ritual hierarchies. The two faces of the state school are, on the one hand, an egalitarian institution and, on the other, the place of a ritual gathering of masses of young people.

DIORTHOS: Like in the platonic cave.

PARLOMURS: The platonic myth represents normality in the governmental circumstances, and from this perspective the state school is no exception. Instead, the egalitarian condition that constitutes exceptions entails major comings and goings through the cavern without allowing the belief in the reality of shadows to prevail.

PRUDENTIA: Therefore, it is not a matter of one class against the other, but it is about egalitarian exceptions *versus* ritual normality. Today normality reigns because egalitarian political inventions are weak.

PARLOMURS: However, this normality is not just the usual normality; instead it has contemporary characteristics, it emerges as a reaction to something new, to the ensemble of the previous political inventions, and to their effects in education.

DIORTHOS: That ensemble of inventions was communism.

PARLOMURS: Communism was the name of the general horizon of the egalitarian invention.

DIORTHOS: However, communism was also the name of the lasting governments in the twentieth century.

PRUDENTIA: Some of those governments are still quite sprightly.

DIORTHOS: Yet the majority collapsed in the eighties.

PARLOMURS: That was the result of a crisis that dated back to the sixties, which had already started in the second half of the fifties.

PRUDENTIA: The crisis of the socialist states coincides with the crisis of the state school.

PARLOMURS: The socialist version of the state school claimed to be the best possible one. Here too, one needs to think back to the sixties in order to grasp its decline.

DIORTHOS: Does the impasse of the socialist state school start in the sixties?

PARLOMURS: Yes, but at the origins of this impasse there is a series of political inventions that deeply impacted the socialist state school. During the Cultural Revolution there were many experiments in the field of education – all were widespread and very controversial.

DIORTHOS: But they were stopped fairly soon.

PARLOMURS: It needs to be said that many of those experiments emerged and developed outside, or at the margins of, the state school.

Their effective influence on the transformations of the state school was met with stubborn resistance, precisely because the socialist school presented itself as the *ne plus ultra* of egalitarian education. The opening of self-managed public schools in the countryside and of 'workers' universities' in the factories, which Mao greatly supported, was seen, from the 'historical' perspective of the state school, as . . .

PRUDENTIA: 'Historical?' We should ask Demoval.

PARLOMURS: Historically, precisely, those experimental schools were at best tolerated as complementary, as a rough remedy that was useful in those areas that the state system couldn't reach. But at the origin of those experiments there was the question of the egalitarian value of the socialist school beyond its own state supremacy. On the contrary, its own bureaucratism was a recurring target, and that in turn caused those experiments to gain little credibility. And what was one of the main conflicting issues? Exams.

PRUDENTIA: Well, in imperial China exams were a sort of religious cultism.

DIORTHOS: Evaluation, then.

PARLOMURS: Well, yes. There were heightened disputes for and against exams. On the one hand, they were abolished because they were considered only disciplinary tools, completely unfit for egalitarian experiments; on the other hand, without regularly approved standard assessments, the Ministry of Education was reluctant to give them the status of proper schools. At the origin of the opening of new schools there was a strong will to experiment with new forms of education that insisted on self-assessment and even questioned the normality of the state school.

PRUDENTIA: The socialist school aimed to be the perfect balance between state norm and egalitarian exception.

PARLOMURS: That is what socialism as a whole aimed to be. And the state school had to be a major evidence of that.

DIORTHOS: However, the Cultural Revolution starts in universities and in schools.

PARLOMURS: In 1966 what emerges in education is a diffuse will to create politically independent forms of organisation. For a couple of years there are thousands of them, everywhere, that are independent not only of the scholastic organisation but also of the whole structure of the class party.

PRUDENTIA: Actually, the questioning of the political value of the class party begins with the Sino-Soviet dispute, although that looks like a dispute about socialist orthodoxy.

PARLOMURS: Certainly, the texts criticising the Soviet Communist Party already impacted the political formation of the 'Red Guards'. In truth, the Cultural Revolution also has some kind of preamble in the historiographical field – an initial dispute on the political value of a certain historical drama. The relationship between history and politics had been debated for the whole decade.

DIORTHOS: Obviously, from a Marxist perspective.

PARLOMURS: Yes, but with issues that impacted the thorniest questions in the whole history of China.

PRUDENTIA: Also, global modern politics. From the dispute with the Soviet Union up until the end of the Cultural Revolution, for two decades the key problem of all the attempts at political experimentation in China was the issue of the assessment of the history of socialism, or 'the historical experience of the dictatorship of the proletariat'.

PARLOMURS: Ultimately, the very concept of the 'dictatorship of the proletariat' went through great mass movements and many original political experiments. The problems they faced not only concerned the form of government but also the organisation of the whole cultural space that revolved around that concept.

DIORTHOS: As a matter of fact, the 'dictatorship of the proletariat' was also a very structured conceptual space.

PRUDENTIA: The 'class party' worked as 'ideology and organisation'.

PARLOMURS: The Cultural Revolution was indeed extremely 'cultural'. It is remarkable that it had a historiographical dispute as a 'prologue' and that the mass movements started in schools and universities immediately afterwards. In truth, that dispute never reached a conclusion. On the contrary, it revealed that the whole picture of the relationship between history and politics in socialism was precarious and ambiguous.

DIORTHOS: Where was the ambiguity?

PARLOMURS: In the 'class party', specifically in its promise of being the historically most advanced form of government, which contained every possible egalitarian invention. The Cultural Revolution demonstrates experimentally that the 'class party' – that is, the kernel of the 'dictatorship of the proletariat' – is essentially a variation of the modern government and as such it has no intrinsic inclinations towards political invention.

PRUDENTIA: In 1965 the Chinese socialist school was as disciplined as a Jesuit College: an individualised and capillary control of students' behaviours. The autobiography of Rae Yang – a Chinese writer who attended one of the most prestigious high schools in Beijing in the sixties, the elite '101 Middle School' – is a case in point . . .

DIORTHOS: Did they call Beijing's schools by number?

PRUDENTIA: 101 meant that, if 100 is the maximum score, they had to reach beyond that. Endless competition.

PARLOMURS: Democratic evaluation!

PRUDENTIA: The students had a sort of personal 'spiritual guide'. The professor in 'political knowledge' required each student to confide the 'third level' of conscience: the first level couldn't be made public, the second couldn't be shared even with friends, the third couldn't be told even to oneself.

DIORTHOS: Perhaps that obsessive control also explains some of the subsequent anarchism of the Red Guards.

PARLOMURS: In part it does, but that wasn't the only reason. Nevertheless, in the middle of the sixties, that disciplinary obsession was also the symptom of an acute difficulty in keeping everything together on the basis of a certain organisation of the transmission of knowledge.

DIORTHOS: How?

PARLOMURS: The socialist school wasn't only a disciplinary *dispositif*. Its pride was to teach the whole of modern knowledge, organised in a more compact and unitary way than the 'capitalist' school, and to be inspired by egalitarian tendencies.

PRUDENTIA: Equality as in: 'all men are equal before the votes', as the Red Guards said later.

PARLOMURS: Sure, but even in the case of China, what kept together the socialist school was the pride of having an even more compact didactic organisation . . .

PRUDENTIA: . . . that was founded on the superiority of a general unity of knowledge embodied in the 'class party'.

DIORTHOS: That the Cultural Revolution started in universities and schools is usually explained by the fact that those students were naïve teens bewitched by the cult of Mao.

PARLOMURS: One needs to be an unwavering Weberian to maintain that that storm was the result of 'charisma'. The fact that the political crisis – which eventually marks the beginning of all the other Communist Parties – was so strongly felt in universities and in schools depends precisely on the unifying role of the 'class party' even in the cultural and scholastic spheres. When its egalitarian value is questioned, when the 'class party' is subjected to mass experimentation – that is the meaning of 'bombard the headquarters' – the 'epistemic' unity of socialism disappears.

DIORTHOS: Therefore the crisis of the socialist state school is a manifestation of the crisis of the class party?

PARLOMURS: This question opens up a whole new long dialogue.

DIORTHOS: So, is the epistemic and political crisis of the socialist school at the origin of the crisis of the state school in general?

PRUDENTIA: Is it there that the modern university discourse jams?

PARLOMURS: That's another immense topic. We should get back to this discussion when we have more time. The sun is already too high in the sky and there isn't enough shadow on this hill. We should meet again.

DIORTHOS: Let's walk towards that fresh forest. It looks as if it is time for me to go back to the boat. Would you like to come with me and keep talking as we walk?

PRUDENTIA: With pleasure.

PARLOMURS: Of course, let's go.

(*As they are about to leave, Demoval walks in visibly annoyed.*)

DIORTHOS: President Demoval, we weren't expecting you here. What is going on?

DEMOVAL (*looking troubled*) Nothing . . . Nothing.

PARLOMURS: But didn't you dissolve the commission? We kept working without you nonetheless.

DEMOVAL: You did well! I came here to conclude the meeting.

PARLOMURS: Actually, we just finished.

PRUDENTIA: Excuse me, Demoval, do you mean that our commission was restored *ex officio*? Was it still on the basis of your personal approach or was that decided (*points the finger towards the sky*) 'upstairs'? Tell us, all our cognitive abilities are faltering.

DEMOVAL: I ended in a trap, that's what happened. The Department Committee eventually approved another project, basically identical to mine, copied from mine from start to finish, only they called them Local Units of Production and EduInfoTainment, LUPEIT, which sounds very bad. And anyway, apart from the fact that LoBEIT sounded great, they are identical to the local businesses that I proposed.

PARLOMURS: This is incredible – a fox like you, letting the project be stolen from under your nose. But hasn't the project been approved *motu proprio* by the minister?

DEMOVAL: (*irritated*) That was a conspiracy against me, against my party 'Us for Communicative Democracy'. We have always been fair to the New Tribunate, and all of a sudden we have suffered a schism. This was a conspiracy plotted at the last minute by a maximalist current, which became a parliamentary group and managed to put their men in the committee.

PRUDENTIA: What is the name of the splinter group?

DEMOVAL: They are called Democratic Communication.

PRUDENTIA: I see, that is a very subtle cut-off. Do you think it is a breakdown beyond repair?

DEMOVAL: They got their project approved by one vote only – you see? – one bloody vote! Their project was exactly the same as mine, they even used my acronym EIT.

PRUDENTIA: How come someone like you didn't manage to stop the split and react to this despicable plagiarism?

DEMOVAL: They even asked me to move to the new group, assuring me of my project's approval, but I refused.

PRUDENTIA: Good on you, that's appropriate.

DEMOVAL: The minister called me in person to beg me to stay with the party, saying that everything was under control and swearing that if I didn't move to Democratic Communication my project would be approved for sure.

PRUDENTIA: Well, you decided to emphasise democracy in the name of your party. Perhaps they are more up to date with the times?

DEMOVAL: What does that have to do with it? The votes of the committee are what count. If I had moved to Communication my project would have won by a margin of three votes. One was their vote, one would have been mine, and one vote that I would have taken away from Democracy. You see, a margin of three votes counts a lot in evaluation scores.

PRUDENTIA: Your moral rectitude counts too, don't be so upset.

DEMOVAL: The evaluation counts more. And I am here precisely to conclude the work of our commission and to allocate the scores to each of you.

PARLOMURS: But you didn't hear anything of what we have been discussing. How can you assess our performance?

DEMOVAL: Let's cut the procedure short. How long did each of you speak?

PRUDENTIA: We didn't time each intervention.

DEMOVAL: OK, so who spoke more and who spoke less?

PRUDENTIA: I think Parlomurs spoke quite a bit.

DEMOVAL: I thought so.

PRUDENTIA: Diorthos and I spoke less than him, but more or less the same.

DEMOVAL: Prudentia, you certainly spoke more than the international commissary, I know you. Therefore, the score is very straightforward:

the one who spoke the most wasted time in useless ideological chatter, therefore he gets 0. You Prudentia get 1. Diorthos 2.

PRUDENTIA: I can't believe it! Parlomurs, I beat you one–nil.

PARLOMURS: But I beat you in forward-looking cognitive abilities.

DIORTHOS: Well, that was a very precise forecast. Demoval is back, and in full force.

PARLOMURS: (*folds his hands as for prayer*) *Dixi et salvavi animam meam.*

DEMOVAL: (*looking worried, he tries in vain to answer a call from his phone*) That's him, or his secretary . . . This is an important call, but there is no reception here. (*moves around looking for the right spot*)

DIORTHOS: I think we can go now. I'd better get to the boat that will take me back to Crete.

PARLOMURS: That is a long journey, Diorthos, hopefully we will see you again.

DIORTHOS: I hope so too.

PRUDENTIA: Let's go, we will walk you to the harbour. We can let Demoval finish filling in his register with the scores.

(*Demoval manages to answer the call while the three teachers walk away slowly.*)

DEMOVAL: Hello, Mr Minister . . . Yes, I am here, I came back to see the commission, we concluded the survey and assigned the scores. Anyway, as for today's accident, look, I am truly disappointed, after so much loyalty and so many reassurances . . . (*listens carefully*) A bump in the road? Really? I see . . . So you are saying that the game is still open? Really? Well, I am glad to hear that . . . A new parliamentary group? Excellent. (*listens visibly relieved*) Sure, the name sounds perfect: Valuation and Communication! We will reach a historical milestone! Count me in, I will be at the department immediately. But no tricks this time!

8 When Shall We Go . . . ?

Judith Balso
Translated from the French by Robert Boncardo

It is not my intention here to write from the perspective of some sort of reform or transformation of the existing school, nor to comment on what should be subtracted from it or added to it. My objective is to try to think the creation of 'something else', of its absolute necessity, and to indicate what the first lineaments of this 'something else' could be. At each stage I will justify this commitment through my own analysis of what, today, the school institution as a whole is, what it has become, in particular in a country such as France.

1

In the 1960s, teaching was the object of an extremely extensive mass critique, both in the West, where the student youth did serious damage to it, and in the course of the Cultural Revolution in China, where the separation between intellectual labour and manual labour was at the heart of immense discussions and attempts at transformation, as much in the factories and among workers as in the universities. The ruin of the Western teaching apparatus resulted above all from this uprising of the youth against a figure of knowledge [*connaissance*] that it judged to be cut off from life and from the real, and founded more on institutional authority than on the competence of those who were baptised 'mandarins' in '68. This challenge to a knowledge [*savoir*] identified as being largely inert, arid and dead was in part related – in a more or less conscious manner according to the country and situation – to the revolt of a fraction of Chinese workers against the equally inert and fixed character of the relations of production in their factories, even though the country and the state declared themselves to be socialist.

Their failure to durably transform the factories in this regard has weighed heavily ever since on the labour of workers and on labour in general – a failure whose consequences affect not only the labour conditions of workers, but also the ensemble of teaching and educational apparatuses. In terms of work, it has meant a progressive destruction of the limitations imposed upon the augmentation of labour time; an almost generalised destruction of the limitations imposed upon reductions in wages; a fanatical use of the introduction on a global scale of competition between working fractions of the population; and a systematic dislocation, under the constant pressure of employers' associations, of all the legislative and juridical apparatuses for the protection of salaried employees. In terms of teaching, it has meant a refusal to treat the educational apparatuses as being open to a future of thought and invention; a presentation of knowledges [*savoirs*] as a finite stock of knowledges [*connaissances*] whose renewal is not seriously on the agenda; a transformation of educational institutions into places for the repetition and transmission of dominant opinions; and the identification, from the youngest age, of children and young people who do not conform to this institution, with various kinds of coercion and repression directed against them.

Also in the 1970s, Althusser elaborated a theory of 'Ideological State Apparatuses'. The objective of this theory was to understand the way in which the 'relations of production' – that is, the general consent given to wage labour and to the entire social organisation that flows from it – were reproduced, alongside the means of production themselves (the machines) and productive forces (the workers). Althusser concluded from his researches that the school – and in this function it was the successor to the Church – had unquestionably become the most powerful ideological state apparatus.[1]

It is precisely this that concerns me today: how do the relations of production (that is, the organisation by the wage system of the division of labour) and, even more importantly, the current state of subjective relations to this division of labour impact upon the very nature of the school? I would like to recall here a crucial statement from *Capital*: '*capital is not a thing, but a social relation between persons* which is mediated through things'.[2] That capitalism is first of all this – a relation instituted by wage labour between the ensemble of people – is, in effect, a truth that has almost been lost sight of today, almost forgotten, and replaced by the idea – which is false – that capitalism can be identified above all by its financial power. '[T]he means of production and subsistence, while they remain the property of the immediate producer, are not capital. They only become capital under circumstances in which they serve at the same time as means of exploitation of, and domination over, the worker.'[3] For it is then that 'the workers are changed into proletarians, and *their means of labour into capital*'.[4] Contra what is drummed into us each and every day, capital is not, therefore, the money held by the banks, the financial profits of stock market speculation, nor is it even the owners of industry. It is *the conditions and relations of labour, that is, of wage labour*, insofar as these are the conditions of the immense majority of the populations of all countries.

It is equally forgotten that Marx's principal adversary is political economy as a homogeneous science for the bourgeoisie: *Capital* nevertheless clearly presents itself as a *critique of political economy*, and in no way as a book of alternative political economy. For Marx, it is a matter of destroying, point by point, the foundations of political economy as a proposition of thought about the world, and in no way a matter of replacing it by another political economy. It is necessary to recall these things in order to measure to what extent 'Marxism' subsequently sank (today included) into an economism, an economic determinism that is entirely foreign to Marx's vision. For it is from inside this economism that the category of 'capital' itself was disfigured and corrupted.

At the heart of wage labour, Marx certainly established the existence of the production of surplus value, which alone sustains social wealth. But next to this theory of exploitation, what Marx identifies as being at the heart of this social relation between persons that constitutes capital is the division of labour. This point regarding the division of labour is crucial: the division of labour is the root of all inequalities. Rimbaud did not forget this, writing in 1873: 'I abominate all trades. Craftsmen and workers, all of them serfs to a man, and despicable. The hand that guides the pen is just as good as the hand that guides the plough – What a century made hands! – I'll never get my hand in. Besides, there's no end to "service".'[5]

Marx takes great care in describing the gigantic process by which this division of labour is established, from the accumulation and concentration of instruments and of workers that precedes and makes possible the development of the division of labour inside the workshop, up to the general division of labour, which (as he writes as early as the middle of the nineteenth century) has assumed 'such dimensions that large-scale industry, detached from the national soil, depends entirely on the world market, on international exchange, on an international division of labour'.[6] '[T]he first big division of labour', he also points out in this book, is 'the separation of the towns from the country'[7] – with its twofold impact: 'Capitalist production, therefore, develops technology, and the combining together of various processes into a social whole, by sapping the original sources of all wealth – the soil and the labourer.'[8] Contemporary environmentalism would regenerate itself if it linked a concern for the exhaustion of the labourer with its concern for the exhaustion of the earth.

Moreover, there can be no wage labour, and not even unskilled labour, without a minimum of training for the men and women who will have to accomplish this labour. This is why this minimal training (reading, writing, counting, access to some elementary techniques and knowledges) is an obligatory component of modern educational apparatuses. There is nothing surprising, then, in the fact that the collapse of blue-collar work in Europe – accompanied by the generalised development of a new figure of the worker who has everywhere become the 'worker of the world' – has had major repercussions on the educational system of all countries.

At the same time, the absence of any consideration for the work of labourers [*le travail ouvrier*], the confinement of manual labour in its own sphere, the absence of any thought of its singularity, including in the field of thought itself, in turn has had devastating effects on the possible contemporary figures of intellectual labour.

2

The demographers Jean-Joseph Boillot and Stanislas Dembinski have convincingly established that there exists a close relation between the appearance in a country of a large population of young people entering the labour market, their degree of education, and the possibility of a leap in the local development of an economy. This relation, which they identify under the category of a 'window of demographic opportunity', describes situations in which there exist, in large numbers within a population, 'more active young people who are better educated, innovative, and consume more, particularly in order to establish their family, but who save more and more as they approach the second half of their professional lives (after 40/45 years)'.[9]

Between 1980 and 2010, the working-age population in China went from being more than half to more than two-thirds of the Chinese population. At the same time, the China of Deng Xiaoping benefited from the results of Maoist policies with respect to the education and literacy of its huge, poor, peasant population, as well as from a rapid fall in the mortality rate, which flowed from 'a social and health policy among the most advanced in the world' in this same historical period. Contemporary Chinese capitalism draws relentlessly on this youth (including the female youth) who know how to read, write and count – an enormous proletariat that it gathers together in gigantic factories, industrial concentrations of a size without precedent, and such as the world has never before known.

India presents a very heterogeneous profile, with enormous, persistent poverty in the Northern States – an extreme poverty, accompanied by a very low degree of education. However, at the level of India as a whole, the working-age population represented 60 per cent of the population in 2005, and the growth of this percentage is expected to continue up until 2035. Moreover, India compensates for the weakness of early education among the large masses of its population by the extreme attention it accords to higher education. In this way, it has available to it an active and competitive youth in the domains of scientific research and technological innovation.

Conversely, African countries have privileged primary and secondary education, while higher education remains weak. It is no less the case that, in the period 2000–2030, young Africans between 15 and 24 years of age will represent almost four-fifths of the new arrivals at the global level in this age bracket, and the constant effort provided by the most impoverished of the current generation in the instruction of their children allows us to predict that, in just fifteen years, the African continent will have available to it an enormous human potential in productive capacity. We can even predict that, in 2050, Africa will surpass on its own all of the other zones of the world 'with a stock of human capital superior to ten billion years of study' – that is, three times that predicted for the United States in the same period.

From the third decade of the twenty-first century, 'the world', the authors of *Chindiafrique* predict, 'will have to manage the conjugation of three windows of demographic opportunity of an exceptional scale'.[10] In these three regions, the total number of 15–34 year olds will in effect rise to 700 million (as opposed to 120 million in Western countries), with this number representing half of the 'educated human capital' in the world. I hypothesise that it is at the level of these gigantic phenomena – where the centre of global gravity shifts from old Europe to China, India and Africa – that the question of the school, of new places and institutions of teaching, will reconstitute itself according to parameters that are today largely unpredictable, just as the future of a world in which the conditions for general war incessantly multiply – even in this short timeframe – is unpredictable.

In the immediate future – between the blow struck against all emancipation of work with respect to wage labour by the failure of the Chinese Cultural Revolution; the withering away of the ensemble of apparatuses of education, begun at the end of the 1960s with the critique of the student and youth revolts; a moribund educational system, which is openly inefficacious yet ever more aggressive and repressive – I can see nothing to save in any of this. It is already necessary to depart elsewhere, to think elsewhere, and to invent elsewhere. Such is, in my view, the context within which the question of the school must be examined and rethought from now. I note that whoever attempts to act, and succeeds in acting, from inside these existing apparatuses of teaching, is already departing from elsewhere in order to do so – whether they know it or not. The objective of this text is also, therefore, to help consolidate this 'elsewhere'. On this point, I resolutely adopt what I will call 'the Robin Blaser method', such as he defines it in these lines extracted from a seminar he held in Vancouver in the 1970s: 'it is an elsewhere from future past, it is not now, it is elsewhere. Where it is I don't know, but it is that place where I am now, I am elsewhere. And then my past and my future are the things I must honour . . . but that zero is elsewhere.'[11]

3

I think moreover that it is essential to meditate on the fact – which is proven – that only great emancipatory sequences in thought have been able to give birth to new figures of the school and to render obsolete the preceding obscurantist apparatuses. I will therefore have recourse here to history: on the one hand to refute all continuity in the processes by which teaching has been organised; and on the other hand to enlarge our capacities for invention, which are always limited by a sort of dictatorship of existing forms, by an excessive influence of the present and of the recent past. From the French Revolution, I will retain not so much the decisions taken – which were necessarily limited by reason of the brevity of the political sequence – as the scope and depth of the debates which surrounded the project of creating a teaching capable of breaking with the weight of traditions, the influence of the Church and of unequal social origins, and the possible negative role of the family. Everything was to be re-examined and re-thought.

From the vast political debates that took place up until 1795, there resulted a very original apparatus of *Ecoles centrales*, one for each *département*, in which all of the new sciences were to be taught and where the student could compose for himself the body of lessons that he would follow. Between 1795 and 1802, a hundred of these schools intended to ensure secondary teaching across the entirety of the territory had been opened. Not only did the freedom of the curriculum in the *Ecoles centrales* indicate the will to place the student at the heart of questions of knowledge [*connaissance*] – it was he who had to define how to educate himself in accordance with what he intended to study – but it also announced that he who does not yet know is as important in the elaboration of knowledges [*savoirs*] as he who already knows [*celui qui est déjà savant*]. Teaching must give to he who does not yet know the future of thought.

In the notes that make up his *Projet d'institutions*, which was interrupted by his death, Saint-Just brings together a certain number of ideas and principles drawn from these debates in the Convention with a view to creating new bodies necessary for the safeguarding and pursuit of the Revolution. I will include here a few extracts from these notes, grouped together by themes, to allow us to measure what was being sought and what was not accomplished:

'Children are neither to be caressed nor struck. They are taught the good. They are left to nature.'
'Whoever strikes a child is banished.'
'They are dressed in fabrics in all seasons.'
'They sleep for eight hours.'
'They live on bread, vegetables, dairy and water.'
'Children will be raised in a love of silence and of terseness and in a contempt for rhetoricians.'

We see here the inspiration of Rousseau, the significant influence of *Emile* – in the frugality and the refusal of luxury, in a new vision of children, in whom it is necessary for a love of the good to be constituted, and whom it is necessary to render insensible to the eloquence of demagogues.

'There are schools for children from five to ten years of age. They are in the countryside. There is one in each department and each district.'
'From five until ten years of age children learn to read, to write, to swim.'

Here, then, was the vast project to cover France with a network of primary schools, created by the state, in order to ensure instruction for all children, without exception, whatever their social origins or the resources of their parents. It would not be realised by the Convention, and even less so by Napoleon, who preferred to return, with the apparatus of the high schools and the imperial university, to a military organisation of an education destined for an elite.

'There are schools for children from ten to sixteen. There is one in each department and each district.'
'The education of children from ten to sixteen is military and agricultural.'
'They are distributed into companies. They learn the manouevres of the infantry and of the cavalry. They learn languages. They are distributed to the farmers at harvest time. They never return to their parents before the age of twenty-one.'

The principle proposed here is that primary, basic teaching be immediately followed by the participation of adolescent children in agricultural labour and in the defence of the revolutionary Republic: they are sent to the countryside at harvest time; they are taught the basic exercises of soldiers at the same time as they discover languages (and no longer only French). Familial influence should be limited in the course of these years, which are so important in the formation of a self-image in adolescents. Likewise, the negative effects of clothing, whose differences reflect social inequalities, would be reduced through the following measures:

'All children will have until the age of sixteen the same dress. From sixteen to twenty-one, the dress of the worker. From twenty-one to twenty-five, that of the soldier, if they are not magistrates.'

Beyond the age of 16, what interests me is the clear separation that is proposed between the time at school and the time of the effective apprenticeship of work. Between 16 and 21 years of age, in fact, what is at stake is for everyone to learn a trade and to carry it out effectively:

'From sixteen to twenty-one, the children enter into the arts [= technical apprenticeships].'
'From sixteen to twenty-one, all of the youth are required to learn a profession

and to carry it out in his father's place, or to work in the factories or on ships, whether they are married or not.'
'The farmers, the manufacturers, the artisans, the merchants are teachers.'

This idea that the teachers should be the very same people who carry out the trades in which the young people are to be trained would be taken up a century later by the Paris Commune. This is enough to indicate that it, too, had not been put into practice in the intervening period.

It is worth recalling that the majority of the great transformations in teaching that are commonly attributed in France to the regime of the Third Republic – in particular free, secular and compulsory education, which our governments delight in using as a war machine against an entire segment of the population – were inventions brought about by the Paris Commune, which was massacred by those very same 'republicans' who are so extolled by the political class today. In the sixty days during which it lasted, the Commune in effect found the means for decreeing that teaching be free, secular and compulsory for all children from six to fifteen years of age. It decided on the creation of schools for girls, and invented the first professional schools, where workers were called upon to teach. Defying the powers of order, family, religion and private property, which were united in the French and Prussian armies it faced, the Commune wanted teaching to be based on scientific and experimental methods and for it to draw on the observation of the real, that is, on the ensemble of physical, intellectual and moral facts. It also affirmed that each person had to be able to pass from the classroom to labour, and that it was necessary to reduce the gulf between intellectual labour and manual labour: 'The wielder of a tool must be able to write a book [. . .] without for all that thinking themselves obliged to abandon the vice or the workbench. The artisan must be able to rest from his work through the culture of arts, of letters or of sciences, without for all that ceasing to be a producer.'

The emergence of the university in the Middle Ages interests me here for a different reason. At root, we can perceive the situation in which it arose as being very close to our own. The movement that gave birth to it was above all an intellectual movement, a profound change in the parameters of intellectuality. In effect, at its origin the university is structured on the basis of a few masters around whom are grouped people of all ages and all origins, drawn by the development of thoughts that are courageously liberating themselves from the weight of tradition and calling for a rejection of all authority founded on belief. Bernard de Chartres states this magnificently: 'I refuse to follow as a captive the chain of a fabulating authority.' Abélard attracts crowds through his will to found his arguments and demonstrations solely on the dialectical capacity of thought. A powerful movement of intellectual emancipation unfolds around these new convictions, which are summed up perfectly by Gilbert de Tournai: 'We will never find the truth if we content ourselves with what has already been found.' And: 'truth is open to all, it has not yet been possessed in its entirety'.

These declarations and this ardour to know are obviously opposed to the confinement of thought in the restricted orbit of faith and of revelation transmitted by the Church; but they also go hand-in-hand with the considerable enlargement of the contents and processes of teaching. Moreover, the places of teaching are not fixed, for this nascent university does not possess any of its own buildings: the lessons take place in churches, convents, public squares. The masters themselves go from city to city, with the best among them being authorised to teach wherever they find themselves. Another decisive trait is the unity affirmed between artisans and peasants, artists and intellectuals. On this basis, new disciplines – physics, mechanics, economics and dialectics – come to be added to older disciplines – grammar, rhetoric, arithmetic, music, geometry and astronomy. Their reunion under the name of Liberal Arts signifies that what is at stake is the elaboration of a general thought of what it is to 'do' [*faire*], and underscores that thinking and doing should not be separated.

When this intellectual current was exhausted, the nature of universities was profoundly transformed. In the fourteenth century, states, popes and kings multiplied the creation of places for universities, but the creators and thinkers deserted them. Rabelais mocks the 'Sorbonagres' and the 'Sorbonicoles', figures who incarnate the ossification of knowledges [*savoirs*] and the domination of false knowledges [*connaissances*]. Villon or Montaigne can only exist outside of these spaces that have been reconquered by tradition and by the absence of all freedom and invention. Now, have we not once again found ourselves the prey of the Sorbonagres and the Sorbonicoles? And without being able to believe again that one day that there will be realised Wallace Stevens's otherwise ironic and sceptical wish, from his great poem 'Notes Toward a Supreme Fiction': 'They will get it straight one day at the Sorbonne.'

These elements of history bring out a number of issues that to my mind are encouraging with respect to the situation in which we find ourselves: first of all, it is always from great intellectual and political innovations that a new apparatus of teaching emerges. We must therefore interrogate where the contemporary novelties in this double register are to be found and to draw some consequences from them. Then, when an established form enters into crisis and withers, it is always a matter of enlarging once again the field of teaching: to expand access to it by reducing the gulf separating manual labour from intellectual labour, but also girls from boys, men from women; to expand its contents by incorporating into it the latest sciences and the latest arts which have arisen; and even more so to open up again and to subordinate the apparatus of what is known to what is unknown, and to discover, as Mao clearly says, 'everything that we do not yet know'.

4

What are, today, the major new orientations in thought that could and should be points of attraction for any project of teaching or of schooling? I think, first of all, that we can absolutely not base ourselves on the apparatus of the 'humanities'. These disciplines – biology, economics, sociology, linguistics, literature, academic philosophy – were supposed to constitute a unified vision of humanity, of a 'full' or 'fully human' humanity. Now this figure is completely dead. At the beginning of the twentieth century, humanity without doubt discovered that it is, like the man of Musil, 'without qualities'. 'I carry within me a sign of hollowness', Mandelstam writes. This sign is inscribed in humanity itself, which must today construct itself around this void. An immense freedom and an immense risk.

Alain Badiou suggests, on the basis of an inquiry into politics, the same imperative:

Is it the case that all forms of humanity or of society are not ultimately inhuman, is it not precisely and positively the formless [*l'informe*] that is the form of humanity? It does not go without saying that it is always necessary to make an apology for form. Now, the idea that gregarisation is by itself negative has for its foundation the idea that humanity should present itself as form. But is humanity not rather the incessant movement of the dissolution of its form? Should man not be constantly worked on by the idea that any man, insofar as he is, is strictly equivalent to any other, which is necessarily a principle of the formless [. . .] *Perhaps the essential political gesture is the dissolution, in any case the recomposition, of forms.*[12]

It is extremely strange that, more than a century after the Freudian invention, which displaced the centre of gravity of the knowledge that man could have of himself, psychoanalysis is today at the furthest point from being, not only a knowledge, but also a shared good. But the thought of what a truth is is just as absent or disoriented, despite the distinction established by Heidegger between knowledge and truth – a distinction deepened by Lacan and which is at the heart of the entire apparatus of the thought of Alain Badiou. Now, today, truth is no longer opposed only to opinion, as it was for Plato. The gulf is between the ensemble of what circulates as information/communication and the constitution of stopping points that are places with the capacity to produce truths and thought.

Physics in its most recent developments has also not succeeded in establishing contingency as the absolute figure of the natural world; on the contrary, it cohabits with various obscurantist speculations. The infinite is recused as a dimension immanent to every universe in favour of repetitive refrains to finitude as the only horizon of the human. The tolerance of differences: no society can raise itself up above the lamentable incapacity to affirmatively think multiplicities, ignoring Pasolini's warning: 'it is intolerable to be tolerated'. Hatred, murderous, warlike subjectivities, solicited by states and the most abject political parties, fill the world with their noise, without the terms of any new friendships that would ward off the general descent into war being discernible or audible.

I can only sketch here what should be inscribed in our hearts and should work our hands: void, truth, thought, contingency, infinity, multiplicity, friendship. All future schools must orient themselves on these newly opened paths, of which contemporary humanity has the strongest need in order to grow, if it is not to sink.

5

I would like to develop another notion: all educational institutions, everywhere, and insofar as they belong to the general apparatus of the state, are characterised by being 'double'. They simultaneously ensure, in effect, the functions of the apprenticeship of some knowledges [*savoirs*], and the functions of engagement in the general social apparatus of the division of labour. More precisely, the functions of apprenticeship are commanded by this social apparatus and by the necessity that flows from it to engage in a differentiated way with the youth in this apparatus. The distinction between private and public schooling does not enter into this, for both of them today share the same field and assume the same functions – according, of course, to hierarchies and nuances proper to them.

In France, a periodisation focused on the Haby reforms and the creation by this latter of the *collège unique* allows us to distinguish two successive modes of articulation inside this always double functioning of the school. The school of the Third Republic had for its central task to give the youth of the countryside access to reading, writing, arithmetic and (against *patois*) the French language. It was a matter of making workers and soldiers (who would go on to be capable, guided by non-commissioned officers who were their teachers, of stoically supporting the senseless massacres of the First World War), and also little colonisers, susceptible to implanting themselves in Algeria, Madagascar or Black Africa. (I recall on this occasion that the first great mass world migration was colonial migration, which saw, for example, 40.9 per cent of the total population of the British Isles spread out across the surface of the Earth, and 11.1 per cent of the total population of Europe and Japan. And they brought with them infamous, arrogant contempt, pillage and rape, wars and destruction. The figures with respect to which we dare to name, abjectly, the refugee 'crisis' today represent negligible quantities. This does not stop us from trembling at the idea of welcoming the peaceful and exhausted crowd of the unfortunate that war and hunger chase from their destroyed countries.)

To this end, the school of the Third Republic ensured a quality primary education – the *certificat d'études*, which validated elementary but very real knowledges and capacities. The separation between technical teaching and general teaching was effective from the beginning of secondary studies and created a distinction between children destined to become workers, technicians or employees, and those destined for the tasks of leadership at different levels – those who took up in the countryside the labour of their parents most often stopping their studies at the end of primary school.

Established at the end of the 1970s, the apparatus of the *collège unique* presents itself as having for its objective the delaying of the moment of selection and the 'democratising' of secondary teaching by giving all children the possibility of pursuing their studies in one and the same framework up until the age of 16. According to Haby, the promoter of this reform, it was a matter of reducing the separation between technical teaching and general teaching by giving to all a teaching that would in some sense be polyvalent, that is, as technical and manual as it was classical. In reality, this ambition would be limited to the introduction of a single lesson in 'technology', as inconsistent as it was superficial, and in any case stripped of all educational virtues with respect to the relations between manual labour and intellectual labour; and to the imperative of a week as an intern in a company, which was generally just as void and empty of meaning. By contrast, in the course of the interminable years of *collège*, which are years as heavy as lead, a selection does indeed take place through the more or less overall rejection by the students of what is taught to them. At the end of this, an ever-growing number of students either abandon all schooling and disappear from the school system, or interiorise the fact that their 'personal nullity' predestines them to having no future in higher studies, or even a future worthy of the name.

One can easily conclude that this is a matter of an even more violent mode of selection, under its democratic appearances, than the selection that distributed students, from the outside, according to criteria of class and according to a technical stream or a classical stream, from the end of primary classes. In my view, this is a much more violent mode of selection because the children must interiorise at length that they alone are responsible if they find themselves rejected by the school apparatus. In truth, however, the school system has nothing to do any more with forming and educating young boys and girls, for whom the general social apparatus of work has nothing to offer at the end of it all except massive unemployment or repeated imprisonment for various delinquencies.

We find here again the 'double' character of the school, except that today it is no longer a matter of crossing the acquisition of some knowledge with engagement in an apparatus of labour, but rather of making students interiorise the absence of pseudo-competencies or the incapacity to acquire them as in some sense the 'natural' cause of the massive exclusion of youth from the existing apparatuses of work. In other words, the immense population of people that capitalist apparatuses leave outside all figures of labour would itself be a 'natural' given of the world, tied to the weak personal capacities of these people. But we know, do we not, that capitalism is a great return to nature, that it is itself nothing other than an emanation of human nature in its most profound truth! It remains true that, in this case, the school inevitably transforms itself into a monstrous childcare centre, where masses of young people are persecuted and destroyed subjectively, for reasons that are totally foreign to them.

The doctrine that prevails, in the higher years of secondary school as in the universities, can itself be described as a reinforcement of the double character of the educational institution, to the benefit this time of a pseudo-function of 'professional formation' – to great cries of 'we must educate high school and university students for their future careers'. Now, it is not thus that students are trained for a profession. Listen to the persistent choir of bosses: 'the youth know nothing when they come out of university, or when they obtain their baccalaureate'. And for good reason: these same bosses have always known that, if we want to train people in a profession, it is necessary to make apprentices of them in the places of work or in the schools tied to production, and in no way to make students of them. This, moreover, is what the companies that really need people trained for specific professions do (thus Free, the French telecommunications company, has opened a school of digital programming).

For me, it follows from this analysis of the contemporary school that a school worthy of the name cannot and must not be double. It must be 'simple': that is, it must devote itself to what it claims to teach, and it must teach it equally to all without selecting anybody with respect either to their competences or with a view to professional training. The time of schooling must be a time of formation and of maturation, which permits each person to accede to their own capacity for thought, to discover their own centres of interest, whatever that domain may be, and to discover the world in all of its dimensions. This time must be separated from the question of their profession. This does not mean that the time of school should be cut off from manual labour – quite the contrary. The school must also be a time for the discovery of the singularity and grandeur of manual labour, including what it demands in terms of thought. It is absolutely necessary that manual labour, whatever it may be, be practised and known in its proper intellectual richness. And I would add, that the intellectuality of all labour be reflected on and identified.

6

There exists no school that does not pronounce upon what it is to think, including on what it is to think the world, to think the real. On this point, the contemporary school pronounces that it works on cutting children and young people off from the real, that it renders them incapable of thinking the world otherwise than through the abstruse filter of dominant opinions. A majority of teaching bodies are today in conformity with, rally to, and are subjectively engaged in this aim, and develop not only a fear but sometimes even a hatred of their students – insofar as these latter precisely belong to the real of this world!

It is not by chance that, in France, the educational institution was the site for the exercising of the will to repress or exclude young girls who had courageously decided, by wearing the headscarf, to have recognised their existence as young Muslim women who were born here and were determined to live here without hiding their religious convictions. At the first contact with a real, that of their students, many teachers reacted with denial and with a call for repression, and they were encouraged in this by the government and political parties. After the murders of January 2015, governmental directives were to use 'secularism' [*laïcité*] as a war machine against this very same youth. It is necessary to underscore the extraordinary corruption of the category of 'secularism', which today allows one to use it merely as part of the integrationist and assimilationist policy directed against the minority Muslim population of this country, which is an important component part of its worker and poor populations. At the beginning of the twentieth century, 'secularism' meant the obligation that the state, its administration and its personnel be strictly neutral with respect to religion, in particular in schools – a neutrality that was, moreover, entirely relative: fish, not meat, was served every Friday in the school canteen, and in the high schools there were Catholic chaplaincies in which the catechism was taught. Yet in the end the teaching itself was at least separated from the influence of religion, whatever that religion may have been. Today, 'secularism' has for its sole content no longer the regulation of the state and the personnel of the school, who for their part do not hold back from proffering declarations hostile to Islam, but rather the imposition of silence, opprobrium and discrimination on people of the Muslim religion. Thus, mothers wearing the headscarf are banned from accompanying their children during school trips; women asking to be examined by a female doctor rather than by a man are prohibited access to hospitals; recently, young girls wearing skirts judged to be too long were stigmatised, with the newspapers making quite a story of it. All of this is not only abject, but constitutes the ferment of a subjectivity of war directed at an entire fraction of the population of this country, causing terrible damage to the youth in particular.

In this respect, the contemporary school is not only, as Althusser analysed it, a place that ensures the reproduction of the relations of labour,
but a place that develops the generalised ascendancy of dominant opinions and the incapacity to subtract oneself from them – and does so, if
necessary, by encircling and breaking those who do not submit to it. It
has also become a place of separation: between students, between students and teachers, between teaching and the real.

In my view, from this situation flows, more so than novel disciplines,
something that must orient all new projects of teaching today, namely,
the question of thought, of the conditions of a thought that is a thought
of the real. And this must occur in an apparatus in which the collective
is not a negative pressure, but on the contrary a point of support and
expansion; not a limitation, but the deployment of unprecedented possibilities. Here lies the heart of the difficulty, but also the beauty of the
project. What I can add to these first elements for orientation arises from
a new and recent invention, whose creation and existence I have participated in for three years now – that of the *Ecole pour penser*.

The *Ecole pour penser* is a collective proposition addressed to whomso-
ever wants to be part of it, and which counts everyone in terms of their
capacity for thinking (without distinction of age, and even in fields that
the person does not know). What is at stake in the work undertaken
there is to give each person the possibility of creating for themselves a
new capacity with respect to the world. It is a matter of putting to the
test the possibility of constructing a thought on the basis of the thought
of each person, and to do so by working, not around questions, but
around initial, strong affirmations that are to be worked on, validated or
transformed, in any case expanded. We have verified that it is absolutely
necessary to set out from affirmations, and to carefully choose the initial
affirmation for the following reason: all affirmations always already
belong to thought and sketch out a path in thought – the beginning of
an orientation. On the other hand, to set out from 'questions', or from
themes, leads us inexorably back to knowledge and to the encyclopedia.
The first four workshops thus created named themselves: '*On peut lire les
poètes*', '*Français, françaises, ça n'existe pas*', '*On peut penser la folie en intériorité*',
'*Il faut rencontrer le roman*'.

The ambition of each workshop is considerable. Take the case of
'*Français, françaises, ça n'existe pas*', whose title was, after two years, sup-
plemented by this new declaration: '*Je suis ici, je suis du monde*'. This workshop accomplished an immense trajectory, which I cannot retrace here

in all of its detail, but whose scope can be measured by the three new workshops to which it is in the process of giving birth:

- the implementation of a collective inquiry into work on the basis of our own declarations on the subject;
- the establishment of a place of historical and political study, on the basis of an initial assessment of the 1960s and of the counter-revolutionary turn of the 1980s and of a putting-at-a-distance of the economy, above all of its parameters for the evaluation of the common good;
- refugees, displaced peoples: to declare and to constitute a place of interlocution with them.

Another case, which is different again, is that of the workshop '*On peut penser la folie en intériorité*'. In fact, this workshop was created without anybody having any particular competencies at the beginning, but at the intersection of two points of subjectivisation: the desire of a young female student in psychology to compensate for the absolutely immobilising and obscure, indeed inept, character of the teaching that she received at university, and the conviction of many of us that the mode according to which the mad of today are treated, and the absence of any thought in interiority of madness, is a particularly alarming and barbarous symptom of the world we live in.

On the basis of this, it is clear that we are going to build from top to bottom an apparatus of novel knowledge and thought. Here are a few of the first elements with which we set to work:

- to constitute a collective capacity for reading Freud (including by looking at Zweig's text on what the appearance of psychoanalysis signified for the youth of his time);
- to find our bearings in Lacan's texts, beginning with the great text from *Ecrits I*, 'The Function and Field of Speech and of Language in Psychoanalysis';
- to examine the theses of Canguilhem on the normal and the pathological, and to determine whether Foucault's *History of Madness* is still illuminating today, and on what points;
- to work on the basis of the way in which artists today think the question of madness and the situation of the mad: thus Henry Bauchau's book *L'enfant bleu*, a notebook of relations with a young psychotic, and

the recent film by Wang Bing, *A la folie*, on an internment centre in China;
- to know and to revisit the progressive experiences of the 1960s and 1970s: anti-psychiatry in Italy, the La Borde clinic in France, the asylum according to François Tosquelles during the Spanish Civil War and, later, in France;
- to undertake interviews on the state of psychiatric practices in hospitals today and to examine the apparatus of existing laws;
- to include summaries of experiences (work in CLIS classes – dedicated to so-called 'problematic' children – internships in psychiatric structures, etc.) and their discussion.

Inside this vast programme, each person decides, according to their own will, to engage themselves in the possible, collective creation of a work of unprecedented thought. Subjectivity therefore does not pass through the filter of pedagogy – a register that articulates 'competency' and its transmission. These workshops are in principle trans-generational, trans-national and also 'trans-historical' (in the sense that we also speak and work with the mighty dead). We envisage the possibility of workshops (for example, around cinema) in which children are the principal protagonists, on the condition that the initial affirmation is elaborated among themselves. We would also like to institute a 'nomadism' in this school, and we wish for it to be able to be held in places in which, currently, no work of thought is proposed.

All situations that truly put into play the possibility of collectively constructing a thought depend on people themselves, and in a very concrete fashion. I would like to include here elements of an analysis which emerges from the text of a group of young people, one of whom is one of the co-founders of the school:

Thought can be shared, subjective and concrete, in which it is necessary to have confidence. Confidence in the collective possibilities that it institutes. Confidence in the processes, which are made up of stages and of ruptures, of advances and of impasses, of deployments and redeployments. Determined also by the composition of each workshop in terms of histories, of lives, of multiple experiences.

Thus the workshop '*Français, françaises, ça n'existe pas*' has constituted a place of inquiry on the basis of its own interiority, and in particular on what the youth had to say with respect to the state of the university, and the absence of orientation and of interlocution that reigns there. The work of thought is not totalising; it is above all an open process (which runs counter to the idea of 'results', and of individualism, which is promulgated by the school). Nor does it consist in the transmission of the true and the false, but rather of the capacity to explore an unknown. We make our own Mandelstam's wish (in *De l'interlocuteur*) 'to exchange for good signals with Mars'. For his remark is profound: 'if we address ourselves to the known, we can only express the known'. And, similarly: 'only the real can call the real into existence'.

What is at stake is to make the common, but in no way compromises, emerge. Resistance is therefore not only accepted but welcomed, for all contradiction or discord can be appropriated as part of the work of thought. It is therefore not a question of being good or bad, of being in truth or in falsity, but of understanding how such or such a proposition participates, including as an obstacle, in the elucidation of the orientation of thought, and is susceptible to leading to a new truth. Confidence and patience are capacities that the process of thought creates by itself, if we watch over it scrupulously.

That the contributions of individuals nourish a collective process is easily represented, even if a real mastery of this trajectory is, in fact, rarely at work. But the true challenge is to create a trajectory of thought going from the collective towards the individual, and enlarging the apparatuses of thought of individuals.

It is striking in this respect that even people who are relatively well learned in the contents put to work in a workshop are newly enlightened by the process itself and by the contributions made by each person. The reciprocal thesis has a crucial importance: one can come 'virgin' of all instruction (about poetry, politics, madness, etc.) and constitute for oneself one's own knowledge and thought. This new relation to thought and to the world, subjectively invested and traversed by the condition of the collective, opens up a liberating path outside of opinions. Here resides the great force of what one could call a 'collective subject'. This collective does not count individuals, but brings them into existence; in this, it is opposed to the 'false collectives' that the family, and voting, can be . . . Its existence is under the condition that each person has a place in it, that nobody be left aside, and constantly ensuring that the only authority is that of the thought that is taking form.

One could claim that this school for thinking puts to the test, but also verifies, a hypothesis on the possible superiority of the collective over the individual that Alain Badiou, in his seminar from 2014–15, articulated in these terms:

A point that has been rigorously demonstrated by Cantor is that, in a given multiple, the parts are infinitely more numerous than the elements. This signifies that the resources of the collective offer infinitely more possibilities than the resources of the individual. If you take voting, it is a determination that is founded on the capacity of individuals and of numericity – the number counted is a number of individuals. By contrast, if you take the question of political movements, of mass strikes, of gatherings, the approach is entirely different, because you found yourself on collective resources whose foundation and immanent development immediately creates more numerous possibilities. In other words, *individualism, often taken to be the ultimate enrichment of the evolution of humanity, is an impoverished doctrine; it considerably restrains the possibilities with respect to that which collective groupings are capable of in terms of potentialities.* (emphasis added)[13]

I confirm: all true collective thought emerges from a decisional ensemble and returns to each person as an unprecedented personal capacity. There is much, here, to put one to work – thinking, with Rimbaud once again: 'When shall we go beyond the shores and the mountains to greet the birth of the new work, the new wisdom, the rout of tyrants and demons, the end of superstition, and become the first worshippers to celebrate Christmas on earth!'[14]

Notes

1. L. Althusser, 'Ideology and the State', in *Lenin and Philosophy and Other Essays,* trans. B. Brewster (New York: Monthly Review Press, 2001).
2. K. Marx, *Capital, Volume 1. A Critique of Political Economy* (London: Penguin, 1990), p. 932 (emphasis added).
3. Marx, *Capital,* p. 933.
4. Marx, *Capital,* p. 928 (emphasis added).
5. A. Rimbaud, 'Bad Blood', in *A Season in Hell,* in *Selected Poems and Letters,* trans. J. Harding and J. Sturrock (London: Penguin, 2004), p. 141 (translation modified).
6. K. Marx, *The Poverty of Philosophy: Answer to the 'Philosophy of Poverty' by M. Proudhon* (Moscow: Progress Publishers, 1975), p. 129.
7. Marx, *The Poverty of Philosophy,* p. 119.
8. Marx, *Capital, Volume 1,* p. 638.

9. J.-J. Boillot and S. Dembinski, *Chindiafrique: la Chine, l'Inde et l'Afrique feront le monde de demain* (Paris: Odile Jacob, 2014), p. 36.
10. Boillot and Dembinski, *Chindiafrique*, p. 35.
11. R. Blaser, 'The Metaphysics of Light', talk given in Vancouver, 1974.
12. A. Badiou, *Séminaire sur Heidegger / 18 Novembre* (Paris: Fayard, 1986), pp. 56–7 (emphasis added).
13. See http://www.entretemps.asso.fr/Badiou/seminaire.htm or http://lacommune-aubervilliers.fr/medias/seminaires-alain-badiou (accessed 9 January 2017).
14. Rimbaud, 'Morning', in *A Season in Hell*, p. 183 (translation modified).

Bibliography

Abelhauser, A., Roland, G., and Sauret, M.-J., *La folie évaluation*. Paris: Fayard, 2011.

Agamben, G., *The Kingdom and the Glory: For a Theological Genealogy of Economy and Government*, trans. Lorenzo Chiesa. Stanford: Stanford University Press, 2011.

Alam, M., Haque, M. S., and Siddique, S. F., *Private Higher Education in Bangladesh*, ed. N. V. Varghese. Dhaka: International Institute for Educational Planning, 2007.

Althusser, L., 'Ideology and the State', in *Lenin and Philosophy and Other Essays*, trans. Ben Brewster. New York: Monthly Review Press, 2001.

Anscombe, E., and Geach, P. T., 'Descartes, "Meditations on First Philosophy", Meditation 1', in *Descartes Philosophical Writings*, trans. and ed. E. Anscombe and P. T. Geach. London: Nelson's University Paperbacks, 1954.

Arendt, H., 'The Crisis in Education', in *Between Past and Future*. New York: Penguin, 1977.

— *The Origins of Totalitarianism*. Cleveland: Meridian, 1958.

Aristotle, *The Complete Works of Aristotle*, ed. and trans. J. Barnes. Princeton: Princeton University Press, 1985.

— *Nicomachean Ethics*, trans. D. P. Chase. Mineola, NY: Dover, 1998.

Badiou, A., 'Art and Philosophy', in *Handbook of Inaesthetics*, trans. A. Toscano. Stanford: Stanford University Press, 2004.

— *Being and Event*, trans. O. Feltham. London: Continuum, 2005.

— 'Can Change Be Thought', in *Philosophy and its Conditions*, ed. G. Riera. New York: SUNY Press, 2005, pp. 237–61.

— 'The Democratic Emblem', in *Democracy in What State?*, trans. W. McCuaig. New York: Columbia University Press, 2011.

— *Happiness*, trans. A. J. Bartlett and J. Clemens. London: Bloomsbury, 2017.

— *Logics of Worlds*, trans. A. Toscano. London: Continuum, 2007.

— *Second Manifesto for Philosophy*, trans. L. Burchill. London: Polity, 2011.

— *Séminaire sur Heidegger / 18 Novembre*. Paris: Fayard, 1986.

— *Theory of the Subject*, trans. B. Bosteels. London: Verso, 2011.

Bartlett, A. J., *Badiou and Plato: An Education by Truths*. Edinburgh: Edinburgh University Press, 2011/15.

— 'Refuse Become Subject: The Educational Ethic of Saint Paul', *Badiou Studies*, 3(1) (2014), pp. 194–216.

Bensaïd, D., 'Permanent Scandal', in G. Agamben et al., *Democracy in What State?*. New York: Columbia University Press, 2010, pp. 16–43.

Bergson, H., *Bergson: Key Writings*, ed. K. A. Pearson and J. Mullarkey. London: Continuum, 2002.

— *Creative Evolution*, trans. A. Mitchell. Lanham: University Press of America, 1983.

— *The Creative Mind*, trans. Mabelle L. Andison. Totowa, NJ: Littlefield, Adams and Co., 1965.

— *Laughter: An Essay on the Meaning of the Comic*, trans. Cloudeseley Brereton and Fred Rothwell. Copenhagen; Los Angeles: Green Integer, 1999.

— *Mind-Energy*, trans. H. Wildon Carr. Westport, CT: Greenwood Press, 1975.

— *Oeuvres*. Paris: Presses Universitaires de France, 1959.

Block, F., and Somers, M. R., 'Beyond the Economistic Fallacy: The Holistic Social Science of Karl Polanyi', in Theda Scokpol (ed.), *Vision and Method in Historical Sociology*. Cambridge: Cambridge University Press, 1984.

Bollier, D., and Helfrich, S. (eds), *The Wealth of the Commons: A World beyond Market and State*. Amherst, MA: Levellers Press, 2012.

Bouloumie, A., *Michel Tournier. Le roman mythologique*. Paris: Jose Corti, 1988.

Bourdieu, P., and Passeron, J. C., *The Inheritors: French Students and their Relation to Culture*, trans. R. Nice. Chicago: University of Chicago Press, 1979.

Bowles, S., and Gintis, H., *Schooling in Capitalist America: Educational Reform and the Contradictions of Economic Life*. New York: Basic Books, 1976.

Brandt, R., 'On Restructuring Schools: A Conversation with Fred Newman', *Educational Leadership*, 53(3) (1995), pp. 70–3.

Brecht, B., *Life of Galileo*, trans. John Willett, ed. John Willett and Ralph Manheim. London: Methuen, 1980.

Brown, W., *Undoing the Demos: Neoliberalism's Stealth Revolution*. New York: Zone Books, 2015.

Bulut, E., 'Labour and Totality in Participatory Digital Capitalism', in C. McCarthy, H. Greenhalgh-Spencer and R. Mejia (eds), *New Times:*

Making Sense of Critical/Cultural Theory in a Digital Age. New York: Peter Lang, 2011, pp. 51–69.

Boillot, J. J., and Dembinski, S., *Chindiafrique: la Chine, l'Inde et l'Afrique feront le monde de demain*. Paris: Odile Jacob, 2014.

Caffentzis, G., 'A Critique of Cognitive Capitalism', in M. A. Peters and E. Bulut (eds), *Cognitive Capitalism, Education and Digital Labor*. New York: Peter Lang, 2011, pp. 23–56.

— 'The International Intellectual Property Regime and the Enclosure of African Knowledge', in C. B. Mwaria, S. Federici and J. McLaren (eds), *African Visions*. Westport, CT: Praeger, 2000.

— 'On the Notion of a Crisis of Social Reproduction: A Theoretical Review', in *Letters of Blood and Fire: Work, Machines, and the Crisis of Capitalism*. Oakland: PM Press, 2013, pp. 95–125.

— 'The World Bank's Africa Capacity Building Initiative', in Silvia Federici, George Caffentzis and Ousseina Alidou (eds), *A Thousand Flowers: Social Struggles against Structural Adjustment in African Universities*. Trenton; Asmara: Africa World Press, 2000, pp. 69–82.

— 'The World Bank and Education in Africa', in Silvia Federici, George Caffentzis and Ousseina Alidou (eds), *A Thousand Flowers: Social Struggles against Structural Adjustment in African Universities*. Trenton; Asmara: Africa World Press, 2000, pp. 3–18.

Calvo, A. G., '¿Qué es un niño?', prologue to Isabel Escudero, *Cántame y cuéntame. Cancionero didáctico*. Madrid: Ediciones de la Torre, 1997.

Châtelet, G., 'A Martial Art of Metaphor: Two Interviews with Gilles Châtelet', https://www.urbanomic.com/document/gilles-Châtelet-mental-ecology/ (accessed 4 January 2017).

— *To Live and Think Like Pigs: The Incitement of Envy and Boredom in Market Democracies*, trans. R. Mackay. New York: Urbanomic/Sequence Press, 2014.

Chaudhuri, B., 'Agrarian Relations: Eastern India', in Tapan Raychaudhuri and Irfan Habib (eds), *The Cambridge Economic History of India* (Cambridge: Cambridge University Press, 1983), 2, pp. 86–176.

Clemens, J., and Grigg, R. (eds), *Jacques Lacan and the Other Side of Psychoanalysis*. Durham, NC: Duke University Press, 2006.

Cornford, F. M. (trans.), *Plato's Theory of Knowledge: The Theaetetus and the Sophist*. Mineola, NY: Dover, 2003.

De Angelis, M., 'Marx and Primitive Accumulation: The Continuous Character of Capital's Enclosures', *The Commoner*, 2 (2001), pp. 1–22.

— 'Separating the Doing and the Deed: Capital and the Continuous Character of Enclosures', *Historical Materialism*, 12(2) (2004), pp. 57–87.

Deleuze, G., *Bergsonism*, trans. H. Tomlinson and B. Habberjam. New York: Zone Books, 1988.

— 'Bergson's Conception of Difference', in *Desert Islands and Other Texts 1953–1974*, ed. David Lapoujade, trans. Michael Taormina. New York: Semiotext(e), 2004.

Deleuze, G., and Guattari, F., *What is Philosophy?*, trans. H. Tomlinson. London: Verso, 2004.

Del Rey, A., *La tyrannie de l'évaluation*. Paris: La Découverte, 2013.

De Romilly, J., *The Great Sophists of Periclean Athens*, trans. Janet Lloyd. Oxford: Clarendon Press, 1992.

Derrida, J., *Glas*, trans. J. P. Leavy, Jr, and R. Rand. Lincoln: University of Nebraska Press, 1986.

Dewey, J., *Democracy and Education*. New York: The Free Press, 1966.

Diogenes Laertius, *Lives of Eminent Philosophers*, trans. R. D. Hicks. London: Heinemann, 1925.

Durkheim, E., *The Evolution of Educational Thought*, trans. P. Collins. London: Routledge and Kegan Paul, 1977.

Federici, S., *Caliban and the Witch*. New York: Autonomedia, 2004.

— 'The Debt Crisis, Africa and the New Enclosures', *The Commoner*, 2 (1992), pp. 1–13.

— 'Education and the Enclosure of Knowledge in the Global University', *ACME: An international e-journal for critical geographies*, 8(3) (2009), http://ojs.unbc.ca/index.php/acme/article/view/843 (accessed 2 February 2017).

— 'The New African Student Movement', in Silvia Federici, George Caffentzis and Ousseina Alidou (eds), *A Thousand Flowers: Social Struggles against Structural Adjustment in African Universities*. Trenton; Asmara: Africa World Press, 2000, pp. 87–112.

— 'The Recolonization of African Education', in Silvia Federici, George Caffentzis and Ousseina Alidou (eds), *A Thousand Flowers: Social Struggles against Structural Adjustment in African Universities*. Trenton; Asmara: Africa World Press, 2000, pp. 19–24.

Federici, S., and Caffentzis, G., 'Chronology of African University Students' Struggles', in Silvia Federici, George Caffentzis and Ousseina Alidou (eds), *A Thousand Flowers: Social Struggles against Structural Adjustment in African Universities*. Trenton; Asmara: Africa World Press, 2000, pp. 115–50.

— 'Commons against and beyond Capitalism', *Community Development Journal*, 49(1) (2014), pp. 92–105.

— 'Notes on the Edu-Factory and Cognitive Capitalism', *The Commoner*, 12 (2007), pp. 63–70.

Fischer, M., *Capitalist Realism*. London: Zero Books, 2009.

Foucault, M., *Discipline and Punish: The Birth of the Prison*, trans. A. Sheridan. New York: Pantheon Books, 1977.

Freire, P., *Education for Critical Consciousness*. New York: Continuum, 2005.

— *Education: The Practice of Freedom*. London: Writers and Readers Publishing Collective, 1974.

— *Pedagogy of the Oppressed*. London: Bloomsbury, 2000.

Giroux, H., and Aronowitz, S., *Education under Siege: The Conservative, Liberal, and Radical Debate over Schooling*. London: Routledge, 1986.

— *Neoliberalism's War on Higher Education*. Chicago: Haymarket Books, 2014.

Gramsci, A., *Selections from the Prison Notebooks*, trans. Q. Hoare and G. Nowell-Smith. New York: International Publishers, 1971.

Groys, B., '. . . Our Fate as a Living Corpse . . .: An Interview with Boris Groys', *Theory Culture Society*, 28(69) (2011), http://theoryculturesociety.blogspot.com.au/2011/06/interview-with-boris-groys.html (accessed 6 January 2017).

Grubb, D., *The Night of the Hunter*. New York: Dell, 1953.

Handke, P., 'Child Story', in *Slow Homecoming*. New York: NYRB Classics, 2009.

Hardt, M., and Negri, A., *Commonwealth*. Cambridge, MA: Harvard University Press, 2009.

Harvey, D., 'The Future of the Commons', *Radical History Review*, 109 (2011), pp. 101–7.

— *The New Imperialism*. Oxford: Oxford University Press, 2003.

Haworth, R. H. (ed.), *Anarchist Pedagogies. Collective Actions, Theories and Critical Reflections on Education*. Oakland: PM Press, 2012.

Hill, P., 'Online Educational Delivery Models: A Descriptive View', *Educausereview*, November 2012, http://er.educause.edu/articles/2012/11/online-educational-delivery-models--a-descriptive-view (accessed 1 February 2017).

Hirji, K. F., 'Academic Pursuits under the LINK', in C. B. Mwaria, S. Federici and J. McLaren (eds), *African Visions*. Westport, CT: Praeger, 2000, pp. 67–84.

Hunter, I., *Rethinking the School: Subjectivity, Bureaucracy, Criticism*. Sydney: Allen and Unwin, 1994.

Illich, I., *Deschooling Society*. London: Penguin, 1971.

Ishtiaque, A., Mahmud, M. S., and Rafi, M. H., 'Encroachment of Canals of Dhaka City, Bangladesh: An Investigative Approach', *GeoScape*, 8(2) (2014), pp. 48–64.

Jackson, P. W., *Life in Classrooms*. New York: Holt, Rinehart and Winston, 1968.

Jorgensen, D., 'The Digital, the Virtual and the Naming of Knowledge', *The*

Fibreculture Journal, 10 (2007), http://ten.fibreculturejournal.org/fcj-063-the-digital-the-virtual-and-the-naming-of-knowledge/ (accessed 4 January 2017).

Karim, S. F., *Dhaka Bissobiddaloy O Purbo Bongio Shomaj: Oddhapok Abdur Razzaker Alapcharita*. Dhaka: Dhaka University Press, 1984.

Kittler, F., *Gramophone, Film, Typewriter*, trans. G. Winthrop-Young and M. Wutz. Stanford: Stanford University Press, 1999.

Klein, N., *The Shock Doctrine: The Rise of Disaster Capitalism*. London: Picador, 2008.

Lacan, J., *Ecrits*, trans. B. Fink, H. Fink and R. Grigg. New York: W. W. Norton, 2005.

— *The Seminar of Jacques Lacan, Book XVII: The Other Side of Psychoanalysis*, ed. J.-A. Miller, trans. R. Grigg. New York: W. W. Norton, 2007.

Lanning, R., 'Education against Everyday Life – An Argument against Educational Futures', *Canadian Journal of Education*, 19(4) (1994), pp. 464–78.

Lapoujade, D., 'Intuition and Sympathy in Bergson', *Pli: The Warwick Journal of Philosophy*, 15 (2004), pp. 1–18.

Larrosa, J., 'Dar la palabra. Notas para una dialógica de la transmisión', in J. Larrosa and C. Skliar (eds), *Habitantes de Babel. Políticas y poéticas de la diferencia*. Barcelona: Laertes, 2000.

— *Entre la lenguas. Lenguaje y educación después de Babel*. Barcelona: Laertes, 2003.

— *Pedagogía profana*. Buenos Aires: Novedades Educativos, 2000.

Lenin, V. I., *Imperialism, the Highest Phase of Capitalism, with an Introduction by Prabhat Patnaik*. Delhi: Leftword Books, 2007.

— 'The State', in *Collected Works*, Vol. 29. Moscow: Progress Publishers, 1972, pp. 470–88.

Linebaugh, P., *Stop, Thief! The Commons, Enclosures, and Resistance*. Oakland: PM Press, 2014.

Long, P. D., and Seimans, G., 'Penetrating the Fog: Analytics in Learning and Education', *Educausereview*, September 2011, http://er.educause.edu/articles/2011/9/penetrating-the-fog-analytics-in-learning-and-education (accessed 1 February 2017).

Luxemburg, R., *The Accumulation of Capital*. London: Routledge, 1963.

Lyotard, J.-F., *The Postmodern Condition: A Report on Knowledge*. Manchester: Manchester University Press, 1984.

Mamdani, M., *Scholars in the Market Place: The Dilemmas of Neo-Liberal Reform at Makerere University, 1989–2005*. Kampala: Fountain Publishers, 2007.

Marx, K., *Capital, Volume 1. A Critique of Political Economy*. London: Penguin, 1990.

— 'Critical Notes on the King of Prussia', in *Early Writings*, trans. R. Livingstone and G. Benton. London: Penguin, 1974.

— *Economic and Philosophical Manuscripts*, in *Early Writings*, trans. R. Livingstone and G. Benton. London: Penguin, 1975.

Marx, K., and Engels, F., *The German Ideology*, ed. C. J. Arthur. London: Lawrence and Wishart, 1970.

— *Manifesto of the Communist Party*. Moscow: Progress Publishers, 1986.

— *The Poverty of Philosophy: Answer to the 'Philosophy of Poverty' by M. Proudhon*. Moscow: Progress Publishers, 1975.

— *Theories of Surplus Value*. Moscow: Progress Publishers, 1969.

— 'Theses on Feuerbach', in *Marx, Engels, Lenin: On Historical Materialism*. Moscow: Progress Publishers, 1972.

Masschelein, J., 'El alumno y la infancia: a propósito de de lo pedagógico', *Cuadernos de Pedagogía*, 11 (2003), pp. 123–4.

Matthews, M. R., 'Reappraising Positivism and Education: The Arguments of Philipp Frank and Herbert Feigl', *Science and Education*, 13(1–2) (2004), pp. 7–39.

Meillassoux, Q., 'History and Event in Alain Badiou', trans. T. Nail, *Parrhesia*, 12 (2011), pp. 1–11.

Merleau-Ponty, M., 'Bergson', in *In Praise of Philosophy and Other Essays*, trans. J. Wilde, J. M. Edie and J. O'Neil. Evanston: Northwestern University Press, 1988.

Midnight Notes Collective, 'Introduction to the New Enclosures', *Midnight Notes*, 10 (1990), pp. 1–9.

Mirowski, P., and Plehwe, D. (eds), *The Road from Mont Pèlerin: The Making of the Neoliberal Thought Collective*. Cambridge, MA: Harvard University Press, 2009.

Mwaria, C. B., Federici, S., and McLaren, J. (eds), *African Visions*. Westport, CT: Praeger 2000.

Nancy, J.-L., *The Creation of the World or Globalisation*, trans. F. Raffoul and D. Pettigrew. Albany, NY: SUNY Press, 2007

Nash, A., 'Affect and the Medium of Digital Data', *The Fibreculture Journal*, 21 (2013), http://twentyone.fibreculturejournal.org/fcj-148-affect-and-the-medium-of-digital-data/#sthash.4DrDyJKs.dpbs (accessed 4 January 2017).

Nietzsche, F., *Beyond Good and Evil*, trans. R. J. Hollingworth. London: Penguin, 1983.

— *On the Future of Our Educational Institutions*, trans. Michael W. Grenke. Indiana: St Augustine's Press, 2004.

Noble, D. F., *Digital Diploma Mills: The Automation of Higher Education*. New York: Monthly Review Press, 2001.

Oksenberg-Rorty, A. (ed.), *Philosophers on Education: New Historical Perspectives*. London: Routledge, 1998.

Ostrom, E., *Governing the Commons: The Evolution of Institutions for Collective Action*. Cambridge: Cambridge University Press, 1990.

O'Sullivan, S., 'A Diagram of the Finite-Infinite Relation: Towards a Bergsonian Production of Subjectivity', in J. Mullarkey and C. De Mille (eds), *Bergson and the Art of Immanence*. Edinburgh: Edinburgh University Press, 2013, pp. 165–86.

Peters, M. A., 'Afterword: Manifesto for Education in the Age of Cognitive Capitalism', in *New Times: Making Sense of Critical/Cultural Theory in a Digital Age* (eds). New York: Peter Lang, 2011, pp. 349–60.

Phillips, D. C., 'After the Wake: Postpositivistic Educational Thought', *Educational Researcher*, 12(5) (1983), pp. 4–12.

Pinar, W. (ed.), *Curriculum Theorizing: The Reconceptualists*. Berkeley: McCutchan, 1975.

Pinkard, T., *Hegel: A Biography*. Cambridge: Cambridge University Press, 2000.

Polyani, K., *The Great Transformation*. New York: Rinehart, 1944.

Plato, *Complete Works*, ed. John M. Cooper and D. S. Hutchinson. Indianapolis: Hackett Publishing, 1997.

Rimbaud, A., 'Bad Blood', in *A Season in Hell*, in *Selected Poems and Letters*, trans. J. Harding and J. Sturrock. London: Penguin, 2004.

Salahuddin Ahmed, A. F., *Bengali Nationalism and the Emergence of Bangladesh*. Bengal: International Centre for Bengal Studies, 1994.

Saltman, K. J., and Gabbard, D. A. (eds), *Education as Enforcement: The Militarization and Corporatization of Schools*. New York: RoutledgeFalmer, 2003.

Scholz, T., 'Why Does Digital Labour Matter Now?', in T. Scholz (ed.), *Digital Labour: The Internet as Playground and Factory*. New York: Routledge, 2013, pp. 1–10.

Seth, S., *Subject Lessons: The Western Education of Colonial India*. Durham, NC: Duke University Press, 2007.

Shuttleworth, J. K., 'The Moral and Physical Condition of the Working Classes of Manchester in 1832', in *Four Periods of Public Education*. London: Longman, Green, Longman and Roberts, 1862.

Silver, H., *Education and the English Radicals, 1780–1850*. London: Routledge and Kegan Paul, 1975.

Silver, B. J., and Arrighi, G., 'Polanyi's "Double Movement": The Belle

Époques of British and US Hegemony Compared', *Politics and Society*, 31(2) (2003), pp. 325–55.

Simons, M., and Masschelein, J., *Rancière, Public Education and the Taming of Democracy*. Oxford: Wiley-Blackwell, 2011.

— 'School: A Matter of Form', in P. Gielen and P. De Bruyne (eds), *Teaching Art in the Neoliberal Realm: Realism versus Cynicism*. Amsterdam: Valiz, 2012, pp. 69–83.

Sloterdijk, P., *Venir al mundo, venir al lenguaje*. Valencia: Pre-textos, 2006.

Strike Debt, *The Debt Resisters' Operation Manual*. Oakland and New York: PM Press and Common Notions, 2014.

Teese, R., and Polesel, J., *Undemocratic Schooling*. Melbourne: Melbourne University Press, 2003.

Tournier, M., *The Erl King*, trans. B. Bray. Baltimore: Johns Hopkins University Press, 1997.

— *The Wind Spirit: An Autobiography*, trans. A. Goldhammer. Boston: Beacon Press, 1988.

Vercellone, C., 'From Formal Subsumption to General Intellect: Elements for a Marxist Reading to the Thesis of Cognitive Capitalism', *Historical Materialism*, 15 (2007), pp. 13–36.

Williams, J., 'The Pedagogy of Debt', in The Edu-factory Collective (ed.), *Towards A Global Autonomous University: Cognitive Labor, the Production of Knowledge and Exodus from the Education Factory*. New York: Autonomedia, 2009, pp. 89–96.

Worsley, P. (ed.), *The New Modern Sociology Readings*. London: Penguin, 1991.

Notes on Contributors

Keith Ansell-Pearson holds a Personal Chair in Philosophy at the University of Warwick and is the author and editor of books on Nietzsche, Bergson and Deleuze.

Judith Balso is a fellow of the Collège International de Philosophie (Paris) and has taught seminars on Pessoa, Stevens, Pasolini, Rimbaud, Mandelstam, Aïgui and Dante. Between 2004 and 2013, she has taught a seminar on 'Poetry and Philosophy' at the European Graduate School and between 2009 and 2014, at the Atelier Théâtre de la Vignette with Marie-José Malis in Montpellier. Books include: *Pessoa le Passeur métaphysique* (Seuil), *Affirmation de la poésie* (Nous) and a monograph on Hölderlin is forthcoming. She is co-founder of the *l'Ecole pour penser* in Paris and between 1997 and 2007 she was a member of the collective *l'Organisation politique*. Currently, she is secretary of l'Ecole des Actes, at the Théâtre de la Commune at Aubervilliers.

A. J. Bartlett is the author of *Badiou and Plato: An Education by Truths*. He is the editor with Justin Clemens of *Badiou and his Interlocutors* and has published widely on Lacan, Badiou, Plato and education. He is Secretary of the Melbourne School of Continental Philosophy and teaches at the Centre for Adult Education in Melbourne.

Justin Clemens is Associate Professor in the School of Culture and Communication in the Faculty of Arts at The University of Melbourne. He has published extensively on philosophy and psychoanalysis, including *Lacan Deleuze Badiou* (Edinburgh University Press), co-written with A. J. Bartlett and Jon Roffe.

Mladen Dolar is Professor and Senior Research Fellow at the Department of Philosophy, University of Ljubljana. His principal areas of research are psychoanalysis, modern French philosophy, German idealism and philosophy of music. He has lectured extensively at the universities in USA and across Europe, he is the author of over hundred papers in scholarly journals and collective volumes. Apart from a dozen books in Slovene his book publications include most notably *A Voice and Nothing More* (MIT, 2006) and *Opera's Second Death* (with Slavoj Žižek, Routledge, 2001). Two books are forthcoming with Duke University Press and Bloomsbury. He is one of the founding members of what has become known as 'the Ljubljana Lacanian School'.

Silvia Federici is a feminist activist, teacher and writer. She is the author of many essays on political philosophy, feminist theory, cultural studies, and education. Her published works include: *Revolution at Point Zero. Housework, Reproduction, and Feminist Struggle* (September 2012); *Caliban and the Witch: Women, the Body and Primitive Accumulation* (2004); *A Thousand Flowers: Social Struggles Against Structural Adjustment in African Universities* (2000, co-editor); *Enduring Western Civilization: The Construction of Western Civilization and its "Others"* (1994 editor). Silvia Federici is Emerita Professor at Hofstra University (Hempstead, New York).

Mushahid Hussain is a research associate at the Fernand Braudel Center, Binghamton University, New York. His research interests are in the fields of historical sociology, labour and the political economy of development, especially in the context of South Asia. Prior to commencing doctoral research, Hussain trained as an economist at Jawaharlal Nehru University in New Delhi and has subsequently taught at universities in Dhaka, Bangladesh.

Jorge Larrosa is Professor in the Department of the Theory and History of Education at the University of Barcelona. He has higher degrees in pedagogy and philosophy from the University of London and at the Michel Foucault Center at the Sorbonne in Paris. The main themes of his work are the relationship between experience and language, subjectivity and education, as well as the formal structure and material functioning of artistic, cultural and educational techniques. Publications include (in Spanish) *La experiencia de la lectura. Ensayos sobre literatura y formación* (Barcelona, 1996 and México, 2004); *Pedagogía Profana. Ensayos* *sobre lenguaje, experiencia y subjetividad* (Buenos Aires, 2000; Belo Horizonte 2001); *La liberación de la libertad (y otros textos)* (Caracas, 2001); *Estudiar/ Estudar* (Belo Horizonte, 2003); *Entre las lenguas. Lenguaje y educación después de Babel* (Barcelona 2003; Belo Horizonte, 2004); *Tremores. Escritos sobre experiencia* (Belo Horizonte 2014).

Alessandro Russo teaches sociology at Bologna University. He has finished a manuscript on *Cultural Revolution and Revolutionary Culture*.